A PILGRIMAGE IN SONG:
UNITARIAN AND UNIVERSALIST HYMNODY

REV. DAVID A. JOHNSON

Rev. David A. Johnson
North Providence, Rhode Island
revdavidjo@gmail.com

First Edition 2016

Published by
KMR & Company
Marlborough, Massachusetts 01752
kmrco@verizon.net

ISBN 978-0-9907269-2-0

To all the UU hymnwriters, known and unknown,
who have kept us singing in our long pilgrimage!

Also by David A Johnson

MC, A Book of Minister's Columns from the 60s
To Preach and Fight, Cincinnati Universalism (1974)
The Disagreements Which Unite Us,
    A UU Adult Education Curriculum (1975)
Chicago Universalism (1978)
In The Beginnings,
    A History of Churches in Tucson, AZ (1980)
To Love, Honor and Shave Twice a Week
    An Inclusive Wedding Book (1980)
A History of First Parish, Brookline 1717-1900
    Brookline, MA (1990)
A Bibliography of UU Women's Hymnody (1990)
A UU Revival Songbook (1995)
Enter Into These Gates With Fear and Trembling
    A Boston Driving Handbook, humor (1995)
John Pierce, His Life as He Lived and Recorded It
    A Biography of Dr. John Pierce,
    Minister of First Parish, Brookline, MA, 1797-1849 (2002)

Chalice Lighting Books
    We Light This Chalice
    The Light Invisible
    The Fire of Ancient Faith

Contents

Acknowledgments

This book would not have been possible without all kinds of people beginning with my parents who loved music and couldn't carry a tune in a bucket. Among those who deserve thanks are Western Reserve Academy whose daily chapel services taught me an entire hymnbook of hymns, the Antioch College Chorus which reminded me to notice the notes, the late Rev. Christopher Moore who taught us fledgling theologues how a hymnal (HCL) was created, and several long suffering congregations who endured my experiments in "singing services."

Somewhere along the way I began to realize that no one talked about "women's hymns" so I spent a year working on a "Bibliography of UU Women's Hymns." It was as if a dam had broken. Colleagues, friends, scholars began to write asking about certain hymns, writers, hymn books. Thanks to all these folk and the UU Women's Heritage Society, Peter Drummey and the staff at Massachusetts Historical Society, the wonderful hymnodic resources of the American Antiquarian Society, Eugene Navias with whom I've worked so long on "Singing, Shouting and Celebrating," and Leo Collins with his thoughtful guidance this book is finally done. As with poetry, such a history is never done really, only "abandoned in despair." All its flaws are mine, and none should be charged to the wonderful folk who helped me along the way!

Rev. David A. Johnson

Introduction

Jane Langton in her Back Bay romp creates a dialogue around the virtues of a particular organ work concluding with this conversation:

> "I guess the moral is," said Barbara, "one person's inspiration is another person's – "
>
> "Hogwash," suggested Homer.
>
> "Crap," offered Mary.
>
> ….
>
> Said Homer, "Music just gives you a sort of unspecified, amorphous, inchoate jolt of something sort of shapeless and unorganized and vague and —"
>
> "But sometimes," objected Barbara, "it can be ecstatic and organized at the same time, I mean —"
>
> "Right," said Martin, "it's the language of the soul, sort of. It's not something you can put into words. It's really kind of —"
>
> "Wonderful," said Mary, "and of course you can put words to it, and then sometimes even the dumbest words can be transformed into something that's really —"

At this point they give up the task of comprehending the inspiration and character of church music and hymns.

This book attempts to trace the history of Universalist and Unitarian hymn writers, hymns and hymn books, and also to continue that dialogue. It is not complete. Hymns and even their writers and hymnbooks are often ephemeral, and disappear quickly from memory. No such work will ever be complete, especially with that prolific author "anonymous" appearing so often, without identification, and early hymns by women and other ignored minorities so easily lost or forgotten. So this is a work in progress.

Musical tastes and certainly tastes in hymnody are often very personal, stemming from life experiences, times, places and persons remembered, endearing or not so endearing songs and hymns. John Haynes Holmes, formative minister of Community Church of New York City, declared that he had learned more about life from poets than theologians. His own poetry was often cast into the form of hymns. It is a truism that all theology is autobiography – if it's any good. Hymns are also autobiography – if they're any good. A long ago friend used to sit on the steps outside the church until the sermon was safely launched before he came in and sat in the back. I asked him why, and he replied with a long story. In short, when he had told his mother he was no longer a Lutheran she said she'd pray for him. He accepted that, until in time she had the whole of his hometown praying for him. From that moment on he cringed whenever he heard church music. Hymns became for him reminders of the relentless faith of his mother, full of guilt and hurt. Hymns are real; they are life.

I grew up in a church with wonderful classic Unitarian Universalist hymnody, played on the best organ in Cleveland, Ohio. I loved it. Oh, there were many hymns I grew soul weary of, many I thought arrogant and triumphalist, many insipid, many just not very good. I have cherished these loves and dislikes all my life and you will find them revealed in this book. I make no apology for them. There's a whimsical but true tale of the good Anglican hymn writer[1] Augustus Montague Toplady's comments on the upstart preacher–hymn writer John Wesley. Wesley's theology is, said Toplady, "an equal portion of gross heathenism, Pelagianism, Mahometanism, popery, Manichaeism, ranterism and antinomianism, culled, dried and pulverized...mingled with as much palpable atheism as could possibly be scraped together." I aspire to Toplady's clarity of expression if not his opinions. I know there are other likes and dislikes different from mine. People have a right to be wrong. Even me – occasionally!

A colleague approached me when I was a theological student frantically seeking to finish the theological course before me, and asked, "Don't you think hymns are dinosaurs?" The "new" Unitarian Universalist hymnal, *Hymns for the Celebration of Life,* was then approaching publication, perhaps fueling the question. I was so non–plused I don't

1 "Rock of Ages" was his great triumph.

think I responded at all. He was sure that hymns were a vestige of the past fated for the dust bin of history when a new generation got around to cleaning house. The only response that came to mind would have been an insult – that perhaps he was the dinosaur fated for extinction. Perhaps he was just thinking of the deadly hymnody "shoveled out four square," as Robert Lowell noted, that besets so many denominations' hymn books, and some Unitarian and Universalist hymnbooks as well. Perhaps he believed that only songs of the living present had any value. Perhaps he hated music. As for me, I agree with Shakespeare's observation that; "The man that hath no music in himself, nor is not moved with concord of sweet sounds, is fit for treasons, stratagems and spoils." And that includes congregational singing. One of my favorite authors quotes a story from the Connecticut woods;

> An old farmer once said that he would not have a hired man on his place who did not habitually whistle….Said he never knew a whistling laborer to find fault with his food, his bed, or complain of any little extra work he was asked to perform. Such a man was generally kind to children and to animals in his care. He would whistle a chilled lamb into warmth and life….He found such a man most careful about closing gates, putting up bars, and seeing that the nuts on his plow were tight before he took it into the field. He never knew a whistling hired man to beat or kick a cow, or drive her on the run into the stable. He had noticed that the sheep he led into the yard and shed gathered around him as he whistled, without fear.[2]

As the son of a hummer and whistler I agree wholeheartedly that none without music in their souls should be trusted. They can whistle, hum, sing, play harmonicas, Jews harps or concert Steinways, or just tap their feet to the music, but relating to folk without music is like riding a buckboard without springs.

For me, certainly, Gabrielle Roth captures the power of song in her *Maps to Ecstasy:*

> …Songs are a vital part of living…; people are listening, night and

---

2 *Hill Country Harvest,* by Hal Borland, J.B. Lippincott Company (Philadelphia & New York, 1967), pp 67–68

day, in their cars and homes, to songs. Once you think about it a little, it's clear that we are dependant on songs and singers to supply us with almost constant emotional energy. Our hunger for songs and our adulation of singers signal our desperate need to share in the raw expression of emotions. Songs are one of the few areas in which the exploration of the full range of emotions is publicly sanctioned and wholly accepted, even in a mass culture where the tendency is to repress real feelings or replace them with pale or cheap imitations.

Feelings get stuck in the throat. We get choked–up with sadness, constricted with fear. But if we could full–throatedly wail our grief... or shout our joy..., we'd begin to feel the pulse of true emotion once more. Singing is a simple, immediate way to free the flow of feeling.

"Awaken the singer in you," she cries, "not with the aim of becoming a professional singer, but just to become a fully functioning human being. If you're afraid to sing, hum." Norman Cousins long ago discovered the power of humor, and song, to heal. Oliver Sachs, Neurologist, among many other researchers, believes that music can open up tightly shuttered personalities. Music and song has been used with nursing home residents, even those suffering from the brutal effects of Alzheimer's disease, to elicit responses when nothing else seems to work. Authors for generations have listened to favored music to free up the creativity locked within.

A song or hymn is not simply words set to a congenial tune. At best the words and music move together, creating something which was not before, something greater than its parts, something deeper and more expressive, a new order of meaning. The words alone are somehow mute without the music. The tune alone seems often incomplete. Together they can move the soul, feed its hungers, capture its hopes and dreams. They can shape a body of people and set them marching, captivate a nation, foment a revolution.[3]

---

3 "Come, come, ye Saints," the great Mormon marching hymn has carried the Church of Jesus Christ of Latter Day Saints across the plains and years, and lives still today in tears and celebration. The Universalists, from whom the Mormon's borrowed the tune, had long

Music attends our lives and our souls. As "Pogo" long ago said "Life without music would be a mistake." A clipping whose author is lost, well declares;

> ...for cooking I adore listening to songs of passionate hunger – traditional Irish music or opera. Soft rock or show tunes keep me moving while I clean, and I love to listen to country music when I carpool. When you crave more than the sounds of silence, there is music for every mood.
>
> Acknowledging your mood swings and honoring their reality with music to accompany the experience is soulcraft.

The power of music and song is manifest in the lives of people in every culture and nation. Surely it requires no defense. And it would be difficult to argue in a culture like ours so vigorous in its musical creativity, so seemingly afraid of silence, so bathed in background music, so enamored with musical entertainment, so prolific in song, that song and music were unimportant. Music in this place and time may often be trivial and lacking in substance and significant message but it is not unimportant.

The late UU minister Kenneth Patton powerfully and pungently put it this way;

> We try to make our words endure by loud shouting, but this only shoves the moment back a little longer. Speak softly, your words will be recalled for their melodies and proportions. If you would speak for the hearing of children in ages to come, train your words to rhythm and resonance.... Would you make yesterday worth remembering, only songs will equip time with immortality.

Hymns and songs imprint new generations with the hopes and dreams of this generation and others before. Perhaps my long ago sour colleague was simply referring to hymns sandwiching the sermon and seeming to do little more. If so, I think he is still on the wrong track. In the history of this nation, strange to say, hymns are a cohesive force. There is a common corpus of hymns in this nation virtually universally recognized in every

---

recognized its power and coupled it with the Thomas Whittemore hymn, "God is Love," a forceful and worthy coupling as well.

social class, among people in every part of our society, even those who never darken the doorstep of a religious institution. Hymns are a cohesive force in times of public crisis and great ceremonial moments. Who can imagine great state funerals, or the civil rights movement, the cries of oppressed people, or the anti war movement, or memorial day events without familiar songs and hymns? Hymns are inherently both personal and affirmations of a larger bonding of people, allowing common public expression that has few other channels.

The late Bruce Chatwin in his magnificent *The Songlines* traces the aboriginal Australian "songlines" that tell the native people where they are, what each place is called, the way forward to the next place with its own song. The native folk would not think of traveling the great, difficult distances of their native land and lives without the songs that keep them on the path and tell them what they need to know to complete the journey. Chatwin says, "I have a vision of the songlines stretching across continents and ages; that wherever [people] have trodden they have left a trail of song." For him no country fully exists unless it can be called up in song. I think that's true, and no religious tradition has a greater or prouder tradition in hymn and song than the Unitarian–Universalists. Our whole heritage is compassed about and celebrated in song and hymn, and we have contributed mightily to the songlines that crisscross this our homeland, that defined moments of crisis, change, courageous confrontation. But, to continue Chatwin's image, where are the connections between ourselves, the UU movement, congregations and those songlines stretching back through all the stories and beyond the boundaries of and history of this land? We can dust off ancient hymnals, choral and song books and point to the songs that marked our way, that shaped our course, that defined and celebrated our grappling with the issues of each new generation. But where are the song lines connecting us to the present? Roman Catholics, the great Eastern Orthodox churches, Calvinist Protestants can point in their hymnals to the "songlines" that link the generations together in clear continuity and succession. We cannot. That deserves attention in this book.

We are not a people of "The Book" any longer. We don't define ourselves as a Biblical people no matter what our respect for Biblical wisdom or for the prophets, or even Jesus. No matter how often we cite scripture in readings and sermons it is not defining, not the ultimate source to which we return for guidance. We have no unifying book of common prayer, no book of discipline to which we turn for guidance on proper forms of worship and proper personal or congregational behavior. So, what does unite us? Beyond the living relationships, the UUA principles, and a very attenuated sense of heritage, not much unites us. We can point to our regnant mythology of historic persons and evens that have formed us, but to a fearsome extent it is really mythology and doesn't go very deep much of anywhere. Our lack of serious knowledge of our own history is deeply embarrassing, or ought to be if we understood it.

It could well be argued that our hymnal is the one unifying document we have – regularly used, helping to define who we are. But, if the hymnal doesn't serve the purpose of linking our stories, our history, our landmark persons and events together over time, across the years nationally and internationally then what does?

We will return to this question as this book unfolds.

In the Beginning

May Music guide you on your pilgrim ways;
May Music bless you; may it caress you;
May Music be your highest joy.
Gerald P. Dyck, composer

Universalist and Unitarian hymnody in North America are two separate strands, representing two long denominational histories, reaching beyond these shores, with fascinatingly diverse roots extending centuries back. On this side of the Atlantic there are 200 years and more of liberal faith set to music. The occasion of a new hymnal is a fundamental and important one, since like the building of a building, you control the outcome through the actual creation, but then the building, as the hymnal, controls you. It is rarely acknowledged the degree to which a hymnal shapes, forms, directs and controls worship of congregations who use it, but it is a powerful, molding force in worship. What is available in the hymnal chosen, or missing, the character, theological language, images, quality and message of its words and music are critical in a congregation's worship life. They are in great degree the face it presents to its people and the community, even its understanding of itself. It is long since time that the story behind Universalist and Unitarian hymnody should be traced and understood. *Singing the Living Tradition*, the latest in a long succession of denominational hymnals, the second congregational hymnal[1] of the Unitarian Universalist Association (the third to be jointly produced) prompts this all too brief book, this overview of Universalist and Unitarian hymnody. Despite a fertile and prolific hymnodic history in both founding denominations there has been no such history ever written before.[2]

---

1 There were also Sunday School hymn and songbooks.

2 Henry Wilder Foote (II) is the great historian of our Unitarian (and some Universalist) hymnody, having written many books and articles relating to and inclusive of the subject, and submitted an unpublished work of review and biography of Unitarian and Universalist hymnody for a revision of Julian's great hymnodic compendium. He also published *Three Centuries of American Hymnody*, Harvard University Press, Cambridge, Massachusetts, 1940,

Nowhere are Universalist and Unitarian hymns so different as in the beginnings and early formative years of the two separate movements. The Universalists began on these shores as a conviction of faith among scattered communities and individuals whose faiths' origins were often in the more mystical and pietist outflow of the Anabaptist wing of the Radical Reformation of more than two centuries before. Much of their early music and hymnody showed its Germanic and Western European origins; and though that influence among American Universalists was limited, some did endure, resonating with and combining with the folk and tavern music that Luther had brought into the church and providing tunes quite unlike those of the Calvinist Reformation. This strand of pietist Universalism and its hymns was quickly succeeded and for the most part replaced in America by the tradition represented by John Murray, and its faith, words and music from Rellyan and Wesleyan rootage, and the enthusiastic Armenian Wesleyan heritage of personal and evangelical hymnody, forged together with Calvinist strains on these shores. Though Murray was in most respects, save universal salvation, theologically a Calvinist his soul moved to the more enthusiastic musical beat of the Wesleys. The Puritan stream of psalmody, brought to Universalism by the early tide of converts from the churches of Calvinist faith in New England had very different characteristics, psalms as the only source of words to be sung, and a history of music tightly confined to received tunes, and those not many. The Universalists, from the beginning in New England, departed from the often deadly though popular Calvinist psalms and wrote hymns prolifically. These were swiftly published in their own hymnals — so ill suited to their worship did the mainstream of traditional psalmody seem to these Universalists. The most vigorous

an overview of American hymnody that contains an amazing and excessive collection of Unitarian and Universalist hymnody including Liberal Christian hymnody that preceded it. Foote drew heavily on Alfred P. Putnam's, *Singers and Songs of the Liberal Faith*, Roberts Brothers (Boston, 1875). Leo R. Lewis, on the Universalist side, worked on hymnal commissions and assisted in the extremely useful hymn writers' biographies at the end of *Church Harmonies New and Old*, Universalist Publishing House, 1905. The Commission that created *Hymns for the Celebration of Life*, Beacon Press (Boston, 1964) also deserves the historian's praise for the detailed hymn sketches and biographies in that volume. Eugene Navias, with a little help from this author, drafted a helpful brief history of Unitarian and Universalist hymnody, included in his *Singing Our History*, UUA (Boston, 1975). These and many others who remembered and recorded the lives and works of Universalist and Unitarian hymn writers made this writer's work possible.

and polemic period of Universalist hymn writing was the earliest when Universalism was its most polemical, theological, apologetic and evangelical. Such hymnody rarely survives its own generation of origin, and for the most part for and among the hymns of the early Universalists it didn't.

A word should be said for the use of musical instruments among the Universalists — so very different from instrumental music among the earliest Unitarians. Universalists did not share the Congregational–Calvinist prejudice against non–Biblically approved instruments in worship. Their forebears did not scour the British countryside to destroy the ancient church and cathedral organs as did some early Calvinistic separatists in England. There is a wonderful notice from the "Columbian Centennial" February 8, 1792, noting the work of Dr. Josiah Leavitt in constructing organs in Boston – the first to do so – and reporting that an organ had just "been purchased by the Universal Religious Society of this town [John Murray's church in Boston], and erected in their house of worship." It is praised by the "Columbian Centennial" for its elegance of construction and "sweetness of sound," "exceeded by but few imported Organs." The Universalists were aggressively and celebratively musical in their worship from the beginning on these shores. They were not self confined as the early Unitarians and their predecessors to using the Bass Viol (and possibly other strings) to accompany hymns.

The American Unitarian movement emerged gradually from the old Standing Order of New England Calvinism through the Evangelical Liberal Christians, who began to threaten the theological purity of the old and new Calvinism of the late eighteenth century and early nineteenth. Their singing heritage in the Standing Order was of traditional psalmody, with all its virtues and faults, but Liberal Christians and proto unitarians had begun to move beyond even the best of the old psalm books by the mid eighteenth century, long before the organization of the American Unitarian Association, and specific "Unitarian" congregations. Progressive ministers and congregations published their own psalm and hymn books in significant numbers, bringing to worship new words, new hymns by men, and women.

Tunes among the Liberal Christians of New England, for the most part, were from Europe, especially England, until the eruption of William

3

Billings on the scene. Billings, often called the father of American music, may have been somewhat plodding and primitive in his musical style but his music was widely used, and some has survived to be appreciated today. His singing was compared by many in his day to loud screeching[3], and some contemporaries thought little better of his music. But his music opened the door to new composition and the adaptation of many pieces of classical music to hymnody, a course vigorously pursued by the Liberals.

Semi–official Universalist hymnody began very early with John Murray's reprint of James Relly's British Universalist hymnal in 1776. There was a tide of Universalist hymnals, mostly without any official standing, in the late 1700s and early 1800s. A much used New England collection, *Hymns Composed by Different Authors, by Order of the General Convention of Universalists of the New England States and Others* was published in 1808 by Hosea Ballou and others. It was a limited mostly living and local collection, as was its successor, The *Universalists' Hymn Book: A New Collection*, gathered a bit more broadly in time and space by Hosea Ballou and Edward Turner, editors. Universalist hymnals, some more and some less official, continued through the 1820s and 30s, culminating in *A Collection of Psalms and Hymns for the Use of Universalist Societies and Families* edited by Hosea Ballou II, and broadly inclusive of the best theologically compatible and useful hymns from every and any source they found available, including British and continental sources. Universalists did edit and adapt others' hymns from the beginning to make the message more theologically congenial. *Hymns for Christian Devotion*, of 1845, edited by the best of early Universalist hymn writers, John Greenleaf Adams, and his friend Edwin Hubbell Chapin finally made Universalist hymnals popularly respectable.

Official Unitarian hymnody did not begin until the *Hymn and Tune Book*, published by the American Unitarian Association immediately following the Civil War. It was drastically reshaped and reprinted for the

---

3 John Pierce, Minister of First Parish of Brookline (1797–1849), a recorder of New England Congregationalism and its music, used the word "screeching" in his Memoirs, held by the Massachusetts Historical Society. The Massachusetts Historical Society, which gave me a grant a few years ago for the study of John Pierce's works, has been unfailingly helpful, especially in tracing biographical information on authors of hymns, and in assisting in searching out libraries with obscure texts that I needed for this work.

rest of the century. *Hymns for the Church and Home* succeeded it in 1895, but its attempt to move toward less formal, more popular hymns and tunes, resonating however gently to the Dwight L. Moody revival spirit, doomed it among mainstream more traditional Unitarian musicologists and hymn book editors. The *New Hymn and Tune Book* of 1914 was indeed new in fundamental ways, including more formal music, and a clear attempt to codify and establish a corpus of great, continuing Unitarian hymns and hymn writers. In 1938 the Unitarians and Universalists, having combined forces, published *Hymns of the Spirit*, affectionately known as "the red book." It is perhaps the greatest hymnal of this lineage, having drawn considerable critical praise and popular acceptance. 1964 saw the next, and first official, hymnal of the Unitarian Universalist Association, *Hymns for the Celebration of Life*. Falling as it did on the cusp of the feminist revolution, and being entirely oblivious to its patriarchal language, its virtues — and there were many — were not properly appreciated. It was half the size of its predecessor and thus also drew in larger measure all the fury of folk whose favorite hymns were dropped for space or other reasons. The latest hymnal is *Singing the Living Tradition* of 1993 is a vigorous new vision of Unitarian and Universalist hymnody. Its 2005 Supplement, *Singing the Journey,* has added a whole new genre of religious expression, and a spirit we have not had in a Unitarian hymnal for a century. Other hymnals proliferated among the Unitarians, mostly local creations — huge numbers in early years, few in the Great Depression — an explosion of titles in the second half of the 20th century, among Unitarian Universalists. This book can only suggest the breadth and depth of this history, especially in local and unofficial hymnbooks. Unusual and landmark Unitarian or Universalist hymnals from whatever source are acknowledged and outstanding Universalist or Unitarian hymn writers are noted. A closing chapter is devoted to brief biographical sketches of those whose work survived into post Civil War hymnals, or was created later, not including new hymnwriters of *Singing the Living Tradition* and *Singing the Journey.*

The Background

> Above all sing spiritually. Have an eye to God
> In every word you sing....So shall your singing
> Be such as your God will approve..., and reward
> You in the clouds of heaven.
>
> *John Wesley,* Sacred Melody, *1761*

We shall never know whether it was "the fighting bishop of Milan," St. Ambrose, who introduced congregational singing into the Roman Church. We do know that at that time "the devout keeping watch day and night in the church, [were] ready to die with their bishop...singing hymns and psalms so they would not succumb to weariness and grief." We also know that virtually every heresy that rent the ancient church came blessed in shared song. It is strange that for so many centuries the clergy and "religious" were the only ones to sing in the formal worship of the Roman Church. But there was a heritage of song outside the mass which burst forth in the Laudi Spirituali of the Franciscan Order in Florence in the late thirteenth century, and outside the church in millenarian sects in the same years and for centuries thereafter.[1]

But the real outbreak of congregational singing was to await the Reformation. The Anabaptists awakened in song as soon as they began to gather. One has only to turn to the Mennonite *Ausbund* (1583) to find hymns from their earliest days. Many believers were, from the same early days, moved by the conviction of God's universal love, to convictions of universal restoration, and this shows in some hymnody. Only a few years after the "95 Theses" Luther turns his thoughts to forms of worship and to hymns. He does not call for the overthrow of the magnificent musical forms of the church, but for hymns like the Te deum Laudamus and Deo Gracias in the vernacular that all could share.[2] His use of new words and popular tunes did not mean, however, that standards of faith and of

---

1   I am indebted for these brief notes to Erik Routley for his cogent discussion of Christian hymnody in the magisterial, *The Music of Christian Hymns*, GIA Publications (Chicago, 1981), p 20.

2   Routley, p 21.

6

musical and singing excellence were not expected for the transcendent beauty of the music of the mass remained with him always.[3]

It was John Calvin who in the middle of the Sixteenth Century set metrical psalmody on its course. The *Genevan Psalter* of 1551 was built on the words of the psalms translated in the vernacular, adapted only to the degree necessary for singing, for the Bible was, to Calvin and his immediate progeny, the only proper source of words for songs of worship, and the words had to be respected. No instruments were to accompany congregational singing, and no other instrumental music was permitted in the service. The *Genevan Psalter*, in its final edition of 1562, 110 meters, 125 tunes remained thereafter long fixed, unchanged. It is not surprising that a Roman Catholic scholar should see Calvin's psalmody with its simple two note values, darkly; "the Lutheran chorale may be likened to a fertile spreading tree, shedding abundant seeds from which other trees were to spring. The Genevan psalm tune remains in its primitive aloofness, like a marble statue; incapable as a statue of propagating its species; pathetic in its frozen grandeur."[4] But Calvinist psalmody was not so sterile. The several subsequent Calvinist psalm books and prolific musical expressions in England, Scotland and America attest to a vitality and progeny that belies this judgment.

Henry Ainsworth (a founder and minister of the English church in Amsterdam, one of three separatist churches in Holland, not the Pilgrim one) created a noteworthy Psalter published in England in 1612, based on the old Genevan tunes, with new and well crafted English words. It was this psalm book which the Pilgrims brought with them on the Mayflower's arduous voyage of 1620 to Plymouth. It was this psalm book that the Plymouth congregation, today First Parish (Unitarian), used until the colony's demise. But it was not this psalm book that the Puritans who settled on up the coast in Boston and close environs brought with them. Thomas Sternhold, groom to young Henry VIII, and John Hopkins had in 1549 collaborated on a more limited psalm book, containing only 44 psalms, and one more later added, named inaccurately the *Whole Book of Psalms*. But no music was included or suggested. "Sternhold and

---

3   Routley, p 21.

4   Sir Richard Terry as quoted in Routley, *The Music of Christian Hymns*, p 33.

Hopkins," as it was colloquially called in the colonies, distinguishing it from the later Massachusetts Bay psalm book of similar name, was the standard, going through almost 200 editions in two generations. It was not the standard for long on these shores. Mass Bay Puritans completed their own *Bay Psalm Book*, a scarce decade after their first settlement. The Puritans, seeking a purer Gospel, judged Sternhold and Hopkins sharply, noting that the "godly learned" were well aware that Sternhold and Hopkins;

> ... have rather presented a paraphrase then (sic) the words of David ..., and that their addition to the words, detractions from the words are not seldome and rare, but very frequent and many times needles ...and that their variations of the sense, and alterations of the sacred text too frequently, may justly minister matter of offense to them that are able to compare the translation with the text...

Seeking a greater purity of text the Mass Bay clergy set out to create "a plain and familiar translation."[5] Several clergy of Mass Bay participated in the translating, each taking on particular psalms. The new printing house in Cambridge, as its third imprint, printed *The Whole Book of Psalms Faithfully Translated into English Meter,* the first English book printed on these shores, commonly called the *Bay Psalm Book,* in 1639.[6] In New England, as in Calvin's Geneva, secular music was suspect and instrumental music often seen "as a snare of the devil."[7] It is often assumed that New England Puritans shared the sentiment that "music was the invention of the devil, to be shunned as worldly and frivolous." But it was not so. Quakers indeed with George Fox, cried "out against all sorts of music"[8]

---

5 As quoted from Bay Colony ministers in Zoltan Haraszti's *Enigma of the Bay Psalm Book,* University of Chicago Press (Chicago, 1956), p 7. (Spelling is in original.)

6 The *Bay Psalm Book* had no tunes with the words. It was not until the 9th edition of the *Bay Psalm Book* in 1698 that thirteen tunes were included in the back of the book. They are set in two parts, not the familiar SATB form of many years later. It was well over a century before music and words appeared together in hymnals, or the SATB form was first established in a hymnal. It was not until the post Civil War era that hymnals regularly included tunes and four part harmony was securely established in mainstream hymnals.

7 Haraszti, p 62.

8 See *The Puritans and Music in England and New England,* by Percy A. Scholes, Clarendon Press (Oxford, 1969), p 52. The surrounding chapter, and indeed the entire book, is an excellent introduction to Puritan music. Resistance to secular music and sacred music in secular

but Puritans did not. No clearer authority need be cited than the stern Puritan Judge Samuel Sewall who regularly recorded his delight in Psalm singing and instrumental music, even at home where his wife played the virginal (spinet).[9] If greater authority is sought Cotton Mather's *Remarkable Providences* notes "the great efficacy" of music "against melancholly discomposures," praising "the sweetness and delightfulness of musick" against such melancholy. Psalmody was diligently studied, as was music itself at Harvard. Psalms were sung in worship and around the hearth, but for long, long years in New England there was no organ accompaniment, often only the Bass Viol or "the Lord's Fiddle" as it was often called. The first organ in New England was reputed to be that owned by Thomas Brattle of Boston in the late 1600s.[10] Brattle's will deeded it to his church in Brattle Square in 1713, but they refused it. Being so refused, the will specified that it go to King's Chapel where it stood for a time in the entryway, denounced by some as the "devil's squeeze box," until at last it joined the congregation in worship. It was many years before another Liberal Christian congregation had the courage to follow the reluctant lead of King's Chapel. The church in Brattle Square took three quarters of a century.

Psalms sung at meeting and at home were not the only songs of the Puritans. Van Wyck Brooks, notes;

> There were popular ballads and folk–songs..., sailors' chanties along the coast, ballads of village murders, rockaby songs, sugar–makers' songs, songs sung by weavers and carpenters, by farm–wives and wandering fiddlers, by hunters, trappers, guides and lumbermen, snatches and refrains and longer pieces, brought from the old world or natural outgrowths of the American soil.[11]

But, in the world of Puritan hegemony there was no migration of tunes

---

settings was widespread and indeed exists in some places today. Evangelicals of many stripes have denounced such usage for centuries. See Scholes, p. 353, for an interesting British example in the 1880s.

9 See *Diary of Samuel Sewall*, 1674–1729, Vols. 1–3, Massachusetts Historical Society (Boston, 1878).

10 See *The Annals of Kings Chapel*, by Henry Wilder Foote (Boston, 1882) for more of the tale of this organ's reception and use.

11 Van Wyck Brooks, as quoted in *Enigma of the Bay Psalm Book,* p 63)

from the secular world to the religious. The Pilgrims drew from the rich music of English psalms, many of them drawn from Dutch and French, including Huguenot sources. The Puritans were much more limited in tunes, clearly, the *Bay Psalm Book* recognizing only "neere fourty common tunes." Difficult meters in the *Bay Psalm Book* had alternate common meter texts, so that all could be sung by the musically challenged in the simplest meter, and to familiar psalm tunes. By the end of the seventeenth century there were only thirteen tunes recognized as in common use among the Standing Order in the Colony. Psalm singing was clearly troubled, for the *Bay Psalm Book* then included instructions for proper singing that there might be no "squeaking above, or grumbling below." Psalms were commonly lined out by a Deacon, sometimes a clergyman, eventually a precentor or chorister. This was needed in the early days when many had no resources, or desire, wherewith to purchase psalm books, as they were then privately owned. Further, the tune for a given text might be different from meeting house to meeting house, or even Sunday to Sunday, depending on the taste of the clergy (visiting or settled), chorister or congregation.

John Calvin and his American religious descendants thought that printed music was not the work of God and that lining out was a godly practice, but that practice began to draw serious criticism from the early eighteenth century in New England. The Rev. Thomas Symes published a not so tongue in cheek dialogue in Boston in 1722 that laid out the objections to singing by note and meter:

(1) That it is a New Way, an Unknown Tongue.

(2) That it is not so Melodious as the Usual Way.

(3) That there are so many Tunes, we shall never have done learning.

(4) That the Practice of it give Disturbance; Roils & Exasperates men's Spirits; gives sundry good People, and causes them to behave themselves indecently & disorderly.

(5) That is Quakerish & Popish, and introductive of Instrumental Musik.

(6) That the Names given to the Notes are Bawdy, yea Blasphemous.

(7) That it is a needless way, since their good Fathers that were

Strangers to it, are got to Heaven without it.[12]

It promised to be, and was, a long hard battle in each individual congregation on ending lining out, on whether there should be choirs (another assumedly "popish" imposition), or instrumental accompaniment, or organs (not mentioned in the Bible as an instrument for worship, surely, and thus religiously suspect). It was more than 200 years after the appearance of the *Bay Psalm Book* before congregations in the Puritan tradition chose to publish common and familiar tunes with the old familiar words or new ones so that there was regularity in whatever church they might worship.[13] This cumbersome, idiosyncratic practice of lining hymns out, the limited musical repertoire of the typical congregation, and the differing musical tastes and talents of parishioners created no end of problems and complaints. The Rev. Mr. Thomas Walter of First Church, Roxbury (later Unitarian) lamented in 1721 that;

> The tunes are now miserably tortured, and twisted, and quavered, in some Churches, into an horrid Medley of confused and disorderly Noises, [leaving] to the Mercy of every unskillful Throat to chop and alter, twist and change, according to their infinitely divers and no less odd Humors and Fancies.[14]

It was far from rare for people to bellow out the same words to different tunes at the same time, and to strive to outsing others. Some churches struggled to maintain some commonality and standards; in others no two singers seemed close to the same tune. It could sound "like Five Hundred different Tunes roared out at the same time," said Walter.[15] Singing schools were quickly instituted in several churches to establish a common and respectable standard, a practice that existed on and off for more than a century suggesting how resistant the Standing Order was to standards and regularity of practice. The tanner become musician, Wil-

---

12 As quoted from Thomas Symes, *Utile Dulci*, of 1722, in "The Regular Singing Controversy: The Case Against Lining Out," by Linda R. Ruggles, Lecturer at the University of Maryland (unpublished paper).

13 Even then there were often multiple choices of tune, to recognize a diversity of taste and tradition.

14 As quoted in Haraszti, *The Enigma of the Bay Psalm Book,* p 70.

15 Haraszti, p 70.

liam Billings, for all his faults, began the task of composing new tunes and gathering and arranging others, publishing *The New England Psalm Singer* in 1770, the first of a prolific tide of choral song books, himself the first of a heady band of new composers. And the psalms, once so fixed, began to change.

Isaac Watts' hymns long existed in England, and had long been used there especially by the General Baptists, but not in rock ribbed New England, not in Puritan congregations anyway. Watts psalms became immensely popular among the Standing Order of New England, but long not for worship, for devotional literature.[16] American reprints of British Psalm and hymn books began to appear by the mid 1700s, some coupled with an appendix of recommended tunes, but they were slow to find approval, though many of the Liberal Christian congregations destined to be Unitarian made the change to Watts hymns in these years. The Great Awakening and the advent of American Methodism brought an awakening to Watts, with Wesley and the Moravian hymns and tunes which so moved John Wesley. The spreading revival movement among Methodists and Baptists brought new revival songs and music but it hardly touched the Standing Order of New England. Real change, beyond individual congregations, had to await the American Revolution which set many freedoms in motion. Appropriately New Englanders felt driven to edit Watts psalms where they seemed to laud British Royalty, and to substitute triumphal references to the Revolution. It was difficult to maintain textual purity in such an age, not that Watts psalms ever did.

William Bentley of East Church in Salem, who created a bright new hymnal (without music) in 1788, noted in his Diary of April 3, 1801, a letter he had sent to a German hymnodist reviewing the changes in New England psalmody. The letter reviewed:

> The history of our psalmody. From the single part in our old Bibles, and the tunes to every psalm in Sternhold & Hopkins till the New England Version then mentioning Increase Mather's measured prose, Prince's poetic version & Barnard's of Marblehead. The introduction of Tate and Brady by Dr. Coleman and of Watts by Mather Byles, the Collection for West Boston by Dr. Howard,

---

16 See Foote's *Three Centuries of American Hymnody*, Chapter 5.

my own Collection in Salem, Dr. Belknap's Collection in Boston, introduced into several churches. [John] Relly's hymns among the Universalists…I then noticed the progress of music from the single part to Tenor, bass and medius…[17]

He went on to note the changes in hymn music and instrumental music in New England, furthered by this prolific change toward new hymnals.

The aged and honored Samuel M. Worchester took the next step in the path toward creating an American hymnal with music among the sons and daughters of the Puritans. In 1815 he published his edition of the *Psalms, Hymns, and Spiritual Songs of the Rev. Isaac Watts, D.D. to which are added Select Hymns From Other Authors; and Directions for Musical Expression,* Crocker and Brewster (Boston, 1834) including not only suggested tunes but also notations on how loudly and at what pace the tune was to be played. Unfortunately this innovation was too radical for the time. Few other hymnals in New England printed or even suggested music until after the Civil war. The local congregation's absolute rule over its choice of tunes for worship continued.

We must return to England. It is an old and honorable prejudice that Isaac Watts led the way into hymnody not based on the sparest and most careful rendition of the psalms, but David Wykes, Director of Dr. William's Library in London makes a compelling case for widespread, if deeply controversial, hymn (as differentiated from psalm) singing among dissenters and non–conformists in the wake of the 1689 Toleration Act, swiftly spreading among dissenting chapels (some of them also moving toward unitarianism) by the first decade of the eighteenth century, before Watts psalms and hymns were in print.[18] The use of such hymnody

---

17 Rev. John Barnard of Marblehead, Massachusetts, published a new psalm book, matched to old and popular tunes in 1752. Thomas Prince of Old South Church in Boston created a psalm and hymn book in 1758 with 48 tunes. Benjamin Coleman and Mather Byles were ministers of the Hollis Street Church in Boston which took the lead in moving past the Bay Psalm Book. Rev. Simeon Howard published a West Church, Boston, hymnal in 1788 which departed almost completely from the psalms and included hymns by Wesley and Barbauld. William Bentley included 163 hymns in his 1788 hymnal. Jeremy Belknap, William Ellery Channing's predecessor at Federal Street Church in Boston created an excellent hymnal, inclusive of new British hymn writers in 1795, but alas no music. The above is found in *Three Centuries of American Hymnody,* by Foote, Chapter 5 and pp 156–158.

18 "From David's Psalms to Watt's hymns: the development of hymnody among dissent-

became a fiery issue among Independents, Presbyterians and Baptists well before Watts, and several collections of hymns were in print in the 1690s among the non–conformists. It should also be remembered that the British Tate and Brady's *New Version of the Psalms of David*, an immensely popular psalm book in New England, was published in 1696.

It was however the prolific Isaac Watts born in 1674, creator of psalms and hymns, who changed the course of song in worship, breaking in time the stranglehold of Ainsworth on the Church of England, and narrow psalmody over dissenters and Puritans. Watts, a dissenter, was educated at one of the vigorous dissenting academies in Stoke Newington. Some of these academies were clearly superior to Oxford and Cambridge at that time, those schools being then and for many years closed to dissenters, a powerful motive for "conforming" among dissenting families in England. Many learned scholars refused to conform to the faith and practice of the Anglican Church and settled in towns sufficiently distant from London to be relatively safe following the great expulsion of 1660. Thus, to a degree, the Anglicans "blew their brains out" with the expulsion of scholarly dissenters (as a Congregationalist historian was later to say of the American Unitarian expulsion) creating creative aggregates of scholars to found and person the dissenting academies.

As the son of a non–subscribing Congregational clergyman Isaac Watts had already in his youth tried his hand at hymn writing, rejecting the popular conviction that the psalms were the only source of holy song, and noting that the psalms were often full of unchristian sentiments like vengeance. He became a scholar, preacher and linguist, but his more than 800 hymns sealed his fame. His first hymnbook was *Hymns and Spiritual Songs* published in 1707, followed later by *The Psalms of David imitated in the language of the New Testament,* the "Watts Psalms" which became a standard, and which amended several of the psalms with added Christian verses. Not being a musician he matched his creations to familiar and popular folk tunes, and thus a revolution in hymnody was set in motion on both sides of the Atlantic. But it required in New England giving up the theological prejudice that only the purest psalms were proper for worship, a prejudice that Liberal Christians and Unitarians fairly quickly found natural to give up. Thus Watts became quickly popular among

---

ers following the Toleration Act," unpublished paper, (London,1999), by Dr. David Wykes.

liberals, but in opening that door set hymn writing ablaze, just as quickly throwing his own works, and political and theological particularities into shadow among the liberals. If one could faithfully edit and create hymns then Watts could be edited, as John Wesley immediately set out to do, and new hymns and hymnals were everywhere possible.

Watts opened up a world of worship, but it was the Wesleys who put hymn singing in the center of it. Charles Wesley, prolific poet and hymn writer, with more than 6500 hymns to his credit, breathed into his hymns a radiant and personal faith. Though an Anglican clergyman with no interest in creating a separate church, he was with his brother, however reluctantly the founder of The Methodist Episcopal Church, and his fervent evangelical zeal moved within and without his movement through the grace and power of his hymns. Who can imagine a hymnal without, "Love Divine, All Loves Excelling, Joy of Heaven to earth come down?" Few, certainly, except the Unitarian Universalist hymnal commission that created *Singing The Living Tradition*. John Wesley, a competent if much less prolific hymn writer, a stirring evangelist and theologian, beautifully edited both Watts and his brother, among many others, while bitterly protesting those who would lay vile hands on another's sacred work. Universalists James Relly, and soon John Murray, began their religious careers surrounded by this fountainhead of spiritual song.

We have referred to the Anabaptist heritage, and the enduring Mennonite hymnal, *Ausbund*. That heritage continued in several religious bodies including the Mennonites, Moravians, Dunkers, Schwenkfelders, Bretheren and eventually the Baptists, though much attenuated in the latter. But it came relatively directly to these shores through all but forgotten German pietists including universalist, Johannes Kelpius (1673–1708), a mystic, musician and hymn writer who settled with his small band of hermits on the Wissahickon in 1694. They may have been the first in the Americas to own an organ, and to accompany their hymn singing with instrumental music.[19] The Organ was used in ordaining one of their own, Justus Falckner, to the Swedish Lutheran ministry in November of 1703. The pietists on the Wissahickon also celebrated this occasion with "viols,

---

19 Charles W. Hughes, *American hymns old and New; Notes on the Hymns and Biographies of the Authors and Composers* (Vol 2), Columbia University Press, (New York, 1980), Vol 2, pp 456 – 457.

hautboys, trumpets and kettledrums."[20] Obviously non Biblical instruments were not a problem to them.

Johann Conrad Beissel (1690–1768), a passionate and persuasive universalist pietist, sought later to join this band, but finding it almost entirely dispersed, became the creator of the Community of Seventh Day Baptists, "Economy," a universalist semi–monastic community in Ephrata, Pennsylvania, on the Cocalico. Beissel, with his amazingly long lasting celibate order set in rural fastness, published his hymns, both words and music, most of his own personal creation, in *Das Gesang der Einsamen und Verlassenen Turtel–Taube*, in 1747.[21] The community sang "not only in four, but also in six, seven, and eight parts at a time" while the *Bay Psalm Book* had only two.[22] The *Turtel–Taube* was "the earliest substantial body of identifiable compositions in the American Colonies," according to Charles Hughes.[23] The *Turtel Taube* and the singing at Ephrata were familiar to George de Benneville who lived nearby in Olney and visited often, and possibly others closer to the rootage of organized Universalism.[24]

---

20 See *Three Centuries of American Hymnody* by Foote, pp 125–126.

21 "The Song of the solitary and forsaken Turtle–Dove"

22 See Hughes, *American Hymns (Vol 2)*, p 224. *American Hymns, Vol 1* includes one hymn by Beissel among the enduring and representative hymns of America. One of Beissel's hymns in his second hymnal, *Paradisisches Wunder–Spiel*, in 1766, contained 215 verses which surely must be a record. See *Three Centuries of American Hymnody*, by Foote, pp 129–132.

23 Hughes, *American Hymns*, (Vol 2), p 309.

24 This subject deserves much more scholarly attention. See David. A Johnson, "George de Benneville and the Radical Reformation," in the *Journal of the Universalist Historical Society*, Vol. XIII, (Boston, 1970), pp 25 – 43 for a discussion of de Benneville and Beissel.

British Unitarian Hymnody

"Where is your God?" they say.
Come not in flashing storm,
Or bursting cloud of thunder:
Come in the viewless form
Of wakening love and wonder;
To every waiting soul
Speak in thy still small voice,
Till broken love's made whole,
And saddened hearts rejoice.
James Martineau, 1805–1900

British Unitarian, and Universalist, history is outside the compass of this volume. We will not review the British hymnals, official and unofficial, but since we share many hymns we must pay attention to a few of the important English Unitarian hymn writers who appear in American Unitarian and Universalist hymnals.[1] Though British Unitarian hymnals of the late 1800s often had music, from 1900 on most such hymnals, until most recent years, have had no music, only suggesting tunes for the organist to follow, or not, as their or the congregation's taste might dictate. Thus British congregations using hymnals of earlier print find themselves where the American Unitarians and Universalists did (and Anglicans and Episcopalians much longer) until the practice of printing music in hymnals became popular following the American Civil War, indeed in some of the same ongoing confusion detailed in the preceding chapter.

---

1 It would be the height of foolishness and ingratitude not to notice *Hymns for Living* Lindsey Press (London, 1998), revised edition, and *Sing Your Faith,* the latest British Unitarian hymnals which gathered hymns from the best of British poets and authors, Unitarian and otherwise, and culled the American Unitarian tradition for current and long forgotten creations by Unitarian hymn writers. John A. Storey's hymns were thus made accessible (in the original 1985 edition) to the editors of *Singing the Living Tradition,* and many old hymns given new life.

Among the Unitarian hymn writers of England who achieved popularity across the Atlantic are these, along with their hymns that appeared in the Unitarian *New Hymn and Tune Book (NTB)*, 1914, the Unitarian and Universalist *Hymns of the Spirit (HOS)*, 1937, and *Hymns for the Celebration of Life (HCL)*, 1964. *Singing the Living Tradition* includes only one of these (Adams), apparently favoring contemporary British authors of limited skill, but untroubling theology:

	NTB	HOS	HCL
Sarah Fuller Flower Adams (1805–1848)			
"Nearer my God to Thee"	287	245	126
Anna Laetitia Aiken Barbauld (1743–1825)			
"Praise to God, Immortal Praise"	176	143	
Rev. Ambrose Nicholls Blatchford (1842–1925)			
"Softly the silent night"	151 vs 2 & 3		
"Within this temple reared of old"	506		
Sir John Bowring (1792–1872)			
"In the Cross of Christ I Glory"	213	190	
"Watchman , tell us of the night"	194	154	283
Rev. Stoppford Augustus Brooke (1832–1916)			
[Anglican–Unitarian]			
"Let the whole creation cry"	61	35	10
Rev. Thomas Wesley Freckleton (1827–1903)			
"O God, who workest hitherto"	227		
Rev. William Gaskell (1805–1884)			
"Calmly, calmly lay him down"	474	452	
"Press on, Press on Ye sons of Light"	370	315	
Rev. Edmund Geldart (1844–1885)			
"When the light of day is waning"	155		
Rev. Thomas Hornblower Gill (1819–1906)			
"We come unto our Father's God"	403	363	15
Samuel Greg (1804–1877)			
"Around my path life's mysteries"	254		
Rev. Henry Warburton Hawkes (1843–1917)			
"Thank we now the Lord of heaven"	197	172	290
"Amid the din of earthly strife"	230		
"Thou knowest, Lord!, thou know'st"	267		

	NTB	HOS	HCL
"Peace! Perfect peace!	275		
"'Thy kingdom come, O Lord,'"	386	333	
"Reveal thy truth, O Lord!	389	335	
"'Give us this day our daily bread'"	476		
"Our hymns are sung, our prayers"	509		
Rev. Brooke Herford (1830–1903)			
"Lead us Heavenly Father"	521		
Rev. John Page Hopps (1834–1911)			
"Father, lead me day by day"	523	479	
"Father, let thy kingdom come"	393	336	
"Hark, hark, my soul"	465	432	
"God of our fathers, hear our prayer"		505	
Rev. John Johns (1801–1847)			
"Come, kingdom of our God"	392	289	
Rev. James Martineau (1805–1900)			
"A voice upon the midnight air"		184	
"Where is your God they say?"	109	71	87
"Thy Way is in the Deep"	250	186	
Hon. Francis Albert R. Russell (1849–1914)			
"Christian rise and act thy creed"	337	282	
Rev. Thomas Saddler (1822–1891)			
"The Lord hath said, 'Seek ye my face"	245		
Rev. William George Tarrant (1853 –1928)			
"The light along the ages"	205	197	
"Draw nigh to God"	274		
"Now praise we great and famous men"	365		
"I saw the city of the Lord"	428	394	204
"With happy voices ringing"	519	478	
"The fathers built this city"	538	395	
"Marching with the heroes"	543	480	
Emily Taylor (1795–1872) [Unitarian–Anglican]			
"God of the changing year"	184		
"O here, if ever, God of love"	481		
John Taylor (1750–1826)			
"Lord, before thy presence come"	31		

	NTB	HOS	HCL
"Like shadows gliding o'er the plain"	180		
"Lord, what offering shall we bring"	336	281	
Helen Maria Williams (1762–1827)			
"While Thee I seek protecting power"	304	255	
Rev. John Reynell Wreford (1800–1881)			
"Lord while for all mankind we pray"	425	390	
"When my love to God grows weak"		189	

Several characteristics stand out on this list of British Unitarian hymns published two generations ago and more, beyond the very religiously traditional character of most of the hymns as suggested in the titles. The list does not include all the then well known British Unitarian hymn writers, leaving out; Joseph Estlin Carpenter (Biblical scholar, Principal of Manchester College, Oxford), Andrew Chalmers (hymnologist and minister), William Johnson Fox (minister, reformer), Thomas Hinks (minister, scientific writer), and a few others, but it misses few. But the number of British Unitarian hymns even in the *New Hymn and Tune Book* is very small in comparison with the total number of hymns in that and in the successor American Unitarian hymnals, especially in *Hymns of the Spirit* (with 576 including extra tunes). And, as is clear from the listing, the number of British Unitarian hymns drastically falls through the century, except that *Singing the Living Tradition,* is enamored of one fairly pedestrian recent British Unitarian hymn writer. The British, on the other hand include more American Unitarian and Universalist hymns and hymn writers, especially in the recent *Sing Your Faith* than they do of their own, as well as including a hearty selection from Anglican and other sources in the British Isles and on the continent. Perhaps W. Garrett Horder who gathered the delightful *Treasury of American Sacred Song,* Oxford University Press [Amen Corner] (1900) was on the right track in quoting American Unitarian Rev. Thomas Wentworth Higginson in his preface, noting the need for "something with a little more buoyancy than the Englishman.... Put in one more drop of nervous fluid, and make the American." There was a special enthusiasm and appeal to the young new American Unitarian hymn writers which made some at least almost at once popular across the "big pond." But no one should slight the classic strength and beauty of the hymns of many British Unitarians. Earlier generations of Universalists and Unitarians vigorously valued these virtues and used British Unitarian hymns in significant numbers.

In the *New Hymn and Tune Book* and *Hymns of the Spirit* (1937), of course, are several of the most prominent British Unitarian hymnwriters, including Anna Laetitia Barbauld,[2] poet, writer, prolific hymnwriter of the Aiken family; John Bowring, linguist poet, MP, Governor of Hong Kong; William Gaskell, minister, writer, reformer; Thomas Hornblower Gill, vigorous hymnwriter who later left the Unitarians; Henry Warburton Hawkes, writer of "evangelical" hymns "admired by some sections of the Unitarian community."[3] Also included were John Page Hopps, minister, reformer, controversialist; John Johns, minister and reformer; James Martineau, Unitarian leader, minister, academic, Principal of Manchester New College, London; Francis Albert Rollo Russell, aristocrat and meteorologist; William George Tarrant, minister and prolific writer of hymns for adults and children; John Taylor, hymnwriter and wool merchant; and John Reynell Wreford, minister and popular hymnwriter. It is clear that the hymnbook commissions which created the *New Hymn and Tune Book* and *Hymns of the Spirit* were trying to create hymnals that recognized a wider liberal religious world than just the United States (though they included only one Canadian Unitarian, Hon. Robert Stanley Weir, who wrote "Oh Canada" and adapted "O Come all ye faithful."). And *Hymns of the Spirit's* creators clearly took a new look at British Unitarian hymnody — including two hymns not in the *New Hymn and Tune Book*, though old enough to have been included. This looking back for what might have been missed is something later Unitarian Universalist hymnbook commissions have hardly done — to their detriment. The heady assortment of classic British Unitarian hymns listed above in *Hymns of the Spirit* shrinks, as is painfully apparent, to seven in *Hymns for the Celebration of Life*, and all but disappears in *Singing the Living Tradition*, except for Sarah Fuller Flower Adams' "Nearer my God to Thee."[4] There is also in *Singing the Living Tradition* a much too large new collection of Andrew

---

2 We look forward to a proper biography of her at the hands of Judith Walker–Riggs who has worked for years on Barbauld's story.

3 Notes on Authors in *Hymns of Faith and Freedom*, Chalice Press (London, 1991), p lii.

4 "Part in Peace" is also in *Singing the Living Tradition*, edited and submitted by this author.

Storey's mediocre work, and little else of the hymnodic creativity of Unitarians in the British Isles. This seems especially unfortunate given new and old hymnodic efforts in Scotland, Ireland, and the large newer Welsh Unitarian hymnal. The vision of this newest hymnal commission was in no way the large, inclusive liberal religious vision of *Hymns of the Spirit* or of the British *Hymns of Faith and Freedom*, or its predecessor *Hymns of Worship* (revised), though it does include some world Unitarian and other sources, mostly edited and changed beyond recognition, or left untranslated in tongues unknown.[5]

---

5   Translations were promised but did not appear in *Between the Lines; Sources for Singing the Living Tradition*, Skinner House Books (Boston, 1995). The new *Singing the Journey* includes hymns with both verses in the original languages and translations.

American Universalist Beginnings

Yes, while adoring hosts proclaim
Love is the nature, love the name,
My soul, in rapture cries the same;
God is Love, God is Love.

Thomas Whittemore, Universalist leader,
hymn writer, composer

The first hymnal in the mainstream of American Universalism was a reprint of James and John Relly's British Universalist hymnal, *Christian Hymns, Poems and Sacred Songs, sacred to the praise of God, our Savior,* printed in Burlington, New Jersey in 1776, reprinted again in 1782 by Noah Webster in Portsmouth, New Hampshire with five hymns added, authored by John Murray (1741-1815). William Billings composed several tunes for Relly's texts. How many were in the limited repertoire of tunes played on the old barrel organ (ten, was their total reported repertoire) in Gloucester, Massachusetts, is not known. Murray and his new wife, Judith Sargent Murray continued to write hymns for many uses and occasions, but none survived into common Universalist or other hymnody.

Elhanan Winchester, Junior, (1751-1797) early fiery and persuasive preacher of Universalism, was also a competent hymn writer. His *Thirteen Hymns Suited to the Present Time* (1776) contained popular patriotic hymns attuned to the revolutionary cause.[1] Silas Ballou (1753-1837), a Universalist layman, hymn writer of the soon to be prominent Universalist family of Ballous, published his early hymnal under the all inclusive title of; *New Hymns on Various Subjects, viz: On the Creation of the World; and the Formation of Man - the State wherein He was Created, and his Sad and Shameful Fall. On the Early and Extensive Promises of God - the Coming of Christ, and the Completion of the Father's Promises: or, the Eternal Redemption and Victorious Salvation of Mankind Through Him,* published in Worcester,

---

1   One, "Let tyrants shake their iron rod," matched appropriately with a Billings tune, appears in Eugene Navias, *Singing Our History,* UUA (Boston, 1975), a useful resource for many of the older Universalist and Unitarian hymns, reset generally to familiar and singable music.

23

Massachusetts in 1785, a hymnal of his own authorship and creation. It went into a second edition twelve years later, and some hymns endured to other hymnals. This tour de force was followed by two hymnals published in 1792, one by Elhanan Winchester Jr's Philadelphia Universal Baptists, *Evangelical Psalms, Hymns and Spiritual Songs, Selected from Various Authors,* and published by a Committee of the Convention of the Churches believing in the "Restitution of All Men," (Proverbs CXVII) met in Philadelphia, May 25, 1791, Thomas Dobson (Philadelphia, 1792), including 35 of Silas Ballou's hymns. The second was *Psalms, Hymns and Spiritual Songs: Selected and Original: Designed for the use of the Church Universal, in public and private devotion,* edited by George Richards, Munroe & Francis (Boston, 1802) including 52 hymns by the prolific Universalist schoolmaster and minister, George Richards (1755-1814) who briefly served the church in Boston in 1791. The hymnal has no attributions to its 417 hymns. It seemed personal and inappropriate aggrandizement to label hymns with their authors, as if holy worship was somehow sponsored by persons, or a contest of favorites. Richards also published another hymnal, *A Collection of Hymns designed for the use of Universal Churches,* and a, second enlarged edition in 1806, in Dover, New Hampshire. The departure of Universalists from an exclusive use of psalms shows in every hymnal, as does the search for American tunes to match the words. There was no hunger for the excellence of British and European liturgical music, but on the contrary a hunger for music rooted on these shores, enthusiastic and moving, more akin to the Methodists and Baptists than the Unitarians.

The first somewhat official Universalist hymnal was the *Universalist Hymns composed by different authors, by order of the General Convention of Universalists of the New England States and others,* of 1808, edited by Hosea Ballou (109 hymns included), Abner Kneeland, Edward Turner, and, according to hymnologist, minister, historian Henry Wilder Foote (II), Sebastian Streeter.[2] Abner Kneeland, before his departure from the Universalists and before his blasphemy conviction, edited a hymnal for the Philadelphia Church called simply, *The Philadelphia Hymn Book; or a Selection of Sacred poetry*

---

2 "Catalogue of American Universalist Hymn Writers and Hymns; Compiled for the Hymn Society of America," by Henry Wilder Foote (II), Cambridge, Massachusetts, 1959, p 4.

consisting of Psalms and Hymns, Clark & Roger (Philadelphia, 1819). It contained 731 hymns, mostly grounded in good British authors and American liberal contemporaries, including Barbauld, just recently published. It was followed in swift succession by a host of others. Ballou and Turner created a large new hymnal, *The Universalist Hymn Book: A New Collection of Psalms and Hymns for the use of Universalist Societies,* in 1821, intended to meet the theological need of Universalists not to be oppressed by hymns with theological affirmations far from the loving Gospel they declared, yet full of evangelical fervor and hope. Here are 578 hymns, broadly gathered from existing Universalist hymnals, and both Isaac Watts and Jeremy Belknap, including proper attributions. It went through many printings. Henry Wilder Foote's list of Universalist hymnals (with this author's notes) continues:

> *Christian Hymns adapted to the worship of God our Savior*
> Boston, 1823.

> *The New Hymn Book designed for Universalist Societies*
> by Sebastian and Russell Streeter, Boston, 1829. This book
> reached a 35th edition in 1845. The brothers Streeter were
> evangelical enthusiasts and sought to create a hymnbook of
> joyful hymns, fully expressive of the hopes of Universalist
> faith.

> *A Collection of Psalms and Hymns for the use of Universalist Societies
> and Families,* by Hosea Ballou, 2nd, Boston, 1839. This book
> was widely used in Universalist circles.[3]

This last one was also the first of the hymnals in this list that broke away from the practice of publishing a long complement of one's own hymns, and began more aggressively to look to the wider world of hymn writers, within and outside the Universalist fold. Including all the obvious Universalist hymn writing contemporaries, and a thoughtful culling of wider American hymnody, Hosea Ballou II drew carefully and well from the best British hymnody past and present. There is a heady collection of Watts, of course, and Phillip Doddridge (1702-1751), William Cowper (1731-1800) and Timothy Dwight (1752-1817). Unitarians like Sir John Bowring, and Anna Laetitia Barbauld are well included, as are many other women on both sides of the Atlantic. Ballou's preface bespeaks

---

3 Foote, p 4.

the polemical era of this hymnal: "It has been my wish to exclude, on the one hand, all effeminate, insipid nicety — Every thing in which cordiality and fervor are sacrificed to formal correctness; and on the other, all downright awkwardness, fondling endearments, puerile sentimentality, and rant." The aggressive evangelical era of Universalism was still in full swing in this hymnal, despite its conventional appearance to later eyes. It should also be noted that Ballou, like his prominent namesake, continued to select verses and edit texts to serve the theological and worship needs of Universalists, but noted as others often did not hymns in which he had made changes, except where the author was unknown.

Hosea Ballou II (1796-1861) was a minister, scholar, editor and sometime hymn writer. A popular editor of Universalist papers and journals, he urged formal ministerial education, an unpopular cause among some Universalists - and Methodists and Baptists - and became President of Tufts University, where a Universalist theological school was finally established in 1869. His authorship of the *Ancient History Of Universalism*, in 1829, gained him membership on the Harvard Board of Overseers and an Honorary Doctor of Divinity from Harvard, not bad for one whose father forbade him to go to college because of feared religious proselytizing.[4] He also served on the Massachusetts Board of Education in the heady Horace Mann era.

---

4 *American Hymns Old and New*, Vol II, p 304. This delightful volume contains biographical and hymn sketches for the writers, composers and hymns in Vol. 1. It is an invaluable resource.

American Unitarian Beginnings

Now to the Lord a noble song!
Awake, my soul, awake my tongue!
Hosanna to the eternal name,
And all his boundless love proclaim.

Isaac Watts, 1674
(who late in life became a Unitarian)

American Unitarian hymnody began quite differently. The Liberal Christians of the post revolutionary era were well aware of British sources, and much new hymnody there was already long in print. Count Zinzendorf and Rev. John Gambord printed an English version of their hymns, *A Collection of Hymns of the Children of God in all ages, from the beginning until now,* in London in 1754. John and Charles Wesley in 1756 published their *Hymns and Spiritual Songs, intended for the use of real Christians, of all denominations,* including some of the beautiful Moravian hymns and music of which they had become aware. The Brethren put their *English Collection of Hymns* to the press in 1769. The *Olney Hymns,* edited by John Henry Johannson followed a decade later. And Unitarian Theophilus Lindsey had sent *A Collection of Hymns and Psalms for Public Worship* to the press in London in 1774. The transformation of psalmody to hymnody was well underway in England before Evangelical Liberal Christians (and proto Unitarians) across the Atlantic struggled with the change. It was not without missteps though. *A Selection of Psalms and Hymns for Private and Social Worship* created by Thomas Belsham and J. Kentish for the Gravel Pit Meeting, Joseph Priestley's old congregation was initially turned down by the congregation in 1798. Perhaps its wide cast net of sources was a bit frightening, including as it did many hymns by six different women, almost all of Anna Laetitia Barbauld's hymns, the largest number of hymns by Anne Steele. There were many hymns from Doddridge, a couple from Samuel and John Wesley, but not Charles, by far the better hymn writer, others from new sources of many kinds, including an irenic hymn against war and for the growth of mutual love by

Dr. Aiken. Thus English dissenters were already well along the path New England liberals began to follow in the closing years of the eighteenth century.

The first to break the mold of psalms alone in New England as we have noted, in print at least, was the small *Collection of Hymns - designed for the use of the West Society of Boston,* in 1783, including psalms, and hymns by authors domestic and British, none identified. The editor is assumed to be Simeon Howard, minister of the church since Jonathan Mayhew's untimely death. Anna Laetitia Barbauld, the excellent and popular British Unitarian hymn writer appears, along with other well known British dissenters. This hymnal was followed among the Liberal Christian, proto Unitarians, in 1788 by Salem East Church's *A Collection of Hymns for Publick Worship,* edited by William Bentley, the minister. It was an excellent selection of hymns then available in English. Jeremy Belknap (1744-1798), minister of Federal Street Church in Boston, predecessor to William Ellery Channing, was the next to challenge the prevailing prejudice. Belknap was the respected author of the *History of New Hampshire* in three volumes (1784-1792), and a forceful opponent of the slave trade. Having written a biography of Isaac Watts, he turned to publish a new book of *Sacred Poetry: consisting of Psalms and Hymns adapted to Christian Devotion in public and private,* in 1795, a hymn and psalm book that achieved wide currency, several editions, among Liberal Christian congregations in and around Boston. He introduced the already vastly popular British hymn writer, Anne Steele including a moving tribute — to her alone — in his preface, and "hymns by Addison, Cowper, Newton, Doddridge,"[1] Merrick, a good group of hymns from the *Liverpool Collection* and most other extant recent British hymnals. His preface well reveals the difference in spirit between the proto Unitarian Liberal Christians and the Universalist Hosea Ballou II - discussed in the last section. Belknap criticizes Watts for using earthly imagery, "epithets and allusions...applied to the Savior, with a license disgusting to the spirit of devotion." Belknap carefully edited out such things to serve more wholly "the chaste and awful spirit of devotion."[2] He also carefully separated psalms from hymns, even sep-

---

1   "American Unitarian Hymn Writers and Hymns Compiled by Henry Wilder Foote (II) for the Hymn Society of America," Cambridge, Massachusetts, 1959, p 2.

2   *Sacred Poetry: Consisting of Psalms and Hymns Adapted to Christian Devotion in Public and Private, Thomas and Andrews and West and Blake,* (Boston, 1812) by Jeremy Belknap,

arate indexes. Some editions included a supplement, *Hymns for the Lord's Supper, selected and original,* later a separate hymn book, by Thaddeus M. Harris, minister of First Church in Dorchester (very soon Unitarian). Communion hymns, interestingly, were a driving force behind the creation and use of new hymnals, as differentiated from psalm books, for there were no psalms at all that seemed appropriate for the Lord's Supper (or Christmas and Easter), and thus even in some churches opposed to hymnody, new hymns for this purpose could be introduced, or psalms rewritten with Christian interpolations, as by Isaac Watts and others.

Henry Wilder Foote (II) tells of the impatient vestry of Trinity Church Boston, tired of waiting for the new hymnal of the General Convention of the Protestant Episcopal Church in America, in 1808 turning to create a hymnal of their own, leaning on Jeremy Belknap's work. They noted in their preface, "In this selection we are chiefly indebted to Dr. Belknap, whose book unquestionably contains the best expressions of sacred poetry extant."[3] Belknap himself contributed several hymns, well wrought but sufficiently antique in expression not to survive long in common usage. James Freeman (1759-1835), minister of King's Chapel during and for long after the American Revolution, turned to the creation of a *Collection of Psalms and Hymns,* to succeed the ancient version in use there for almost a century, in 1799. Freeman was a very competent hymn writer though few of his hymns have endured. Both of these hymnals drew heavily on the psalms, as recast by Tate and Brady whose psalm book was probably the most used in churches of the Standing Order in the first third of the 19th century.

Henry Wilder Foote, the second's, comprehensive list of Liberal Christian and Unitarian hymnals for the next few decades can only be summarized here,[4] with a few notes by this author.[5]

A Collection of Psalms and Hymns, by Rev. William Emerson, First Church Boston, Boston, 1808.[6] The father of Ralph Waldo Emerson was

---

Preface.

3   Quoted in Foote, "Unitarian Hymn Writers and Hymns," p 2.

4   See Foote, "Unitarian Hymn Writers and Hymns," pp 1 - 36.

5   Many of these hymnals suggest that they were created for the use of a single local church, but almost all were in fact used in several churches, as churches sought hymnals that met the religious needs of their people.

6   It included the name of a suggested tune for each selection, the first to do so. Foote, in "Unitarian Hymn Writers and Hymns" includes the collections of tunes and where the

sharply denounced for omitting "most of the capital doctrines of the Gospel," a common criticism as Liberals recreated texts to less narrow use.

A Selection of sacred Poetry consisting of Psalms and Hymns from Watts, Dodderidge, Merrick, Scott, Cowper, Barbauld, Steele and others, edited by Ralph Eddowes and James Taylor of First Unitarian Church in Philadelphia, 1812.[7]

Hymns for the Lord's Supper, by Thaddeus Mason Harris, Boston, 1821.

A Collection of Psalms and Hymns, for social and private worship, edited by Dr. Henry D. Sewall, New York, 1820.[8]

A Selection of Psalms and Hymns, for social and private worship, edited by Jonathan Peele Dabney, Andover, 1821.[9]

A Collection of Psalms and Hymns for Social and Private Worship, compiled by a committee of the West Parish in Boston, Boston, 1823.

A Selection from Tate and Brady's Version of the Psalms: with Hymns by various authors, for the church in Brattle Square, Boston, 1825.

Sacred Poetry and Music reconciled, or a Collection of Hymns original and compiled, by Samuel Willard, Boston, 1830.

A Collection of Psalms and Hymns for Christian Worship, edited by Francis William Pitt Greenwood, King's Chapel, Boston, 1830. Known as "Greenwood's Collection," it went to 50 editions, introducing many new American and British hymnwriters, and Charles Wesley appears here to the Unitarians for the first time.

The Springfield Collection of Hymns for sacred worship, edited by William Bourne Oliver Peabody (whose twin brother William Oliver Bourne Peabody was also a hymnwriter), Springfield, Massachusetts, 1835. Included many new Unitarian authors. This collection was very popular among Unitarians.

---

suggested tune might be found, p 8.

7   The lay editors of this hymnal for the historic church of Joseph Priestley, then led by Rev. William Henry Furness, an outspoken opponent of slavery, drew heavily from the published British collections of prominent dissenters. It went through several editions for more than 30 years.

8   For what is today All Souls Church, New York City. It is remembered for having included 5 hymns by later member, William Cullen Bryant, without his permission. It has been known as "The New York Collection." It went through several editions, that of 1845 enlarged significantly.

9   There were two subsequent editions.

The Christian Psalter: A Collection of Psalms and Hymns for social and private worship, edited by William Parsons Lunt, Boston, 1841. Lunt, minister in Quincy included 22 pieces by parishioner John Quincy Adams, who had completed a full metrification of the psalms.

A Manual of Prayer for public and private worship, with a collection of hymns, edited by William Greenleaf Eliot, Unitarian minister in St. Louis, Missouri, Boston, 1842.

A Collection of Hymns, for the Christian Church and Home, edited by James Flint, minister of East Church in Salem, Boston, 1843. Much borrowed from Dr. James Martineau's British Unitarian hymnal of 1840.

The Social Hymn Book: consisting of psalms and hymns for social worship and private devotions, edited by Chandler Robbins, minister of Second Church in Boston, Boston, 1843. Begins to draw from the Oxford Movement's recapture and translation of hymns from the Roman breviary. Has a brief appendix of tunes.

The Disciples' Hymn Book; a collection of hymns and chants for public and private devotions, prepared for use of the Church of the Disciples, edited by James Freeman Clarke, Boston, 1844. Introduces recent English hymns including Sarah Flower Adams, "Nearer, my God, to thee," and some of Clarke's own workmanlike hymns.

Christian Hymns for public and private worship. A Collection compiled by a committee of the Cheshire Pastoral Association, edited by Abiel Abbott Livermore, Levi Leonard, William Whitwell, Curtis Cutler all of New Hampshire, 1844. It was an amazingly inclusive collection, with much new and many hymns by women. It was also one of the most popular hymnals for more than a generation.

A Collection of Psalms and Hymns for the Sanctuary, edited by George Ellis, minister in Charlestown, Massachusetts, Boston, 1845, including psalms for responsive reading.

Hymns for Public Worship, edited by George Briggs, Boston, 1845. Hymns of inner spiritual life.

Service Book: for the Church of the Savior, with a collection of Psalms and Hymns for Christian Worship, edited by Robert Cassie Waterston, Boston, 1845. This was Greenwood, with several new additions.

This exhausting list is not complete for the gathering and printing of hymnals was easy in an era that had not yet thought of writers' properties and royalties and when printing was relatively cheap. One should not assume too easily that the many hymn books created for a given congregation were only used there. Most of the hymnals that appear local above traveled to other congregations and influenced the larger course of Unitarian hymnody. Many clergy, especially Universalists, created hymnals for local use and for sale on itinerant journeys, and there were hymnals for special purposes. One of these that Foote missed in his list above is *Coldwater Melodies* by John Pierpont, Theodore Abbott printer (Boston, 1843) a small, paperbound, surprisingly well chosen and written, albeit fiery temperance songbook, of which there were many, but not many Unitarian creations. There was also one *Anti-Slavery Hymns*, a small book edited by George Stacy, who preached to both Universalist and Unitarian congregations, printed at the Hopedale Community of Adin Ballou.

What stands out from Foote's intimidating list is not easy to generalize. One is instantly aware of the tremendous resources that individual churches with their ministers poured into these collections, almost all directed initially toward a single church or small group of congregations. One wonders if these hearty individualists could not have made common cause a bit more often and combined their efforts. But most cut some new ground the others did not entirely see. There is a swift and progressive transformation from the preponderance of psalms toward hymns, first from abroad, later inclusive of local and living authors, still later culling carefully British and Continental collections of Christian hymns. Hymns created by women, present from the outset, begin to multiply swiftly, most especially in the *Cheshire Collection*. What was in the environment up there in the hills of New Hampshire that made them so progressive?

Meters, and occasional musical instructions are given. Where tunes are mentioned only one is suggested for each hymn. Indexes appear and hymn writers not at first identified at all have last names, and eventually full names, making identification much easier. Many of the earliest hymnals did not note authors, for this seemed an arrogant personalizing of the Godly work of writing hymns. Sources broaden geographically, historically and in the contemporary era.

Less visible in Foote's simple chronological listing is the increasing editing occurring among the hymns, the removal of verses and conflating others, the change of phrase, the re-creation of hymns. It is an old Unitarian and Universalist prejudice, widely shared by religionists of other persuasions, that Unitarians and Universalists are particularly shameless in their recasting hymns in new and unwonted directions. Isaac Watts, no Unitarian or Universalist in his early years, took his recasting of psalms in new directions their authors surely never intended and interpolated Christian verses.[10] More serious recasting is hard to imagine. Henry Wilder Foote was wont to observe that *The Book of Psalms* was perhaps the most thoroughly tinkered hymnbook in all history."[11] Watts was one of a mighty host. Sarah Flower Adams' "Nearer, my God, to thee" has been reprinted by generations of Christian hymnodists with a narrowly Christian verse she never wrote. "Praise to the Living God" or "The God of Abraham, Praise" is in even the newest hymnals reprinted with Christian verses, far from its Jewish origins. The trinity began to disappear from hymns in Liberal use, as did fierce threats of an unfortunate fate in the life to come for impenitent and recalcitrant unbelievers, especially among Universalists of course. We may on occasion lament with John Wesley the heavy hand of the editor, and cry for others to leave hymns alone, as he pled;

> ...I desire, they would not attempt to mend them: for they really are not able. None of them is able to mend either the sense or the verse. Therefore, I must beg of them one of these two favors: either to let them stand just as they are, to take them for better or worse; or to add the true reading in the margin, or at the bottom of the page; that we may no longer be accountable either for the nonsense or the doggerel of other men.[12]

Sadly, such counsel, at least in noting clearly amendments, is not regularly taken much of anywhere; nowhere is it less taken than in *Singing the*

---

10 Watts toward the end of his life moved toward Unitarian convictions, and fruitlessly sought to return his psalms to their Jewish origins, removing Christian interpolations. The publishers were not interested in his changed convictions.
11 "Henry Wilder Foote, Hymnologist," by Arthur Foote 2nd, in *The Papers of the Hymn Society*, XXVI, Rev. Alfred B. Haas, Editor, Hymn Society of America (New York City, 1968), p 15.
12 *A Collection of Hymns*, by John Wesley (London, 1779), preface, p 5.

Living Tradition. But no more forceful editor existed than John Wesley, who did not take his own counsel. Nor did James Montgomery, another contemporary who bitterly complained of incompetent hymn editors till he became one. The Wesleys, he angrily declared, "used a very free hand in altering, rearranging and amending the verses of other writers."[13]

By the early eighteen hundreds, the Standing Order showed "an increasing disfavor for American compositions," musicologists suggest, "and a steady desire for the latest importations from Europe is in vogue."[14] But, as John Andrew Johnson, Harvard Musicologist suggests, there were other voices. "John Pierce, a well educated and musically astute minister in the Commonwealth of Massachusetts in the first half of the 19th century, mentions several American composers in his Musical Diary" from his Harvard student days; Samuel Holyoke, James Lyon, Lewis Edson, Sr., Daniel Read and Samuel Arnold, whose works comprise half of the compositions he records, the other half being European.[15] The diary appears to have been created to preserve tunes Pierce wanted for singing in worship, for at that time he could countenance no other instrumental music in worship, and was deeply suspicious of secular music. He apparently, as others of his day and faith, championed "both European music of 'good taste' side by side with the most rough hewn of American compositions."[16] There is much for the musicologist to research here.

---

13 Arthur Foote (II), p 15.
14 "John Pierce's Musical Diary (HUD 6793), *An Example of 'Reform' Psalmody at Harvard, 1789 - 1793,*" by John Andrew Johnson, April, 1994, (unpublished paper), p 3.
15 John Andrew Johnson, p 6.
16 John Andrew Johnson, p 10.

Mid 19th Century Universalist Hymnody

We sing the bright and Morning Star,
The dayspring of eternal love!....
More bright and beauteous it will grow,
As onward still [its] way [it] wends:
In heav'n its beams forever glow,
Where light with life in glory blends.

Abel Charles Thomas,
hymn writer and publisher

Organized Universalism dates in institutional form from 1793 and the Convention of Universalists of the New England States, who had a semi official hymnal created by committee in 1808, and a flood of ideosyncratic hymnic creations soon thereafter. But Universalist hymnody's coming of age was not until the 1830's and 1840's. We have already noted the more inclusive hymnbook of Hosea Ballou II of that day, but two concerns were coming into play for the Universalists that would take them in quite new and different directions. One was the Sunday School movement, so passionately forwarded by Universalists, involving a tide of Sunday school songbooks, some of them by leading Universalist hymn writers[1]. The other was the eruption into Universalist life of a competent musician, minister who became a Universalist leader and editor as well. Thomas Whittemore, editor of "The Trumpet" labored with recalcitrant Universalists towards singing societies, choirs, anthems and other "popish impositions," as some called them. Seven Universalist Sunday School songbooks were published between 1837 and 1850, and more thereafter. Most of the songs sound moralistic and sentimental, sometimes theologically heavy handed and morbid. Some of the songs however are good, and even fun, and once in awhile the songbooks introduce hymns that later migrate to regular hymnbooks. Sylvannus Cobb, Universalist min-

---

1   See the listing of Sunday School song and hymnbooks in the Appendix.

ister, evangelist, scholar, trainer of young ministers, also produced his *Family Singing Book,* in 1848, one of many hymnals for home and conference use to appear through the rest of the century, among Universalists, and to a lesser degree, Unitarians. The most popular Universalist children's collection was *The Sabbath School Melodist: A Collection of Hymns and Tunes designed for the Sabbath School and the Home,* by John Greenleaf Adams, a very competent hymn writer, and published – as noted – with music, much especially for children by the Universalist Publishing House (Boston, [1870]). Much music was from the "Sweet Singer" and there are some gentle pieces by Sarah Flower Adams, and Phebe Hanaford among others.

Thomas Whittemore (1800–1860), was a forceful, opinionated minister, editor, denominational leader, controversialist, musician, hymn writer and composer, publisher. He published the Streeter brothers' hymnal in 1828, before publishing his own works, which include;

> *Songs of Zion,* 1837.
>
> *The Gospel Harmonist,* 1841 – hymn and anthem music and texts for choirs and musicians.
>
> *Conference Hymns and Tunes,* 1842 – an evangelical songbook for Universalists. And a second Conference Hymns and Tunes, 1843, often bound together with the First.
>
> *The Sunday School Choir and Superintendent's Assistant,* 1845 – a first for Universalists.

Whittemore became a tireless evangelist of Universalist faith and Universalist singing. As editor of the Universalist's major paper, The Trumpet, he had a "bully pulpit" for pressing his love of evangelical Universalist song, and all of his other religious passions and convictions. He was an editor with an agenda and he didn't mind a little censorship to keep the peace. Naturally it didn't work very well in the long run with independent minded Universalists.

The next public hymnal of Universalists was by Quaker born Abel Charles Thomas[2] that first included tunes on the page with texts, *Hymns of Zion,* with appropriate music designed as an aid to Christian devotion in families, social circles, and meetings for public worship, by An

---

2 See hymn – quote at the beginning of this chapter for a taste of Thomas' elegant hymn style, from his Hymns of Zion.

Evangelist, Thomas, Cowperthwait & Co. (Philadelphia, 1839)[3]. Going through six editions, it did include music of a wide variety, mostly domestic (much with rousing choruses, for every hymn), placed at the top of the page or on the facing page. Since it was unique among Universalists, indeed Christians at large, in this, the very presence of the music may have been an impediment to the book's usage, coercing congregations to use Thomas' choices of tunes (for many Thomas gave multiple choices). Few hymns beyond the compiler's 33 contributions are even initialed as to authorship. And the editor proudly claims in the Preface that he had "disregarded the originals wherever departure from them appeared desirable. Extensive alterations have been made," he declared, "in imagery, expression, rhythm and rhyme." He also excised verses in his disfavor and composed new ones – all of which makes the identification of authorship of these hymns often a bit dicey. The hymnal includes a vigorous collection from other collections; Wesley, Watts, Tate & Brady, Rippon, surely the best of the British including on the liberal end Helen Maria Williams, Anna Laetitia Barbauld, Sir John Bowring, and in the Christian mainstream; Heber, Montgomery, Grant, Toplady, Seagrave and Newton, and the Welshman William Williams. Rev. John Fawcett's, "Blest be the tie that binds is here and Robert Robinson's "Come Thou fount of every blessing" and a heady collection of Americans, with lots of contemporary Universalists among the 578 hymns crammed into this tiny volume. The *Hymns of Zion* also includes the Thomas Olivers version of the old Jewish "Yigdal" to the traditional tune Leoni without Olivers' Christian verses. This hymnal unfortunately suffered from bad timing. It responded well to the heady new British authors of many religious connections, and the first generation or so of enthusiastic hymn writers on these shores, but it was sent to the printer on the cusp of some of the most vigorous domestic hymn writing, not yet available to him. Further, the about to be most popular of pre Civil War Universalist hymnals was already in the works – *Hymns for Christian Devotion*. Abel Charles Thom-

---

3   Thus, unfortunately, Denis M. Weber's otherwise excellent, "The Transition of the Cantus Firmus from the Tenor to the Soprano in Anglo–American Hymnody," in The Hymn, A Journal of Congregational Song, Vol. 51, No. 3, July, 2000, The Hymn Society in the United States and Canada, is incorrect on page 20 in claiming that the first hymnal to print words and music alongside each other was W.H. Blew's Congregational Hymn and Tune Book of 1852.

as was barely thirty when he assembled his labor of love, having been in the ministry already a decade, and a leading controversialist, theologian and evangelist. His own hymns here are crisply drawn, well shaped, and in these early years somewhat polemical and directed toward the larger heavenly faith and hope of Universalists. In later years his hymns cast a wider net.

Also, later, by Abel C. Thomas there was an unusual volume printed under the "direction of the General Convention of Universalists, *The Gospel Liturgy*; a Prayer–Book for Churches, Congregations and Families, Henry Lyon (New York, 1858). It was not really a prayerbook but a comprehensive book of liturgy for worship, public anniversaries, funerals, weddings, christenings, dedications of teachers, and more. Others had published pieces of liturgy, but this was the first comprehensive creation of liturgies for Universalists. It was also a hymnal containing close to 300 hymns and some excellent recommended tunes in the back. It showed a rich mining of British hymn sources including particularly Unitarians Barbauld and Bowring, and others as well, and, of course, some of Thomas' own best later hymns.

The great Universalist hymnal of the first half of the nineteenth century was *Hymns for Christian Devotion,* Boston, 1845, edited by John Greenleaf Adams (1818 – 1887) and William Hubbell Chapin (1814 – 1880), distinguished ministers and respectable hymn writers. It was a large and inclusive volume with some 1008 hymns, but no music. A volume that size with music for all its hymns would be hard to lift on a Sunday morning. It included hymns of its editors and other popular Universalist hymn writers, but reached out to include several Unitarian hymns from the *Disciples Hymn Book*, just published, and the *Cambridge Unitarian Hymnbook*, "handed to us in sheets." James Russell Lowell, Timothy Flint, Theodore Parker, William Furness, Andrews Norton, William C. Bryant, Ralph Waldo Emerson, John Pierpont and John Weiss (still a Harvard Divinity School student), all relatively young Unitarians, some radical, appear in the hymnal, an amazingly inclusive spread of American Unitarians. John Bowring and Harriet Martineau (British Unitarians) and Jeanne Marie Bouvier de la Motte Guyon and many others of liberal sentiments were imported from abroad, as was Martin Luther. There are 59 hymns "on such 'philanthropic subjects' as human equality and rights; the care of widows, orphans and persons in public hospitals and asylums; temperance; abolition; the progress of freedom; the rehabilitation of prisoners; and universal peace."[4] "This was perhaps," Henry Wilder Foote wrote, "the most notable American Universalist collection published in the 19th century."[5] Doubtless the judgement is correct, until close to the end of the century when a very different hymnal appeared, I believe contesting the title, *Church Harmonies, New and Old.*

Rev. George Rogers, London born, Cincinnati based perennial Western itinerant evangelist of Universalism published an interesting small hymnal not unlike many others by individual clergy in several places, except in its solid quality, the *Universalist Hymn Book,* in Cincinnati, in 1845, containing some of his own fairly creditable hymns. It was said, by Universalists at least, that the Methodist circuit rider carried in his saddlebags Bibles and hymnbooks to sell, and perhaps a chicken he had purloined from a neighboring farm. Rogers wanted a hymnal small enough to carry in quantity and sell on his many journeys to support himself, like the Methodists (not including purloining chickens). He had to write it himself.

One digression in the story of hymns and hymnals will hopefully be forgiven, to mention the Hutchinson family which began its musical career in their hometown of Milford, New Hampshire, eleven children over parental objections, singing their hearts out with great presence and skill in 1839 – the Singing Hutchinsons. Their real beginning came earlier in the choir of the Milford Universalist Church. The numbers changed as gradually Hutchinson children took to the road, birthed families, conducted businesses, but the Singing Hutchinsons became a force and not just a musical one, stretching eventually over three generations of Hutchinsons. They met Frederick Douglass in Lynn, Massachusetts and had been won to the cause of anti–slavery. When the greatest orators of the day could not quiet the mobs that showed up for abolition meetings at Faneuil Hall in Boston, the Hutchinsons could instantly calm the crowd for as long as they sang. They traveled the country singing for every noble cause of that day, temperance, women's rights, prison reform, mental health reform, peace and more. They found themselves at home in

---

4   Navias, p 10.

5   Foote (II), "Universalist Hymns," p 4.

Unitarian as well as Universalist churches. Through the generations they sang under different names, with new voices of new generations joining. John Hutchinson, the last survivor of the original brothers and sisters sang at the close of his career at the Columbian Exposition in Chicago in 1893, still singing of patriotism, racial harmony, women's rights – he sang for Lucy Stone's memorial service – progress, freedom and peace.[6]

The *Hopedale Collection of Hymns and Songs,* for the use of practical Christians, edited by Adin Ballou, Hopedale, Massachusetts, 1849, was a vigorous and enthusiastic gathering of hymns, many from the Hopedale intentional community itself. Several women, two important women poets of Hopedale, Abby Hills Price and Mary Colburn, and activists of many stripes were well represented. It has a freshness and immediacy that speak through hymns like those of Abby Price, often matched to popular tunes of the day (but not in that hymnal which had no music). The opening verse, of three, of one of Ms Price's powerful hymns reads;

> In sweet southern vales where the orange trees blossom,
> Where fragrance and sun–light are poured over the plain;
> Where blessings are strew'd that might cheer every bosom,
> And beauty is lavished to banish all pain,
> Dark stains of oppression dim ev'ry fair flower,
> And sighs of the weary are heard in each bower,
> While groans of affliction mark ev'ry sad hour
> That passes away in the land of the slave!

"Why streams the rich sunlight o'er man's degradation? Why is mercy held out to this sin–hardened nation, that crushes God's image so low in the dust?"[7] cries the poet, hymn writer. Few took on slavery with such moving, contrasting images, in any hymnal. The Hopedale Collection's headings bespeak an interesting combination of spirituality and activism; devotional, Jesus Christ, warning and invitation, repentance and reformation, personal righteousness, meekness and humility, love, pity and forgiveness, contrite aspirations, joy, gratitude and praise, the glorious future, temperance, anti–slavery, Christian non–resistant peace, new

---

6 See *Harps in the Wind, The Story of the Singing Hutchinsons,* by Carol Brink, The Macmillan Co. (New York, 1947), and *Singin' Yankees,* by Philip D. Jordan, University of Minnesota Press (Minneapolis, 1946) for more about the family, and its long musical career.

7 *Hopedale Collection,* hymn 203.

social state, fidelity, zeal and progress, mournful and consolatory, conference meetings, and dismissions and farewells. The vision and hope, the faith and consolation of that community breath in these headings and the hymns within. Even William Lloyd Garrison appears, with Caroline Weston, one of the abolitionist Weston sisters, as hymn writers, the only place I've ever seen their hymns. Adin Ballou, the Practical Christian Socialist who created this hymnal complained in the preface of "lack of critical ability, leisure and money" to bring forth the hymnal he hoped, and doubtless he was absolutely correct. The day to day demands of running that long lasting and long successful community were a trial of energy, resources and spirit. We can sympathize with his prefatory note that the hymnal "is defective in quantity, quality, adaptation and execution," but, "it has its merits, whatever its defects, and will be useful in its place." Indeed there was never another like it, and it remains a testament and resource. Adin Ballou is usually credited with the enduring hymn, "Years are coming. Speed them onward." At least one verse of this hymn has been found attributed to an obscure English poet, calling this attribution into question – but as far as I know Adin Ballou never claimed it.

John Greenleaf Adams edited another hymnal in 1861, *The Gospel Psalmist, a collection of Hymns and Tunes,* trying to provide tunes which were missing from his great book edited with Edwin Hubbell Chapin. And in 1868 Adams published, *Vestry Harmonies,* matching more words to tunes. It was clear that music and hymns had to be printed together both for the musical neophyte and the musically literate. A ground cutting hymnal that should be mentioned in these years was the *Prayers and Hymns for the Church and Home,* edited by Edwin C. Bolles and Israel Washburne, New England Universalist Publishing House, (Boston, 1865). It was a Universalist take on the *Episcopal Book of Common Prayer* with an amazingly contemporary set of hymns attached. The classic Universalist authors are here, and pieces of the collections of James Martineau, and on these shores – the Presbyterians, the Methodists, the Episcopalians and even the Roman Catholics. Here too are Barbauld, Bowring, William Gaskell, Harriet Martineau (as her brother James), E.B. Browning and of course S.F. Adams. Americans included J.F. Clarke, E.H. Sears, W.C. Bryant, Eliza Follen, Alice Cary, Mary A.R. Livermore, O.W. Holmes, John Weiss and T.W. Higginson. It was an unusual collection. Universalist hymn writing and publishing began to diminish in these years just before, during and immediately after the Civil War as Universalism began to wrestle painfully with its own internal divisions, and struggle for institutional coherence. But, during these tumultuous years there were many popular songs and songbooks for children, families and adults out in the churches, associations (clusters of churches) and State Conventions. One of them was *Goodwill Songs,* first and second editions, by Stanford Mitchell, Universalist minister and musical evangelist from Maine – a one man Dwight L. Moody and Ira Sankey – who wrote his own texts and music as well as using others, travelling around to wake the dead and dormant (Universalists) and give fire and hope to the living. Some of his songs were quite good and his music very singable. There were many such hymn writers and songbooks. I doubt that an accurate count will ever be made or possible.

Another unusual hymnbook was privately printed for Andrew Chalmers in Wakefield, MA, in 1891 (successor to an 1884 book of litanies and hymns). No music was included but it had the best contemporary Unitarian hymnists; Chadwick, Mary Hale, Hedge, Hosmer, Gannett, O.W. Holmes, J.K. Lowell, S.C. Beach, M.J. Savage, O.B. Frothingham, Collyer and the only hymn I've ever seen by Margaret Fuller in a hymnal ("Infinite Spirit, who art round us ever"), and the usual stable of British Unitarians. Chalmers wanted to, he said, "show the way to a new hymnal before the century ends, and he certainly did.

An ideosyncratic creation of a renegade Universalist congregation, the First Free Church of Tacoma, was *Hymns in Harmony with Modern Thought,* compiled by Alfred Martin printed in 1901. It is an amazing gathering of the best of Unitarian and other liberal authors, including the British Ethical Culturists, and outstanding liturgist, Stanton Coit. Martin scoured hymnody for anything he could use or adapt from the Catholic Breviary, a French king, to current scientific thinkers, women included. He took popular hymn tunes, changed the words completely – or as much as he thought necessary – and made fierce new liberal hymns out of them. It is the kind of hymnal that was not to appear widely for another generation.

Hymns of the Unitarian Literary Renaissance

O Word that broke the stillness first,
Sound on! And never cease,
Till all earth's darkness be made light,
And all her discord peace!
Samuel Longfellow

There is much that could be said about the tide of special church hymnals, published by and for leading churches in the Northeast, and increasingly countrywide. These were almost always extremely well chosen, edited and progressive assemblages of hymns, often in sequence with earlier predecessors. Most cut new ground, sought new sources, found new hymn writers, plumbed traditions heretofore ignored. Their efforts were, however, eclipsed by bright new creations, like *A Book of Hymns,* and will be given only limited attention in this chapter.

We pick up the Unitarian story in 1846 with the publication of a hymnal by two theological students at Harvard, invited by a nearby minister to create a new hymnal, since he found "even the recent ones too antiquated." Samuel Longfellow (1816 – 1892) and Samuel Johnson (1822 – 1882) assembled *A Book of Hymns for public and private devotion* that year. It included many British hymns including the obvious two by John Henry Newman and Sarah Fuller Flower Adams, and one by Helen Maria Williams, and several American women as well, among them Harriet Beecher Stowe, Emily Taylor and Eliza Cabot Follen. They introduced Whittier, Stowe, Jones Very and Sam's brother Henry Wadsworth Longfellow (2 hymns) to the American hymnodic repertoire.[1] Their tastes were modern but not narrow on the liberal end, including; John G. Adams, Henry Ware Jr., Nathaniel L. Frothingham, William H. Burleigh, James Freeman Clarke, John Pierpont, John Weiss, Edmund Hamilton Sears and Stephen

---

1 As noted in Foote (II), "Unitarian Hymns," p 16, but they did not introduce James Russell Lowell as Foote also says, since he had appeared in the Adams and Chapin Universalist Collection of the year before, if not elsewhere still earlier.

Greenleaf Bulfinch. It is usually assumed that a large number of their own hymns was included, but this is not so. Three of the seven hymns (including a translation and an arrangement) for which Samuel Johnson is remembered are here, and only four of the thirty six hymns (including an arrangement and a few hymns built on lines of others) Samuel Long-fellow is known for in Unitarian hymnals are here.[2] It was the *Book of Hymns'* "poetic excellence and freshness" that marked it.[3] Johnson's and Longfellow's major personal work in hymn writing for the most part still lay ahead. The *Book of Hymns* was first used in Worcester, Massachusetts in Edward Everett Hale's Church of the Unity, and next in Theodore Parker's Music Hall congregation, going through twelve editions before an enlarged edition appeared two years later in 1848. It was popular, but tunes were not included!

The young Cyrus Bartol (1813 – 1900), somewhat later to be called the grand old man of Transcendentalist ministers, published his *Hymns of the Sanctuary* in 1849, but it cut little new ground, being basically a revision of the old *West Boston Collection's* last edition of more than 35 years be-fore. *Hymns for the Church of Christ*, 1853, by the somewhat conservative and liturgical Transcendentalist, Frederick Henry Hedge (1805 – 1890), and Frederick Huntington (who departed for the Episcopalians shortly, where he became a Bishop) was strikingly inclusive in its 872 hymns. It included, of course, Hedge's masterful translation of Luther's "A Mighty Fortress is Our God," and his enduring "Sovereign and Transforming Grace." Virtually all of the prominent new names covered by the "Sams" and by Adams and Chapin were in this hymnal, plus hymns by Charles Wesley, hymns from Martineau's Collection, the Episcopal Collection, Lyra Catolica, and Moravian and Methodist sources. Identifications are in some cases elusive, tunes still missing, but this was an excellent hymnal. It was followed by three Unitarian hymnals of local interest; Samuel Gilman's *Services and Hymns for the use of the Unitarian Church of Charleston, South Carolina,* in 1854 (obviously certain then popular hymns opposing slavery were not popular there); and Chandler Robbins' (1810 – 1882) *Hymn Book for Christian Worship*, 1854, for Second Church,

---

2   See p (XXX) for a chart of hymns and hymnals which identify hymns by the

3   Foote, "Unitarian Hymns," p 16.

Boston, including many Methodist hymns, and Samuel Osgood (1812 – 1880)[4] and Frederic Farley's *Christian Worship,* 1862, for the Church of the Messiah (Unitarian) New York City, and First Unitarian Congregational Church of Brooklyn, New York.

The Civil War brought several soldiers songbooks including *The Soldier's Companion: Dedicated to the Defenders of their Country in the Field, by their Friends at Home,* published in the Boston Monthly Journal, Oct. 1861; *The Soldier's Hymn Book, containing a supplement of national songs for the use of chaplains and soldiers in the army and navy of the United States,* by Jacob Forman (d 1885) minister of the Unitarian Church in Alton, Illinois, and Chaplain of the 3rd Regiment of Missouri Infantry; and *The Soldier's Hymn Book for Camp and Hospital,* University Press (Cambridge, 1863). Unitarian and Universalist ministers and lay leaders visited the front frequently, and provided hymn and song books for prayers and services.

After a few intervening reprints Samuel Longfellow and Samuel Johnson radically revised and extended their 1846 work, producing *Hymns of the Spirit* in 1864, published by Ticknor and Fields in Boston, the publishing house of the Unitarian renaissance. It was far larger, with vigorous editings and amendments of the hymns of others[5], a simple theism distanced from Christological language, and more hymns by the editors, but still no tunes. They took the leading poets of the New England Renaissance and set their words to music. Samuel Johnson's enduring hymns are all here, and twenty seven of Samuel Longfellow's many creations are here. Their new hymns are more radical, more open and contemporary in their religious language, more inclusive in their religious understanding. This hymnal was not so much bought and used, as copied from for the hymnals of many denominations up to the present day.[6] Henry Wilder Foote (II) suggests that it was "one of the most important" Unitarian hymnals of all time, and he's of course right.[7] Johnson

---

4 Also departed for the Episcopalians.

5 It should be noted that the "Sams," as the later great Unitarian writers Frederick Lucian Hosmer and William Channing Gannett, edited their own works almost life long.

6 See the chart of hymns of Longfellow and Johnson, as they have survived in Unitarian and Unitarian–Universalist hymnals to the present day.

7 Foote, *Unitarian Hymns,* p 30. A later compendium of some of the hymns with music was published.

and Longfellow "together," Foote declares, "made a more important contribution to American Unitarian hymnody than that of any other writers in the middle of the 19th century." Scholars of hymnody speak of this as the "Unitarian Hymnody" or "Harvard School of Hymnody," and naturally so since the "Sams" were students at Harvard when they first began receiving invitations to write occasional hymns. Their hymnals gathered far more broadly than just the Unitarian renaissance, but there were few important hymn writers on the more open, liberal, mystical end of faith that they missed. The Harvard School was a common designation since so many of the new and often Transcendentalist hymn writers were graduates, but not all, so the name is a partial misnomer since so many hymn writers used by the Sams had no connection with the school..

Foote reflects on the poets of this period "of the flowering of New England Literature," naming beyond the names already noted;

> Dr. Oliver Wendell Holmes, (1809 – 1894) with half a dozen fine and widely used hymns, and Prof. James Russell Lowell (1819 – 1891) who, strictly speaking, was hardly a hymn writer at all, but from whose poems two or three have been quarried. Two other writers of this period were Rev. Edmund Hamilton Sears (1810 – 1876) and his niece, Miss Eliza Scudder. Sears wrote two Christmas hymns widely used throughout the English speaking world. Miss Scudder wrote half a dozen hymns in a mystical vein of the highest quality, but in temperament and outlook both writers belong more to the early period of Unitarian thought than to that prevalent in their later lifetime. In this mid-century period should also be included the famous war-time hymn by Mrs. Julia Ward Howe (1819 – 1910), "Mine eyes have seen the glory of the coming of the Lord," written in 1861 to provide worthier words than "John Brown's body" for the popular tune "Glory, Hallelujah," which had been composed a few years earlier for a Sunday school in Charleston, South Carolina.

After this fresh outpouring Unitarian hymnody mostly lay fallow awaiting new voices in the late years of the century.

A Reflection on Unitarian and Universalist Hymnody Post Civil War

Deep, sometimes, as an organ's tone,
An anthem bursts at every touch;
My heart is an Eolian lyre,
That wakes and sings at every breath,
Now touched as with seraphic fire,
Now wailing like the voice of death.

Sarah Edgarton Mayo,
Universalist poet, hymn writer

Episcopalian George Thomas Rider's *Lyra Americana or Verses of Praise and Faith,* from American Poets, D. Appleton & Co. (New York, 1865), which is not properly a hymnal, but precisely what it claims to be, a book of poetry – poetry which can be and often has been set to music – is full of praise (implied not stated) of Unitarian and Universalist hymn writers in this year of the Civil War's conclusion. He identifies those poet, hymn versifiers he believes to be the best America has produced. Since this assessment comes before many of the great late nineteenth century Unitarian hymns and hymnwriters it is an interesting reflection. In the preface to this prescient book Rider declares himself a "Boreal child" who seeks the noonday warmth. He has picked rich and radiant verses, of deep comfort and hope. Thus he included Margaret Fuller's lovely, "Jesus a child his course began;" and his 125 "verses" include more that 50 by Universalist and Unitarian authors. He misses few of the best known names in either denomination and has an excellent ear for good verses others had not yet accepted into hymnals, including poems of William H. Burleigh (four poems), Robert Lowell (six poems) and less well known words by Universalist Alice Cary (author of the enduring "One Sweetly Solemn Thought," though it doesn't endure in UU hymnals). He recognizes Caroline Cheesbro, poet and daughter of poet Sarah Edgarton

Mayo (Universalists), Maria White Lowell, William B. Tappan (Unitarian turned New Calvinist), Christopher Cranch, Caroline B. Sawyer and E.A. Washburn as well. His greats include E.H. Chapin, E.H. Sears, Samuel Longfellow and his brother Henry, T.W. Higginson, Hosea Ballou, N.L. Frothingham, Henry Ware Jr., Ralph Waldo Emerson, Theodore Parker, James Freeman Clarke, John Pierpont, Oliver Wendell Holmes, William Cullen Bryant, John Quincy Adams. This is indeed a heady mix of Unitarians and Universalists. Many of these authors are in hymnals all over the world, just not in ours any longer. The greatness of this list raises questions to the historian of liberal hymns. How can so many of these be "lost" to us? How do we keep our heritage, though almost every word of so many great hymn writers have perished among us?

George Thomas Rider has Frederick Henry Hedge as "T.H. Hedge." Even a careful Episcopalian can't be right all the time! It is an extraordinary compilation, with more Unitarian and Universalist verse for its size than any Unitarian or Universalist hymnal of that day. The question does resonate; How do we keep our heritage when almost every word of all but a few of these figures, many broadly acknowledged great hymn writers, has perished from our hymnals? In Judaism, throughout ages of persecution, they sang the ancient liturgical songs to remind them of who they were, the treasure of faith they carried and embodied. But we have no such musical vessels to remind us of our pilgrimage, or to connect us with our religious siblings around the world. What calls us to remembrance? What reminds us of the gift of our faith, heritage, tradition? The hymns aren't in our hymnal, though many which did for a time carry our faith were written. We seem to feel we have outgrown them.

Of course a few survive. Edmund Hamilton Sears, Samuel Longfellow (many hymns), and his brother Henry are the few survivers in the sadly misnamed *Singing the Liberal Tradition*. What does tradition, heritage, continuity mean with so many disconnects.

A Centenary Spirit — Universalist Hymns in the Second Half of the 19th Century

> Heaven is here. Its hymns of gladness
> Cheer the true believer's way,
> In this world where sin and sadness
> Often change to night our day.
> Heaven is here: where misery lightened
> Of its heavy load is seen;
> Where the face of sorrow brightened
> By the deed of love hath been;
> Heaven is here…
>
> *John Greenleaf Adams, hymn writer, editor*

Judging from the published hymnals, it appears that the Universalists weren't interested in new hymns and hymnals in the years immediately after the Civil War. A local collection, *Hymns for the Church and Home, with a selection of psalms: Portland Collection,* was published in Boston in 1865 by Dr. F.C. Bolles, and Israel Washburn, Jr. one of the seven oustanding Universalist brothers from Maine, all of whom went on to public careers and significant public service, governors, legislators, ambassadors, entrepreneurs.[1] The first Universalist Publishing House imprint hymnal, *Church Harmonies,* was issued in Boston in 1873.

The Universalists were indeed slow in launching an official new hymnal in the years following the Civil War. The War had drawn immense energies from Universalists and their church. Many Universalist ministers were chaplains; huge numbers of young men had fought. The Universalist Church in Salem, Massachusetts, is said to have sent 600 young men to the Union lines alone. Lay people and clergy visited the army encampments and even battlefields, especially from the central Midwest

---

1   See Theodore A Webb, *Seven Sons; Millionaires and Vagabonds*, Trafford Press (Victoria, BC, 1999) for coverage of the children of Israel and Martha Washburn.

where many a young man's Sunday School class went en mass to volunteer – the men anyway. The huge endeavor of the Western Sanitary Commission co-chaired by Mary Ashton Rice Livermore – its fairs, its gathering of supplies and its visits to the troops – gathered large Universalist energies. In the years following much of that organization went into a huge Midwest effort at spreading churches, ministers and enthusiasm in the northern Midwest. It was not until 1873 that the Universalist Publishing House issued *Church Harmonies: a Collection of Hymns and Tunes for the Use of Congregations.* It had more than a thousand hymns, and a helpful set of indexes; first lines, tunes, metrical index of tunes, a subject index. It sold well into the new century.

David Hunter in an unpublished and masterful review of the 1917 Universalist hymnal in 1999 asks an obvious question that applies to much more than that hymnal alone. Why didn't the Universalists appeal to and celebrate the rich pietistic, mystical strain of Universalism in its hymnody as the bitter sectarian battles, debates, challenges wound down in the late 19th century, into the 20th, and orthodoxy seemed – for the most part – no longer interested in defending infant damnation, endless fires of Hell, and fierce particularities of faith? The answer is complex. The pietistic strain of the earliest Universalism on these shores was always a minor instrument in the big brass band of organized Universalism. Its great texts of thought and faith, its martyr stories and battles for religious freedom were vigorously claimed and affirmed until the time of Hosea Ballou and beyond; but from Ballou on Universalism moved in new and different ways.

The Mennonites, Moravians and a host of smaller groups had claimed the pietistic tradition and bound it strongly in often rigid standards of faith and practice. Universalists began to group theologically around the four understandings that George Hunston Williams described in his *American Universalism;*

1. Classical Biblically based proof text Universalism.
2. Universalism as the soul of Christianity.
3. Universalism as more inclusive – Christian in a large embracing sense.
4. Universalism as a world faith that could gather others together in one community of the faithful.

None of these excluded that old Pietist strain, but Universalists had been spooked by two movements on the religious horizon, Transcendentalism which most Universalists rejected as a cheap non-Christian Pantheism; and Spiritualism which grew strongly in their own ranks, persuading, convincing many ministers and many churches.[2] Many saw Spiritualism as a fulfillment of that Pietist strain of Universalism. The denomination did not, emphatically!

The Universalist Centennial of John Murray's arrival on these shores occurred in 1870, with a huge national gathering on the edge of the Atlantic Ocean in Gloucester, Massachusetts, close to the old Independent Christian Church (Universalist) whose congregation he had served. In preparation the Women's Centenary Aid Association had been formed to raise money for extension and ministry. It was quite successful, and became the origin of the Association of Universalist Women. But, more to our interest, the Centennial and the organization of Universalist women created a grand celebration, surely an invitation for hymns and songs of Universalist faith and joy. They were not lacking, including several by prominent women, including Caroline Soule, Universalist women's leader, head of the women's department of Clinton Liberal Institute, Missionary to Scotland and perennial speaker and writer.

Universalists were immensely diverse, with about as much diversity of religious conviction as they could handle in the post Civil War years. They organized for the great Centennial in Gloucester, Massachusetts, in 1870 hoping that a new unity, vision, and energy would flow from these celebrations. But this was just the beginning of a much larger outpouring including hymns, mostly by women, and sadly thus mostly forgotten. The hymns appeared for special services and memorials. They were gathered in small books of poetry, and sometimes of hymns and songs, especially for children.[3]

New energy did flow, but it involved, in part, the suppression of

---

2   John Buescher's *The Other Side of Salvation*, Spiritualism and the Nineteenth Century Religious Experience, Skinner House Books (Boston, 2004) is a good introduction to Universalist Spiritualism.

3   See the author's *A Bibliography of UU Women's Hymns*, Third Edition, Philomath Press (Brookline, MA, 1995) for a fuller discussion of this subject in the Introduction. For an introduction to most of the well known Universalist women poets of this era see *Our Women Workers*, by Eliza R.Hanson, Star and Covenant (Chicago, 1882).

Universalist Spiritualism, and the attempt to provide a new growing center for the faith, clear and strong, somewhere between Universalism as the soul of Christianity and Universalism as an inclusive, not exclusive Christian body. It also involved a new hymnal. That was a harder sell for the still hugely popular Adam's and Chapin's *Hymns for Christian Devotion* reached its 63rd edition in 1867, and went on to a New Edition with multiple printings (1870 – 1875).[4] Obviously not everyone wanted a new hymnal.

Church Harmonies from the Universalist Publishing House in 1873 included many of the old Universalist favorites; six hymns by Hosea Ballou, two by Sebastian Streeter, two by George Richards, two by Menzies Rayner, one by George Rogers (tireless evangelist), one by Adin Ballou (of Hopedale) and one by Abel C.Thomas, two by John G.Adams and three by Edwin H. Chapin. Newer Universalist voices were included; six hymns by Thomas Lake Harris (spiritualist), two by Alice Cary, and one each from Sarah Edgarton Mayo, P.H. Sweetser, Mary A.R. Livermore, and Moses Ballou. The hymnal included a respectable number of hymns from the usable Christian hymnody of the western world. Clearly they had benefited from the new Unitarian *Hymn and Tune Book*, and had also drawn from Sam Longfellow's and Sam Johnson's newly published *Hymns of the Spirit* (1864), from which among others they drew Sam Longfellow's "Soft as Fades" (altered). It was a very servicable hymnal and continued in print well after its successor was published. One interesting omission in this hymnal, which explains itself instantly, is that there was no author – composer index. Clearly they did not want in any clearer way to point out that they had included far more Unitarian hymns, and even composers, than Universalist. It's music was, according to Henry Wilder Foote, uninspired, but then he said the same of the music in the *Hymn and Tune Book*. I have no reason to challenge either judgment. It should also be noted that the fiery "meat axe" and passionately partisan Universalist evangelical hymns and hymn writers of the early years were all missing, even Thomas Whittemore[5].

The end of the century saw *Church Harmonies New and Old*, Univer-

---

4 Music was still missing until *The Musical Supplement*, of 1864.

5 But some of the glorious old Universalist spirit breaks through in hymn 417 by Hosea Ballou and Abel Thomas's "The Gospel of Peace: hymn 376.

salist Publishing House (Boston, 1895).[6] It contained newer hymns by a host of Universalist men and women, an excellent selection of Unitarian authors, including quite recent ones, and classics in Christian hymnody.

Church Harmonies New and Old was virtually a whole new creation, drawing on all the usual Christian and Unitarian sources, but attempting a compendium of the best Universalist hymn writers from the whole of their American experience among its 708 hymns – up to that moment – 1895. Edited by Charles Tenney and Leo Lewis, probably the first professionally trained teacher of music (Tufts) to edit a Universalist hymnal, it was large and inclusive of many of the best known Christian hymns and an extraordinary collection of Universalist hymn writers. Alphabetically it included John Greenleaf Adams, Hosea Ballou, Hosea Ballou II, Moses Ballou, Sanford Fillmore Bennett, Henry Lovell Canfield, Julia Abigail Fletcher Carney, Alice Cary, Phoebe Cary, Luella Juliette Bartlett Case, Edwin Hubbell Chapin, Sylvanus Cobb, Mary Ann Dodd, Cyrus Hyde Fay, Dwight Munson Hodge, Abner Kneeland, Alexander Gretton Laurie, Henry Codman Leonard, Abbie Goodwin Davis, Mary Ashton Rice Livermore, James Lombard, Anna Lippett Marvin, Stanford Mitchell, Adirondam Judson Patterson, Jane Lippett Patterson, Menzies Rayner, George Richards, George Rogers, Byron Russell, Caroline Mehitabel Fisher Sawyer, Otis Ainsworth Skinner, Sebastian Streeter, Sebastian Ferris Streeter, Paul Hart Sweetser, Abel Charles Thomas, Hiram Torrey, Edward Turner, Benjamin Ballou Whittemore and Thomas Whittemore (resurrected). There were also four young Universalist composers who composed tunes for this hymnal. This was not, of course a complete list of Universalist hymn writers in the American experience – but it was an amazing effort. It includes some of the earliest writers from George Richards, publishers of several hymnals (both Hosea Ballou, Abner Kneeland and Edward Turner, Sebastian Streeter, George Rogers (tireless evangelist), Abel Charles Thomas, Thomas Whittemore and Stanford Mitchell – the "sweet singer" of Universalism), and a heady collection of women. There is a full range of indexes and, in some editions, biographical information on all hymn writers but especially on the Universalists. It was a

---

6 Henry Wilder Foote (II) suggests that this is a revision of the *Portland Collection,* but that is clearly not so. It is a revision of *Church Harmonies,* whatever of the *Portland Collection* it included.

strong effort to define a Universalist identity in hymnody, a changing, moving identity, but a clear one. The book remained in print for almost 20 years, but most of those years it continued to overlap its predecessor which was still popular. If, as the antiquarian book experts say, the most used books disappear first and when found are likely to show intense use then this was a well used hymnal. I've almost never seen a pristine copy.

It also gathers in a few of the then popular gospel hymns, and much music in that sweet and sentimental style. Perhaps that is why Henry Wilder Foote, whose musical tastes were decidedly traditional and formal, saw little to comment on in the book, except its excellent brief biographical sketches of authors and translators.[7]

There was also an explosion of youth and Sunday School sonbooks. (See Appendix).

---

7 Henry Wilder Foote II drew on these broadly for his work on "Hymns of American Universalism," unpublished) Foote, "Universalist Hymns," p 5. Not all copies included the biographical material and index.

Unitarian Hymnody, from Old to New, the Late 19th Century

Now on land and sea descending,
Brings the night its peace profound.
Let our vesper hymn be blending
With the holy calm around....
Hope and Faith and Love rise glorious,
Shining in the spirit's skies.

Samuel Longfellow,
from his famous vespers hymn

Following the shattering, yet finally hopeful and heartening struggle of the Civil War, in which Unitarians and Universalists had proved, to themselves and others, their patriotism on and off the battlefield in countless ways, there was a new energy. The Universalists gathered and celebrated it through their Centennial, the Unitarians through the gatherings of the National Conference, the first democratic body representing congregations in the Unitarian movement, in 1865 and thereafter. The National Conference set out to create the structures of participation missing in the American Unitarian Association, an organization based entirely on individual memberships, all gentlemen of course, most ministers. The merger of these two had to wait into the 20th century. A powerful sticking point for the National Conference was, of course, the words of faith and purpose which would encompass and include all Unitarians and their congregations. The exceedingly traditional words chosen for that purpose would be a cause of bitter contention for most of the rest of the century, cast as they were in language that might please the conservatives, but no consolation to the aging transcendentalists and new radicals. What did this have to do with hymnody? Everything!

In 1868 a committee created by the American Unitarian Association published the *Hymn and Tune Book for the Church and Home,* edited by

Leonard A. Livermore (1822 – 1886), the first more or less official hymnal of the Unitarians. It was large – 740 hymns and chants and more – and tunes. The tunes – 299 of them – were placed at the top of the page, with several sets of words beneath and often on the facing page. It "marked no advance over its predecessors, but its tunes were well up to the average level and gave it a great advantage," quotes Henry Wilder Foote (II) from some unnamed source, probably himself.[1] The *Hymn and Tune Book* included many of the usual hymn writers on both sides of the Atlantic, and the best of the work of previous hymnbooks. Charles Wesley was represented by 19 hymns, and John Whittier by 7. Love Maria Williams appears as do Eliza Scudder, Mary Whitwell Hale and both Caroline and Samuel Gilman. Bancroft, Barbauld, Bowring, Bryant, Bulfinch and Furness (in varied meters) all appear with multiple hymns. Its 771 hymns included some good new ones, and the *Hymn and Tune Book* was widely used, but not widely loved or respected, nor did it appeal to the more liberal wing of the denomination who felt it included too much they though long and well left behind. It was substantially rewritten and extended under the editorship of AUA secretary, Rush Shippen, only nine years later. Foote notes the improvement in the quality and music in the *Hymn and Tune Book for the Church and Home*, 1877, however its 871 hymns, 14 chants and many new tunes still contained "only a few examples of the newer English tunes which were being introduced into America by the Choirs of Episcopal churches," and that was to Foote a near fatal flaw. Some of these new English tunes are excellent and survive well in our hymnals to the present, but some are deadly, and Foote's personal preferences are clear. This hymnal, including much more of the newer work of hymn writers of the late Unitarian renaissance, was popular and endured. Another hymnbook, *Hymns for the Christian Church, for the use of the First Church of Christ in Boston* (Unitarian), appeared the following year, edited by First Church's minister Rufus Ellis (1819 – 1885), but its retrospective character and lack of music limited its usefulness. Other individual churches, too many to here record, created hymns and hymnals in various parts of the country through the remainder of this century and into the next, but they usually were of very local and limited use. I don't think any one will ever be able to gather all their names and occasions.

---

1 Foote, "Unitarian Hymns," p 20.

An interesting way to see the flow of the work of outstanding new hymn writers into, and with the passage of years and changing tastes, out of hymnals is to look at the work of the "Sams," Longfellow and Johnson over a century and more. Here are their hymns, as they appeared in Unitarian hymnals and their own:[2]

INDEX
BOH – Book of Hymns, 1846
HOS – Hymns of the Spirit, 1864
NHT – New Hymn and Tune Book, 1914
HOS2 – Hymns of the Spirit, 1937
HCL – Hymns for the Celebration of Life, 1964
SLT – Singing the Living Tradition, 1995

Samuel Johnson	BOH	HOS	NHT	HOS2	HCL	SLT
City of God, how broad		637	451	410		
Come Thou almighty King (arr w SL)	480	16		10	26	
Father, in thy mysterious presence	33	81	268	229		
God of the Earnest Heart	592	242	344	301	224	
Life of ages, richly poured		633	394	337	172	111
Oh Thou whose power (trans/Boethius)		15		67	128	
Onward, onward though the region		584	214	216		

Samuel Longfellow	BOH	HOS	NHT	HOS2	HCL	SLT
A voice by Jordan's shore		641	219	210		
Again as evening's shadows fall		57	138	119	271	48
Beneath the shadow of the cross	564	647	248	187	312	
Come Thou Almighty King (arr w SJ)	480	16		10	26	
Eternal one, thou living God (1875)			441	367		
Every bird that upward springs		585				
Father give thy benediction		127	413			
Go Forth to life, o child		553	372	290		
God of the earth, the sky, the sea		330	49	28	43	25
God of truth! Thy sons		550				
God's trumpet wakes the slumbering		676	366	309	213	
He who himself and God (from Martineau)		438		106		
Holy Spirit, Light divine (after Andrew Reed)		407	98	68		

---

2   Exempting the *Hymn and Tune Book* and revisions.

Samuel Longfellow	BOH	HOS	NHT	HOS2	HCL	SLT
Holy Spirit, source of gladness	483	12	119	3		
I look to thee, in every need		485	284	258		
In the beginning was the word		673				
Life of all that lives below (from Wesley)			93	53		
Light of ages and of nations			453	75	248	189–90
Lo, the earth is risen (1876)			210	200		
Alt by HCL to "Lo the earth awakes again"					318	61
Now on land and sea descending		58	154	111	274	47
Now, with creation's morning song		152	137	102		
O father fix this wavering will		368				
O God in whom we live and move		294				
O God thou giver of all good		73				
O God, thy children gathered here		230				
O God, unseen but ever near		44	475	447		
O Life that maketh all things new (1874)			375	416	54	12
O still in accents sweet		575	490	449		
O Thou, in whom we live and move			83			
One holy church of God appears		638	452	407	261	
Out of the dark, the circling sphere		244	237	99	208	
Sing forth his high, eternal			28	308		
Spirit divine, attend our prayer		9	77	55		
The summer days are coming			167	138		
Recast by HCL to						
"The sweet June days are come again"					326	65
Thou Lord of life, our saving (1886)			255	469		
Cut by HCL to "Bless thou the gifts"					508	
Tis winter now, the fallen snow		193	170	133	301	
With joy we claim the growing life (1875)					246	345
When my love to God (from Wreford)	144				313(alt)	

The list is quite revealing. It is a common perception that Johnson and Longfellow's *Hymns of the Spirit* reveal a much more radical faith in both compiler–hymn writers. I think that is, in fact, not in evidence for Samuel Longfellow, who included in their HOS many of his new hymns across the spectrum. Samuel Johnson has by this edition completed his few great hymns and they are broad in theological brush, though his most radical popular hymn, "Life of Ages, richly poured" is here. What is obvious for Longfellow is that some of his very best and most radical hymns were written still later in life, some at the very end of his life. It is also obvious that he was well acquainted with the best of new English Unitarian hymn writing and authors (ie. Martineau and Wreford).

Johnson and Longfellow edited, rewrote, recast large numbers of hymns to the point where they hardly knew who to credit. Thus the original *Book of Hymns* and the successor *Hymns of the Spirit* include hymns without attribution that were built on a line or two of others, but essentially written by Longfellow or Johnson. Hundreds of familiar hymns by many hymn writers are creations in exactly the same manner from an idea, line, phrase in an earlier hymn. They will not be sorted out before the next millennium. There are also the translations as Frederick Henry Hedge's masterful reworking of Luther's "A Mighty Fortress." It is to a significant degree a new hymn. Another important example is the ancient Jewish liturgical piece known as "Yigdal," authored centuries back, perhaps by Daniel ben Judah Dayan. In the 1880's Rabbi Max Landsberg of Rochester, New York, asked the neighboring Unitarian minister, Newton Mann, to make a better and more accurate translation in English than the Christianized form created by Methodist Thomas Olivers the century before in England. Mann's translation didn't fit well the traditional tune so Landsberg turned to Mann's successor William Channing Gannett, an excellent hymn writer in his own right, to recast Yigdal in the traditional meter. In this large and long collaboration the lovely, "Praise to the Living God" finally achieved a fitting English form. Few hymns are recast in quite such a clear linear collaboration, but most are reformed and recast as years and hymnals come and go. It becomes difficult to properly address authorship, and to give appropriate credits, or even to recognize and acknowledge changes so the student of hymnody is counseled to take care to know the story of any hymn well before passing out credits. The Episcopalians and Methodists are particularly careful in the companion volumes to their hymnals to try to give accurate information and appropriate credits.[3]

---

3 *The Hymnal 1982 Companion,* in three volumes, Raymond F. Glover, Editor, Church Hymnal Corporation, (New York, 1994) is a masterful tour de force on the hymns, both

The work of hymnal commissions is evident in the list of Johnson's and Longfellow's work. The commissions for the *Hymn and Tune Book* (1878), *New Hymn and Tune Book* (1914), and *Hymns of the Spirit* (1937), clearly sought out the hymns of these two most creative Unitarian hymn writers, using virtually everything that Johnson and Longfellow included in their *Hymns of the Spirit*, including even Samuel Johnson's recasting of "Love for all," a pleading Gospel song, but not his gentle editing of "Just as I am," which appears in the next hymnal we address, the Western Conference hymnal. The commission that created *Hymns for the Celebration of Life*, feeling limited to far fewer hymns (327) made some careful judgments and editings, but also reached back to the original *Hymns of the Spirit*, for two hymns ignored by intervening commissions. The new commission that created *Singing the Living Tradition* appears to have played the part essentially of "bean counters" in resting their decisions for heritage hymns for the most part on questionnaires on use and preference, but not sifting the past, as their predecessors had done for what might be newly valuable.

The editorial hand shows too, in the HCL commission's revision of the first line of Samuel Longfellow's "Lo the earth is risen" and using only a piece of his "Thou Lord of life, our saving." All commissions edit, by shortening hymns by one or more verses, by conflating two or more verses to gain one they are pleased with, by altering one or more words or phrases. Henry Wilder Foote (II) points out that the Scotch Presbyterians were once interested in using "Montgomery's hymn containing the lines, 'The mountain dew shall nourish – a seed in weakness sown.'" Mountain dew in Scotland is short for illegal Scotch hootch, and thus would be problematic in a sober hymn to be sung in that land. The phrase had to be changed.[4] The issue, not always so urgent, is a recurring one every hymnal commission has to wrestle with, and there are no easy answers. We shall return to it again.

The next hymnal, a regional hymnal created by leaders of the Western Unitarian Conference, Unity men and women, "ethical basis brethren" as

words and music, in their latest Episcopal *The Hymnal 1982*, The Church Hymnal Corporation (New York, 1982). The latest *Julians* is of course a resource, as is the Hymn Society of the United States and Canada, but there are few other thorough and careful general sources of information on hymns, composers and hymn writers.

4   Quoted in Arthur Foote, p 15.

they were often called to distinguish them from the scripturally Christian or simple theisticly based folk, who were believed primarily to inhabit the Unitarian churches on the eastern seaboard, a not entirely accurate perception but a useful generalization. Frederick Lucian Hosmer (1840 – 1929), William Channing Gannett (1840 – 1923) and James Villa Blake (1842 – 1925), the editors, were all hymn writers, the first two more successfully, and ministers. The book was called *Unity Hymns and Chorals*, published in 1880, with significant revisions additions and enlargement in 1911. It is, even enlarged, a small book due to the split leaf design, with tunes at the top of the page and words at the bottom with the page cut between them so that any words could be matched to any tune (in the same meter, hopefully). "Musically it was mediocre," declares Henry Wilder Foote, reflecting his dislike for Victorian era popular hymn tunes and for the more enthusiastic spiritual tunes popularized by evangelists like Ira Sankey and many others around the turn of the century, some joyfully used by these Western Unitarians. The HCL commission reached back to the early 1800's, to the *Kentucky Harmony* and *Union Harmony* for a few more enthusiastic tunes in the 1960s, doubtless to the scandal of lovers of English Cathedral music. Foote was not entirely right on the issue of tunes, but his judgment that the *Unity* hymnal with its new hymn writers and capturing of contemporary religiously radical poetry "may be compared to the hymn-books by Longfellow and Johnson" is correct. *Unity Hymns* mostly gathered its hymns from the radical wing of the Unitarians, but it especially sought living authors, women and men, and thus included Anna Garlin Spencer (1851 – 1931) and a host of relatively unknown midwesterners. Nowhere is this more obvious than in "Songs of Faith, Hope, Charity, set to old tunes" published separately, and included in some late editions of *Unity Hymns*. These "Songs" adapt, edit and borrow revival hymns, and tunes popular in the evangelical turn of the century world to Unitarian use. Some of the best turn of the century (1900) revival tunes are suggested, but not provided, in this supplement filled with contemporary liberal wordings.

Richard Stanislaw in a magazine column titled "Songs of the sawdust Trail" reflects on the post revolutionary flow of religious music:

While American church music in urban areas was becoming increasingly dignified (European) the rural majority kept colonial musical style alive and expanded it to include an enthusiastic repertoire of folk hymnody.... It was popular with many people in the developing western U.S. (who significantly, were the primary movers in that century for civil liberty, human rights and higher education.) It is that music which was written down by the next wave of singing teachers and used in the frontier singing schools... And it is that music which led to the Gospel song as it is still popular today."[5]

It was this popular and singable folk and Gospel musical tradition that the *Unity Hymns,* editors wished to bring into the chilly halls of Unitarian hymnody because it surrounded them and moved Western people. It was this importation that the editors of the *New Hymn and Tune Book* and *Hymns of the Spirit* fought so passionately and effectively to keep out. Much of the supplement's material and matches are too much of a stretch to be useful, but some, including words like Helen Hunt Jackson's (aka Saxe Holm) are great fun, and just occasionally good hymnody. Many songs like "Work for the Night is Coming" required no theological editing at all. Many Unitarian women and men took up the challenge also to write new words and recast old ones for some of the enthusiastic music. Most don't quite work, but some are hymns that deserve a future, if perhaps with still other music for this generation.

With the *Unity Hymns and Chorals* it was as if the dam had burst once more in creative hymn work. Minot J. Savage (1841 – 1918), minister of Unity Church in Boston created his own *Sacred Songs for Public Worship"* *A Hymn and Tune Book,* in 1883, set to music by Howard M. Dow. Most are Savage's own hymns set to music "akin to the typical gospel song–book."[6] Few of his hymns, and none of his matches survived. Henry Wilder Foote, I, compiled *Hymns of the Church Universal,* edited by Mary W. Tileston and Arthur Foote, which included many excellent English compositions and words as well. This collection, essentially for King's Chapel of which Foote was minister "was influential in setting a standard

---

5   "Eternity" magazine, August, 1976, pp 50 – 51. He overstates the "primary movers" note, but since it is an enduring Western perception, I have left it.

6   Foote (II), "Unitarian Hymns," p 32.

for later books," proudly declares his son and namesake who was to lead in the creation and editing of the next two official Unitarian hymnals.[7] This work was revised by the editors and published as *Hymns for Church and Home,* with 801 hymns, many more than its predecessor. In 1902 it was abridged to only 513 hymns.

Two excellent hymnals by women appeared in the late years of the 19th century, *Hymnal: Amore Dei,* by Velma Williams (1852 – 1941), Boston, 1890 (revised 1897), aided by hymnwriter husband Theodore Chickering Williams (1855 – 1915); and *Hymns of the Ages,* edited by Louisa Putnam Loring (1854 – 1924), Cambridge, 1904. Both show very high standards as to words and music, of traditional and English caste, but neither could seriously compete with the denominational hymnals which contained so many more hymns and tunes. Another unusual hymnal was the *Isle of Shoals Hymn Book* of 1908, edited by Rev. George H. Badger. It includes hymns unique to the Isle of Shoals and several hymns based in nature and environment. It is a lovely hymnbook, including many more women among its hymn writers than was usual in those years.

---

7   Foote, *Unitarian Hymns,* p 33.

Universalist Hymns
for a New Century

> Courage! Let no heart despair –
> Mighty is the truth we bear!
> Forward, then, baptized in love,
> Led by wisdom from above!
>
> *P.H. Sweetser, minister, hymn writer*

There was a millennial moment at the end of the century, especially reflected in the Columbian Exhibition (World's Fair) with its religious congresses (including the Universalist and Unitarian Congresses) and the World Parliament of Religion. Universalists turned out in the thousands to renew and declare their faith (Unitarians were there too in grand numbers, but interestingly more to listen to world religious speakers than to exhibit their own faith). At the Parliament and Fair millennial hopes were paraded, along with a running list of the world's ills. The hopes of the late 19th century had been ripped by the economic roller coaster of boom and bust. Universalists felt heartened and renewed by the World Parliament and their own very successful Congress.

The new century dawned to a Universalist constituency continuing to shrink, to lose membership and churches as the urban world drew the life from rural America and the economics of church survival became more problematic. Once a building could be whitewashed from time to time, the roof patched, the outhouse relocated. Suddenly electric lights were needed, and a heating system and indoor plumbing, and maybe a full time minister (at what a cost) to replace the long gone circuit riders. Rural churches perished and urban churches struggled. *Church Harmonies*, both old and new, seemed dated. Darwinism, Social Darwinism, wrenching urban issues, a renewed sense of social purpose among the Universalists, and the looming signs of what would be World War One seemed to demand a new hymnal.

Hymns of the Church was prepared by Cornelius Alpheus Parker, Stephen Herbert Roblin and Charles Conklin[1] – all ministers and all directors of the Universalist Publishing House. It was about the size of *Singing the Living Tradition*, of many years later, much, much smaller than both its predecessors. In part this was due to the change in putting only one set of words to one piece of music to a page, not a piece of music surrounded by the words to several hymns that could be sung to that tune – as had prevailed before. Almost 73% of the hymns were from *Church Harmonies New and Old* and of those that were not from that hymnal few were new. John Coleman Adams (son of John Greenleaf Adams) wrote three; Julian Stearns Cutler, Katherine Louise Brown, Stanford Mitchell, Thomas Lake Harris and Grace F. White wrote one each - constituting the "new" Universalist hymn writers.. John Haynes Holmes contributed three (strong new social action hymns), Frederick Lucian Hosmer - four, Henry Wadsworth Longfellow and James Russell Lowell – two each, Julia Ward Howe, John Pierpont, Henry Ware Jr., Samuel Johnson, Samuel Longfellow, John White Chadwick, and James Martineau and William George Tarrant (both British) with one each constituted the Unitarians. (The absence of an index showing religious affiliation again suggests that the Universalists did not want to broadcast their heavy leaning on Unitarian hymns.) The rest were mostly by Congregationalists. The new hymns from Unitarian and various Christian sources were well chosen but not unusual in virtually any mainline and liberal hymnal of the time. The hymnal was, in short, a solid traditional one that cut little new ground and embodied no new vision[2] It was published in 1917 on the cusp of our entry into World War One. It was also just ahead of the *New Century Hymnal*, Universalist Edition which cut no new ground and little old ground. Coming so soon after *Hymns of the Church* it could not have helped the slow sales of *Hymns of the Church* which lingered weakly until the joint Unitarian and Universalist publication of *Hymns of the Spirit* in 1937.

---

1   Charles Conklin had tried his talents in the West, in Chicago at Church of the Redeemer, Universalist (Second Church) and was eventually to become State Superintendent of the Massachusetts Universalist Convention, where he urged Universalists where possible to make common cause, with the Congregationalists – believing merger was inevitable and desirable.

2   The music was substantially updated from *Church Harmonies New and Old*, and drew from many other mostly contemporary hymnals. The hymns at least were singable – one of the intentions of the editors.

Unitarian Hymnody
at the Beginning
of the 20th Century

Mysterious Presence, source of all, –
The world without, the soul within, –
Fountain of life, O hear our call,
And pour thy living waters in....

Thy hand unseen to accents clear
Awoke the psalmists trembling lyre,
And touched the lips of holy seer
With flame from thine own altar fire.

That touch divine still, Lord, impart,
Still give the prophet's burning word;
And vocal in each waiting heart,
Let living psalms of praise be heard.
Seth Curtis Beach, 1866[1]

In 1914 the Unitarians published their long awaited new hymnal, *The New Hymn and Tune Book,* whose commission included American Unitarian Association President, Samuel Eliot (1862 – 1950), Henry Wilder Foote, II, (1875 – 1964), Rush Shippen (former AUA Secretary, 1828 – 1911) and Lewis G. Wilson (1858 – 1928) all influential male ministers. A large and more inclusive advisory committee was appointed a year later including several women. The *New Hymn and Tune Book* was not really a revision of the old *Hymn and Tune Book,* but a new book drawing extensively from the profusion of recently published Unitarian hymnody. Henry Wilder Foote, II, had just begun his term of service as Secretary of Education of the American Unitarian Association when the task of chairing the new hymnal commission fell upon him. Samuel

---

1   This hymn with slightly altered theology (unacknowledged) survives in SLT.

Eliot could be quite persuasive. In three short years the work was complete, with services in the front, a psalter for responsive reading (the last
of the movement's hymnals to include this), every prayer sourced and
acknowledged (never done since), and radical changes visible everywhere. Almost 3/4th of the hymns from the previous official Unitarian
hymn book are excised, and 198 of its 300 tunes eliminated. The short
promotional volume done for this hymnal declares that almost all of
the 1877 hymnal's tunes and texts still "in use" are retained in the 1914
hymn book[2]. If this is true then considerably under ten percent of the
much larger (885 to 546) 1877 hymnal was still "in use." It was clearly
more than time for a new hymnal. Foote later reflected:

> The change of religious thought in the intervening thirty–seven
> years is indicated by the retention of only 242 of the 885 hymns
> which the earlier book had included. In reality the new book was
> based much more upon the later Unitarian collections of the eigh-
> teen–nineties.... The Unitarian hymn writers were, naturally, ful-
> ly represented so far as their work still had living value, and the
> book was rich in hymns of public service and social righteousness,
> Musically it was less progressive, presenting the top musical level
> of about 1900, but paying inadequate attention to the new tunes
> which were coming into use in England, though they had not yet
> reached this country.[3]

The *New Hymn and Tune Book* had more than three hundred fewer
hymns, making the carryover seem very small indeed. The carryover of
hymns of Unitarian and Universalist authorship is still more interesting.
From the original 1868 *Hymn and Tune Book* only 42 of the 125 survived
to the *New Hymn and Tune Book,* suggesting that older Unitarian and
Universalist hymns were falling out of favor in large numbers, but being

---

2   *Hymns and Tunes with Services for Congregational Worship,* (selected from the New Hymn
and Tune Book and the New Service Book) – published by the AUA (Boston, 1914). It is of
interest to note what is in this brief promotional piece meant to encourage congregations to
buy the new hymnal. There are few hymns we would find today in *Singing the Living Tradition,* but most of the best hymn writers of that and the preceding generation are included
– suggesting that their popularity was already secure.

3   *Three Centuries of American hymnody,* by Henry Wilder Foote, Harvard University Press
(Cambridge, 1940), p 338.

replaced by a host of new ones, a total of 181 Unitarian and Universalist hymns being found in the *New Hymn and Tune Book*.

The *Hymn and Tune Book* had a count of 16% of its total hymns of Unitarian or Universalist origin; the total in the *New Hymn and Tune Book* rising to 32%, of a considerably smaller hymnal. Thus the disappearance of hymns of other origin and authorship was still more drastic and the new hymnal was "Unitarian" in a way and to a degree that did not exist before in official Unitarian hymnals. This was a revolution in hymnody whether it seemed so at the time or not. Charles Wesley did, at last however, come into his own in Unitarian hymnals, here with eleven excellent and stirring hymns.

Further, it was not so boring a hymnal as it sounds in Foote's remembrances. It introduced to the American Unitarian Association hymn book many outstanding new Unitarian hymns and hymn writers, including six hymns by William Channing Gannett (1840 – 1923) most notably, "The thought of God," and "Bring, O Morn thy Music," written for the 1893 World Parliament of Religions in Chicago. The latter hymn was originally written to a gospel tune with a rousing chorus,[4] but in 1930 recast by Vincent Silliman to the familiar title (above) and the more sober music with which we are familiar. Frederick Lucian Hosmer (1840 – 1929) appears with 34 hymns, many among the most popular among Unitarians for two generations. Hosmer and Gannett worked together and conducted a friendly challenge for 40 years, each seeking to produce a hymn for major holidays, anniversaries, special occasions. The fruits of these efforts were published together in three short volumes, later gathered in the *Thought of God*, replicating in one book the earlier smaller collections, and revealing that some of their best hymn writing occurred in the quiet mutual challenge of these years.[5]

The *New Hymn and Tune Book* included a hymn by John Coleman Adams (1849 – 1922), a popular Universalist minister, the enduring "We Praise Thee God."[6] Ten hymns, representing the corpus of his best writing are here from John White Chadwick (1840 – 1904). Marion Franklin Ham (1867 – 1956) has two hymns in the NHTB, some of his best still to

---

4   Tune: "The Crowning Day."

5   See p 67 for list of Gannett and Hosmer's hymns in recent hymnals.

6   All but unrecognizable in its bowdlerized form in *Singing the Living Tradition*.

be written.[7] Theodore Chickering Williams (1855 – 1915) is represented by several hymns, including his two most enduring, "In the lonely midnight" (a Christmas hymn) and "When thy heart with joy o'erflowing." Edward Everett Hale's "Lend a Hand" song is here, with Felix Adler's version of "Hail the glorious golden city" and single hymns by a host of more or less new Unitarian names; James Villa Blake, Charles Gordon Ames, Charles William Wendte, and Henry Wilder Foote I's only known hymn. Women, too, are introduced, notably Florence Harris' "As pilgrims sailing" and Francis Whitmarsh Wile's gracious, "All beautiful the march of days." There was much new and beautiful in the hymnal, but the music did leave much more to be desired.

The hymnal included four Unitarian composers; Henry Oliver Kemble who composed Federal Street, Mary Phillips Webster who composed Chadwick, Arthur Foote (chant 553), and Benjamin Lincoln Whelpley (Chants 548 & 568). Foote (II) later particularly regretted that Ralph Vaughan Williams 1906 English Hymnal was unknown to them, but it was to be fully attended to in *Hymns of the Spirit* in 1937. He did not regret the near extirpation of the more enthusiastic folk and Gospel tunes that were singing their way across America. Foote moved on to become the Secretary to the Faculty at Harvard Divinity School, where his many historical, musical and intellectual skills could be well employed. It was there that he published many pieces on history and hymnody, and discovered the authorship of Samuel Longfellow in five hymns left anonymous in the original *Hymns of the Spirit*.

---

7   Marion Frankin Ham published two collections of his poetry – hymns, the latter with a sketch of his life, in *The Golden Shuttle*, 1896, and *Songs of a Lifetime*, in 1953.

Hymns of the Spirit – 1937

Bring, O morn thy music!
Night thy starlit silence!
Oceans, laugh the rapture
To the storm winds coursing free!
Suns and planets chorus,
Thou art our creator,
Who wert and art,
And ever more shalt be!

William Channing Gannett, 1893

The Directors of the American Unitarian Association approached Foote in 1927 to chair a new Commission on Hymns and Services to revise the *New Hymn and Tune Book*. The commission included Dr. Curtis W. Reese (1887 – 1961), vigorous humanist minister and Western Conference executive; Dr. Von Ogden Vogt, minister and author of *Art and Religion* and many subsequent works in the field; and Edward P. Daniels, minister, and accomplished musician (a first on such a Unitarian commission). In 1931, well along the way, the Unitarians and Universalists decided that the newly appointed Universalist Commission on Hymns and Services (Professor Edson Miles, Tracy M. Pullman, L. Griswold Williams, – with Professor Alfred Cole added later) should join the other and create a common hymnal. Obviously the hymnbook could no longer be a simple revision of the *New Hymn and Tune Book*, and it needed a new name. It was difficult to meld two traditions which had in recent years both been struggling with their own "gospel," and publishing hymnals fairly disparate, the Unitarians increasingly including more of their own creations, the Universalists having hymnodically moved closer to the liberal Christian mainstream. The task was accomplished, thanks in great part to Henry Wilder Foote's "patience and diplomatic skill, gifted in reconciling differences in taste and experience that ran deep."[1] In the end there were many Unitarian hymns and only 11 Universalist hymns included

---

1   Arthur Foote, "Henry Wilder Foote, Hymnologist," p 9.

(nos. 11, 86, 314, 431, 503, 552, 553, 554), and a caboose of hymns – placed after pages of chants – of "hymns and tunes which do not enter into the general scheme of the book" at the end of the book (including the "Battle Hymn of the Republic" among others in disfavor). Thirty nine percent of *Hymns of the Spirit's* hymns and chants are Unitarian (and Universalist) in authorship, still more than before in a denominational hymnal with almost exactly the same number of hymns. 138 hymns of the 224 total Unitarian and Universalist hymns were carryovers from the *New Hymn and Tune Book*, a somewhat less revolutionary change, for Unitarians at least. But there were significant changes. The old practice of tune above and words, mostly, below was changed, to some verses interlined in all cases, though subsequent verses, and occasional variant texts might be below or opposite.

Arthur Foote proudly noted that;

> Few such collections...can claim a more catholic range of music. Its tunes were drawn from the Jewish ritual, the mediaeval church, the psalmody of the Genevan reform, and the great German chorales. Included were French church melodies, and tunes from Iceland, Finland, Denmark, Hungary, Italy, and the Netherlands; also a wide variety of English and French carols and folk tunes, as well as tunes of the more familiar British and American composers from the time of Oliver Holden through the third decade of the twentieth century.[2]

The tune and text matches, edited by Daniels and young musician composer Robert Sanders, changed drastically, a huge number of familiar words being set to new tunes. Sanders arranged and adapted many old tunes and three of his own tunes appear in HOS. Sometimes the disfavored old tunes were kept nearby, or referred to in hymn notes, but the expectation of the commission was clear, to change many tunes Unitarians and Universalists were familiar with. For good, and ill, it worked. Some hymns matched to new tunes caught on well. Others all but disappeared from use, especially when the old tune was part of the common currency of the culture and not just the denomination. Henry Kemble Oliver's tune survived from the NHTB, and other Unitarian composers

---

2   Arthur Foote, p 9.

were used, Thomas Clarke (English), Robert Sanders (musician with the commission) and Rev. Charles Ellwood Nash. Rev. Edward Perry Daniels, also on the commission, helped match and arrange several tunes. Foote got his new British Cathedral music, getting rid of much but not all of the "intolerable sentimentalities" of Victorian tunes – as expressed so brightly by Ivor Atkins, then organist at Worcester Cathedral in England.[3] The acknowledgments and credits in HOS reflect a large debt to the Oxford University Press (for both words and music), doubtlessly reflecting the newly published *Oxford American Hymnal* for Schools and Colleges (1935) which received so much of the appreciation.[4]

> Henry Wilder Foote sought a large, inclusive hymnbook free of; sectarian dogmatism which harps upon a few of the many strings which give utterance to the religious life....
>
> The editors, therefore have borne in mind the saying that "in the hymn book is the true key to the doctrine of the communion of the saints; for here the saintly ones of all ages meet in their saintliest mood," and have sought to make as catholic a selection as is compatible with the interpretation of religion held by the free churches for the use of which the book is intended. So far as modern hymns express the thought of our day in a reasonably acceptable lyrical form, they have been eagerly accepted.[5]

Though the volume was not a drastic change for Unitarians, except musically, it does reveal some interesting choices and selections. There are new Unitarian hymnwriters, Jacob Trapp, Vincent Silliman, Curtiss Reese, Edwin Wilson. Newton Mann and William Channing Gannett's masterful translation of Yigdal appears. Several Ethical Culture authors were included, Box, Chubb, Quinn. Harry Emerson Fosdick's grand

---

3   *The Oxford American Hymnal*, edited by Carl F. Pfatteicher, Oxford University Press (New York, 1935) preface pp v–vi.

4   It is interesting to note that *The Oxford American Hymnal* changed the doubtless intolerably sentimental tunes to "It Came Upon a Midnight Clear" and "The Battle Hymn of the Republic." At least HOS didn't try that!

5   *Hymns of the Spirit*, preface by Henry Wilder Foote (II) (though signed also by a Universalist), Beacon Press, (Boston, 1937), vi.

"God of grace and God of Glory" is here but not much new from the larger Christian world. Edwin Markham's "Crest and Crowning of all good" presages the passion of the next commission to capture secular poetry for use in hymns.

Hymnal commissions are always seeking balances, a balance between the tastes, expectations and prejudices on the commission, a balance between the commission's collective wisdom and the expectations of the constituency they hope to serve and must please, balances between old and new in music and text, in this case a balance between the new English music Foote so loved and the old chestnuts that congregations adored, and so much more. And always for Unitarians and Universalists a balance must be struck between the theology of past generations as it continues in the present and the growing edges of theology that demand to be served in the contemporary day. Nowhere was this more difficult than in the day of *Hymns of the Spirit*, with Universalist and Unitarian interests, the new and as yet undigested humanist movement clamoring at the doors, and more traditional views barricaded within. The commission did include words by several new secular writers like Markham, and religious humanist writers, most notably Edwin Wilson and Curtiss Reese with relatively triumphal and trivial pieces but immensely popular ones. And the sharp theological edges of some traditional hymns were lopped off to please the age.

It is clear that the commission sought many other balances. There are many hymns by liberal women, but rarely two by the same one. This suggests a decision to see that important women hymn writers be represented, barely. A similar decision shows on some of the men. Surely the appearance of Henry Wilder Foote, the elder's, proper but not great hymn and Henry Wilder Foote II's single hymn also suggest a desire to honor their important gifts to church music. Many great names seem so represented. It is likely that this delicate balancing act in fact worked, for the hymnal was published to excellent reviews and to a considerable approval in the Unitarian movement (and republished into the 1970s) and cautious acceptance among some, not all, Universalists.6 To some, this author included, who grew up with *Hymns of the Spirit*, it often seemed musically plodding and dull, in text often hortatory, whiney or syrupy,

---

6 Arthur Foote, "Henry Wilder Foote," p 11.

sometimes a lethal combination of all of the above regardless of theology. When friends came to church, we ducked our heads, not to be seen when luckless new combinations of tune with familiar words or visa versa were sprung on the unsuspecting. Henry Wilder Foote reveled in the glowing reviews, "far above that of the average American hymnal, and the ethical note is strong. The section on social service and brotherhood is thrilling."[7] But he also heard from a Unitarian minister who called it "an atrocious collection, set to miserable, unsingable music." "Throw it out," the writer said, "and secure a really good hymnal like the Methodists."[8] The gospel and marching hymns of the Methodists were precisely what was missing, as intended! But nonetheless, it was indeed a great hymnal, of amazing breadth, vitality and virtue.

Having arrived at the first Unitarian and Universalist hymnal of the new century it would be useful to look at the corpus of Unitarian Universalist hymnody as it moves through the major denominational hymnals to the present.[9] I have begun with the *New Hymn and Tune Book*, since it did indeed set a new course, as every hymnal that followed also did.

Hymnwriter & Hymn	NHTB	HOS2	HCL	SLT
Adams, Rev. John Coleman (1849 – 1922)				
We praise thee God for harvests earned	371	314	219	294*
Adams, John Greenleaf (1810 – 1887)				
Heaven is here		553		
Adams, Sarah Flower (1805 – 1848)				
Nearer, my God, to Thee	287	245	126	87
Part in Peace				411*
Alcott, Louisa May (1832 – 1888)				
O, the beautiful old story	532			
Ames, Charles Gordon (1828 – 1912)				
With loving hearts	497			
Appleton, Rev. Charles Francis Parker (1822 – 1903)				
The past yet lives	442			

---

7   Arthur Foote, p 12.   * Revised

8   Arthur Foote.

9   I have excluded *Hymns of the Church*, 1911, since it was by any measure not a good or lasting hymnal.

Hymnwriter & Hymn	NHTB	HOS2	HCL	SLT
Thirsting for a living spring		221		
Badger, Rev. George Henry (1859 – 1953)				
O thou who art my king	359			
Ballou, Adin (1803 – 1890)				
Years are coming, speed them onward		554	198	166
Ballou Rev. Hosea II (1796 – 1861)				
Bright those jewels of the skies				132
Barbauld, Anna Laetitia (1743 – 1825)				
Praise to God, immortal praise	176	143		
Barber, Rev. Henry Hervey (1835 – 1923)				
Far off, O God, and yet most near	508			
Bard, Roberta (1940 –)				
Earth was given as a garden				207
Beach, Rev. George Kimmich (1935 –)				
Perfect singer, songs of earth				332
Beach, Rev. Seth Curtiss (1837 – 1932)				
Kingdom of God, the day	443			
Mysterious presence	80	63	130	92
Thou one in all, thou all in one	54	64		
Where is he that came to save	209			
Beardsley, Monroe (1915 – 1985)				
From all the fret and fever of the day			84	90
Belknap, Rev. Jeremy10 (1744 – 1798)				
Give ear, ye children (arr)	402	366		
Belletini, Rev. Mark L. (1949 –)				
Alleluia! sang stars				363
Bring out the festal bread				220
Chant for the seasons				73
Earth is our homeland				309
O liberating rose				130
The arching sky of morning glows				330
When Jesus looked from Olivet				263

---

10 A Liberal Christian, here to show continuity with later Unitarians.

Hymnwriter & Hymn	NHTB	HOS2	HCL	SLT
Blake, Rev. James Villa (1841 – 1925)				
Father, thou art calling	7	18		
O sing with loud and joyful song		420		
Blatchford, Rev. Ambrose Nichols (British)				
Softly the silent night	157			
Boeke, Rev. Richard Frederick (1931 –)				
Mother Spirit, father spirit (trans)				8
View the starry realm (trans)				28
Bonney, Mary B. (1910 –)				
Now the day is over (new verses)				46
Box, Howard (1926 –)				
Bells in the high tower			303	56
Creche flickers bright here				227
Bowring, Sir John (British)				
Within his temple	506			
Father and friend	90	79		
God is love, his mercy		121	83	
In the Cross of Christ I glory	213			
The offer at thy throne	499	154		
Watchman tell us of the night	194		283	
We cannot always trace the way	260			
Brooke, Rev. Stopford Augustus (Irish)				
Eternal peace, whose word of old	290			
In our dark and doubtful strife	257			
Let the whole creation cry	61	35	10	282
Now the wings of day are furled	146	118		
Oft as we run the weary way	186			
The morning walks upon the earth	55	105		
When the Loord of love was born	215	207		
Brooks, Rev. Charles Timothy (1813 – 1883)				
God bless our native land	421			
Bryant, William Cullen (1794 – 1878)				
Look from thy sphere of endless day	89			
Lord, who ordainest for mankind		439		
Thou, whose unmeasured temple stands	498	461		

Hymnwriter & Hymn	NHTB	HOS2	HCL	SLT
Buehrer, Edwin T. (1894 – 1969)				
We sing now together (rewrite)		22	67	
Bulfinch, Stephen G. (1809 – 1870)				
Hath not thy heart within thee burned	84	109		
Burleigh, William Henry (1812 – 1871)				
Abide not in the realm of dreams	346	297	222	
Lead us o father, in the paths of peace		70		
Capek, Rev. Norbert F. (1870 – 1942)				
Color and frangrance				78
Mother spirit, father spirit				8
View the starry realm of heaven				28
With heart and mind and voice				300
Carpenter, Alicia S. (1930 –)				
A promise through the ages rings				344
All people that on earth do dwell,				
sing ye aloud (recast)				370
Here we have gathered				360
Just as long as I have breath				6
Sleep, my child (complete recast)				409
We are children of the earth				314
We celebrate the web of life				175
Where my free spirit onward leads				324
Will you seek in far–off places				356
Cary, Alice (1820 –1871)				
My God, I feel thy wondrous might	57			
Chadwick, Rev. John White (1840 – 1904)				
Another year of setting sins		132		
Eternal ruler of the ceasless round	443	349		
It singeth low in every heart	473	451		
O Love Divine, of all that is	294	51		
O Thou, whose perfect goodness				
crowns	507	463		
Spirit of God, in thunder speak	397	322		
Thou glorious God, before whose face	437	462		
Thou mighty God who didst of old	440	422		

Hymnwriter & Hymn	NHTB	HOS2	HCL	SLT
Thou whose spirit dwells in all	95	65		
Thy seamless robe conceals thee not	112			
What has drawn us thus apart	97	222		
Chapin, Rev. Edwin Hubbel (1814 – 1880)				
Our Father God, not face to face	224			
Cheney, Edna Dow (1824 – 1904)				
At first I prayed for light		275		
Church, Edward Alonzo (1844 – 1929)				
Almighty Builder, bless we pray	487	456		
Clarke, Rev. James Freeman (1810 – 1888)				
Father, to us thy children, humbly kneeling	271	231		
Clute, Rev. Oscar (1837 – 1902)				
To thee, o God, in heaven	516			
Collyer, Rev. Robert (1823 – 1912)				
Unto thy temple, Lord, we come	24	14	252	35
Corrado, Rev. John (1940 –)				
Voice still and small				391
cummings, e.e. (1894 – 1962)				
purer than purest				250
Cutler, Rev. Julian Stearns (1854 – 1930)				
Motherhood, sublime, eternal		557		
D.S. (Universalist) (20th century)				
Holy, holy, holy, O thou Love Eternal		503		
Denham, Shelley Jackson (1950 –)				
Blessed spirit of my life				86
Dark of winter, soft and still				55
Faith is a forest				194
We laugh, we cry				354
Winter night, clear and bright				256
DeWolfe, Rev. Mark M. (1953 – 1988)				
Sing out praises for the journey				295
Dorian, Nancy C. (1936 –)				
Dear weaver of our live's design				22
Dorr, Julie Caroline Ripley (1825 – 1913)				
Heir of all the ages			245	

Hymnwriter & Hymn	NHTB	HOS2	HCL	SLT
Dwight, Rev. John Sullivan (w C.T. Brooks) (1812 – 1893)				
God bless our native land	421			
Eliot, Frederick May (1890 – 1958)				
O thou, to whom the fathers built			116	
Emerson, Ralph Waldo (1803 – 1882)				
No number tallies nature up				79
We love the venerable house		466		
We sing of golden mornings			40	44
Etzler, Carole A. (1944 –)				
We are dancing Sarah's circle				212
Fahs, Sophia Lyon (1876 – 1978)				
Divinity is round us – never gone			58	
Findlow, Bruce (1922 –)				
For all that is our life				128
Flint, Rev. James (1779 – 1855)				
In pleasant lands have fallen the lines	406	370		
Foote, Rev. Henry Wilder I (1838 – 1889)				
O thou with whom in sweet content		289	259	
Foote, Rev. Henry Wilder II (1875 – 1964)				
Thou whose love brought us to birth			193	
Freckelton, Rev. Nathaniel (British)				
O God who workest hitherto	227			
Frothingham, Rev. Nathaniel Langdon (1793 – 1870)				
O God, whose presence glows in all	81	60		
'Remember me,' the Master said	477	443	165	
Frothingham, Rev. Octavius Brooks (1822 – 1895)				
Thou Lord of Hosts, whose guiding hand	376	310		
Furness, Rev. William H. (1802 – 1896)				
In the morning I will pray	126			
Slowly, by thy hand unfurled	128	114		
Unworthy to be called thy son		249		
Gannett, Rev. William Channing (1840 – 1923)				
Bring, o morn, thy music	6	8	5	39
From heart to heart	76	54	251	
God laid his rocks in courses	491	458		

Hymnwriter & Hymn	NHTB	HOS2	HCL	SLT
He hides within the lily	65	29		
He who suns and worlds upholds	326			
I walk amidst thy beauty forth	166	136		
It sounds along the ages (arr)		76	247	187
Not Lord, this ancient	188			
O saints of old (ed)	459			
Praise to the living God (trans)			6	
Praise to God and thanks we bring	178	140	308	
The Lord is in his holy place	111	73		
The morning hangs a signal		90	1	40
To cloisters of the spirit			260	
Walk with the Lord along	353			
Gaskell, Rev. William (British)				
Calmly, calmly lay him down	474	452		
Father, through the coming year	179			
Mighty God, the first, the last	175			
Press on! press on! ye sons of light	370	315		
Geldart, Rev. Edmund Martin(British)				
When the light of day is waning	155			
Gibbons, Rev. Kendall (1955 –)				
From the crush of wealth and power				125
Lady of the season's laughter				51
Gilbert, Rev. Richard Stewart (1936 –)				
Thanks be for these				322
Gill, Thomas Hornblower (British)				
Lord God, by whom all change is wrought	185	359		
Our God, our God, thou shinest here	9	29	36	
Spirit of truth, who maketh bright	57	82		
The glory of the spring how sweet	134	165		
We come unto our fathers' God		363	403	15
Greeley, Rev. Dana Mclean (1908 – 1986)				
Let all the beauty we have known			326	
Greg, Samuel (British)				
Around my path life's mysterious	254			

Hymnwriter & Hymn	NHTB	HOS2	HCL	SLT
Grigolia, Rev. Mary E. (1947 –)				
I know this rose will open				396
Guttormsson, Guttormur J. (Canadian)				
Stillness reigns				49
Hale, Edward Everett (1822 – 1909)				
From city and from prairie	536			
Ham, Rev. Marion Franklin (1865 – 1956)				
As tranquil streams that meet		406	253	145
From Bethany the master		181		
Heir of all the waiting ages			293	
I hear thy voice, within the silence speaking	269	232		
O Lord of life, thy kingdom is at hand	385	332		
O thou whose gracious presence	482	448	125	
Ring, o ring, ye Christmas bells		169		
Songs of spirit, like a prayer				13
The builders toiling through the days			445	
Touch thou mine eyes, the somber shadows	270	230		
Hanson, Heather Lynn (1938 –)				
Gather 'round the manger				229
Harris, Florence (1891 – 1933)				
Like pilgrims sailing through	407	361		
Harris, Rev. Tomas Lake (1823 – 1906)				
O earth, thy past, is crowned		354		
Hart, Connie Campbell (1929 –)				
What wondrous love (new words)				18
Hawkes, Rev. Henry Warburton (British)				
Amid the din of earth	230			
Give us each day	476			
Our hymns sung	509			
Peace, perfect peace	279			
Reveal thy truth, O lord	389	335		
Thank we now the Lord of heaven	197	172	290	
Thou knowest, Lord, thou knowest	267			
'Thy kingdom come, O Lord,' we daily cry	386	373		

Hymnwriter & Hymn	NHTB	HOS2	HCL	SLT
Hedge, Rev. Frederick Henry (1805 – 1890)				
A mighty fortress is our God (trans)	314	304	16	200
'It is finished,' Man of sorrows	203	185		
Sovereign and transforming grace	30	25	127	33
Hereford, Rev. Brook (Britush)				
Lead us heavenly father	521			
Higginson, Rev. Thomas Wentworth (1822 – 1911)				
From street and square, from hill and glen		343		
No human eyes thy face	239			
The past is dark with sin and shame	380	321		
To thine eternal arms	246			
Hodge, Rev. Dwight Munson (1846 – 1906)				
Blow winds of God, and bring us on our way		552		
Holmes, John (1904 – 1962)				
O Lord of stars and sunlight			9	11
Though man, the fiery element, sink like fire			61	
Now give heart's onward habit brave intent			178	
Peace is the minds old wilderness cut down			179	
The peace not past our understanding falls				164
Holmes, Rev. John Haynes (1897 – 1964)				
All Hail the pageant of the years		146	205	
America triumphant!		372		
God of the nations	426	399		
O Father, thou who givest all	132	268		
O God, whose smile is in the sky	68	36		
O'er continent and ocean		400	227	
Show us thy way, O God			437	
The voice of God is calling	541	316	214	
This land of bursting sunrise				82*
Holmes, Oliver Wendell (1809 – 1894)				
Lord of all being, throned afar	50	16	38	
O love divine, that stooped to share	243	188		
Our Father! while our hearts unlearn	212	235		
Thou gracious Power, whose mercy	496	264		

* Revised

Hymnwriter & Hymn	NHTB	HOS2	HCL	SLT
Hopps, Rev. John R. (British)				
Father, lead me day by day	523	479		
Father, let thy kingdom come	393			
God of our fathers, hear	505			
Hark, hark my soul	465			
Hosmer, Rev. Frederick Lucian (1840 – 1929)				
All hidden lie the future ways		440		
Father, to thee we look in all our sorrow	272	227		
Forward through the ages	378	329	215	114
From age to age how grandly rise	455	423	231	105
From age to age they gather	409	566		
Go not, my soul, in search of him	75	58	88	
God that madest earth and heaven (vs 2)	152	100		
Hear, hear, o ye nations	429	398	194	
I came not hither of my will	298	252		
I cannot think of them as dead	231	202	73	96
I little see, I little know	229			
I walk the unfrequented road			277	53
Immortal by their deed and word	228	203		
Lo, the day of days is here	206	199	317	269
Lo, the Easter tide is here		201		
Not always on the mount may we	222	215	90	
Now while the day in trailing splendor	149	121	269	45
"O beautiful, my country"	424	388	240	
O blest the souls that see	399			
O day of light and gladness	204	196	316	270
O lights from age to age the same	503	464	255	
O Lord of life	207	195		
O name all other names above	296	242		
O prophet souls of all the years	457	421	233	272
O thou in all thy might so far	295	241		
O thou in lonely vigil	439	171		
O thou, who art of all that is	293	270		
O thou, whose spirit witness bears	69	52	74	
On eyes that watch through sorrows night		211		

Hymnwriter & Hymn	NHTB	HOS2	HCL	SLT
One thought I have, my ample creed	74	77	50	
Through willing heart and helping hand	497	457		
Thy Kingdom come, O Lord	387	339	210	
Thy kingdom come, on bended knee	458	338		
Today be joy in every heart	190	157		
Uplift the song of praise	404	378		
We pray no more, made lowly wise	342	274	188	
When courage fails and faith burns low		238	95	
When shadows gather on our way	104	125		
Horton, Edward Augustus (1843 – 1931)				
We honor those whose work began	504			
Howe, Julia Ward (1819 – 1910)				
Mine eyes have seen the Glory	410	567		
Ide, Beth (1921 –)				
Creative love, our thanks we give				
(recast of Creation's Lord)				289
Ishola, Bishop Adedji				
Words that we hold tight (based on his words)				179
Johns, Rev. John (British)				
Come, Kingdom of our God		289		
Johnson, Rev. Henry Harrold (British)				
Bring beam of oak, and		459		
Johnson, Rev. Samuel (1822 – 1882)				
City of God, how broad and fair	451	410		
Come thou almighty King (arr w SL)		10	26	
Father, in thy mysterious presence	268	229		
God of the earnest heart	344	301	224	
I bless thee Lord, for sorrows sent	256			
Life of ages, richly poured	394	337	172	111
O thou whose power o'er moving worlds (trans)		128		
Onward, onward, though the region	214	216		
Thou whose glad summer yields	460			
Kapp, Rev. Max (1904 – 1979)				
Far rolling voices				24
I brought my spirit to the sea				4

Hymnwriter & Hymn	NHTB	HOS2	HCL	SLT
Kimball Rev. Richard S. (1934 –)				
Winds be still				83
Knight, Sydney Henry (British)				
The sun at high noon				14
When the summer sun is shining				66
Wild waves of storm				80
Larned, Augusta (1835 – 1924)				
In quiet hours the tranquil soul	318	267		
Lathrop, Rev. John Howland (1880 – 1967)				
Hosanna in the highest		183	309	262
Lehman, Rev. Robert S. (1913 –)				
Within the shining of a star				238
Lewis–McLaren, Grace (1939 –)				
Touch the earth, reach the sky				301
When we are gathered				359
Livermore, Rev. Abiel A. (1811 – 1892)				
A holy air is breathing 'round	480	445		
Long, Hon. John Davis (1838 1915)				
The evening winds begin to blow	143			
Longfellow, Henry Wadsworth (1807 – 1882)				
All are architects of fate		346	175	288
I heard the bells on Christmas day	193	161		240
We have not wings		560		
Longfellow, Rev. Samuel (1819 – 1892)				
A voice by Jordan's shore	219	210		
Again as evening shadow falls	138	119	271	48
Beneath the shodow of the cross	248	187	312	
Bless thou the gifts		508		
Calmly, calmly lay him down (arr w SJ)			26	
Eternal One, thou living One	441	367		
Father, give thy benediction	513			
Go forth to life, O Child of earth	372	290		
God of the earth, the sky, the sea	49	28	43	25
God's trumpet wakes the slumbering world	366	309	213	
He who himself and God (adapt)		106		

Hymnwriter & Hymn	NHTB	HOS2	HCL	SLT
Holy spirit, light divine (adapt)	98	68		
Holy spirit, source of gladness (adapt)	119	3		
I look to thee in every need	284	258		
Life of all that lives below (adapt)	93	53		
Light of ages and of nations	453	75	248	189–190
Lo, the earth is risen again	210	200	318	61
Now, on land and sea descending	154	111	274	47
Now with creation's morning song (adapt)	137	102		
O god unseen, but ever near (adapt)	475	447		
O Life that maketh all things new	375	416	54	12
O still in accents sweet and strong	490	449		
O Thou in whom we live and move	83			
One holy church of God appears	452	407	261	
Out of the dark the circling spheres	237	99	208	
Sing forth his high eternal	28	308		
Spirit divine, attend our prayer (adapt)	77	55		
The summer days are come again	167	138		
Thou Lord of life, our saving health	255	469		
The sweet June days are come (arr)			326	65
T'is winter now; the fallen snow	170	133	301	
When my love to God grows weak			313	
With joy we claim the growing light			246	345
Loring, Louisa Putnam (1854 – 1924)				
O thou who turnest into morning	148			
Lowell, James Russell (1819 – 1891)				
Men whose boast it is that ye		318	173	
All whose boast				150
Once to every man and nation		319	220	
Once to every soul				119
The ages one great minister seem	448	417		
What means this glory round our feet	192	160		
When a deed is done for freedom			168	
Lyon, Carrie Ward (1879 – 1965)				
Praise ye, praise ye the Lord,			31	

Hymnwriter & Hymn	NHTB	HOS2	HCL	SLT
Lyttle, Charles H. (1884 – 1980)				
Bring, o past, your honor				290
Praise God the love we all may share			37	365
Rejoice in love we know and share			42	
Bring, OPast, your honor			254	
MacKinnon, Rev. John G. (1903 – 1983)				
Ye earthborn children of a star				319
Maki, Jeanne (1943 –)				
Has summer come now dawning (trans)				72
Markham, Edwin (1852 – 1940)				
Cherry blooms (English words to "Sakura")				177
Martineau, Rev. James (British)				
A voice upon the midnight air		184		
Thy way is in the deep, O Lord	250	186		
Where is your God they say			87	
Mason, Caroline A.,B. (1823 – 1890)				
O God, I thank thee	38	91		
Masten. Ric (1929 – 2008)				
Let it be a dance we do				311
McDade, Carolyn (1935 –)				
Come, sing a song with me				346
Spirit of Life				123
We'll build a land				121
Michaels, Christine Doreian (1942 –)				
Though gathered here to celebrate				340
Mikelson, Rev. Thomas J.S. (1936 –)				
Sing of living, sing of dying				306
Wake, now my senses				298
Moore, Berkeley L. (1932 –)				
Let love continue long				129
Moore, Rev. Henry (British)				
Supreme and universal light	350	292		
Morgan, Rev. John Hanley (1918 –)				
Let Christmas come				224

Hymnwriter & Hymn	NHTB	HOS2	HCL	SLT
Navias, Rev. Eugene B. (1928 –)				
Come thou fount of every blessing (new verses)				126
Norton, Rev. Andrews (1786 – 1853)				
My God, I thank thee! May no thought	247			
Where ancient forests widely spread	35	27		
Parker, Rev. Theodore (1810 – 1860)				
O thou great friend to all the sons	216	209	120	
Patton, Kenneth (1911 – 1994)				
Brief our days but long for singing			28	
Before the stars a man is small			68	
Feet of the urgent pioneer			232	
Let all men living in all lands			225	
Let all who live in freedom			171	
Man is the earth upright and proud			62	
We are the earth upright				303
Now once again the heaven turns			320	
Ours be the poems of all tongues			138	
Quest of the ages, good of men			203	
The blessings of the earth and sky			256	308
The earth is home and all abundant			56	310
We journey with a multitude			66	
When we have ended searching			181	
Peabody, Rev. William B.O. (1799 – 1847)				
Who is thy neighbor?	339			
Pierpont, Rev. John (1785 – 1866)				
Another day its course hath run	527			
Gone are those great and good	417	364		
O God, I thank thee that the night	526			
O Thou to whom in ancient time	438	15		
Poley, Joyce (1941 –)				
One more step				168
Quimada, Bishop Toribio				
O, the beauty in a life (based on his words)				182
Reese, Rev. Curtiss (1887 – 1961)				
From all that dwell below the skies (arr)			502	381

Hymnwriter & Hymn	NHTB	HOS2	HCL	SLT
Reynolds, Malvina (1900 – 1978)				
O what a piece of work we are ("is man")				313
Robbins, Rev. Chandler (1810 – 1882)				
Lo, the day of rest declineth	34			
Russell, Rev. Byron G. (c1850 – 1930)				
Our Father, unto thee		11		
Russell, Hon Francis A. R. (British)				
Christian, rise, and act thy creed	337	282		
Sadler, Rev. Thomas (British)				
The Lord has said, "Seek ye my face"	245			
Savage, Rev. Minot Judson (1841 – 1918)				
How shall come the kingdom holy		358		
O Star of truth, down shining		246	115	293
Seek not afar for beauty		40	174	77
When the gladsome day		123	272	
Scott, Jim (1945 –)				
Gather the spirit				347
Nothing but peace is enough				167
Tradition held fast				316
Scott, Thomas (British)				
The uplifted eye and bended knee	352			
Scudder, Eliza (1821 – 1896)				
I cannot find thee		72		
Thou Grace Divine, encircling		224		
Thou life within my life		81		
Seaburg, Rev. Carl G. (1922 – 1998)				
Be that guide whom love sustains				124
Find a stillness				352
God who fills the universe				37
I seek the spirit of a child				338
In the gentle of the moon				234
Once in Royal David's city (complete recast)				228
Rank by rank again we stand (new words)				358
When daffodils arrive				62

Hymnwriter & Hymn	NHTB	HOS2	HCL	SLT
Sears, Rev. Edmund Hamilton (1810 – 1876)				
Calm on the listening ear of night	189	159		
It came upon a midnight clear	191	162	287	244
Senghas, Dorothy Caiger (1930 –)				
We gather together in joyous thanksgiving (recast)				349
Silliman, Rev. Vincent B. (1894 – 1979)				
As we leave this friendly place				414
Earth arrayed in wondrous beauty			48	
Faith of the larger liberty (vs 3)			257	287
Morning so fair to see		45	14	42
One world this for all its sorrow			145	133
We three kings (vs 5)			300	
Sills, Edward Rowland (1841 – 1887)				
Send down thy truth, O God			124	
Spencer, Anna Garlin (1851 – 1931)				
Hail the hero workers		330		
Storey, Rev. John Andrew (British)				
Down the ages we have trod				2
Far too long, by fear divided				160
Golden breaks the dawn (second vs)				353
Grieve not your heart (Confucius recast)				186
In the bleak midwinter (recast later verses)				241
In the spring with plow and harrow				71
O earth, you are surpassing fair				174
Our faith is but a single gem				193
The ceaseless flow of endless time				350
The human touch can light the flame				307
The star of truth but dimly shines				297
The sun that shines across the sea				19
We the heirs of many ages				102
Tarrant, Rev. William George (British)				
Come let us join with faithful souls	365	303		
Draw nigh to God	274			
I saw the city of the Lord	428	394	204	
Marching with the heroes	543	480		

Hymnwriter & Hymn	NHTB	HOS2	HCL	SLT
Now praise we great and famous men		365		
The fathers built this church	538	395		
The light along the ages	205	197		
With happy voices ringing	519	478		
Tagore, Rabindranath (1861 – 1941)				
Now I recall my childhood				191
There are numerous strings				197
Your mercy, oh eternal one				185
Taylor, John (British)				
Lord, before thy presence one	31			
Lord, what offering shall we	336	281		
Like shadows gliding		180		
Thorn, Emily L. (1915 –)				
Do you hear, o my friend				112
Trapp, Rev. Jacob (1899 – 1992)				
Let freedom span both east and west				148
The art, the science and the lore		250		
Wonders still the world shall witness	330	191		139
Very, Jones (1813 – 1880)				
Father thy wonders	45	41		
We go not on a pilgrimage	297	265		
Ware, Rev. Henry Jr. (1794 – 1943)				
All nature works his praise	500	454		
Great God, the followers	25	21		
Wendte, Rev. Charles W. (1844 – 1931)				
Not given to us from out the skies		391		
Weston, Rev. Robert Terry (1899 – 1988)				
This is the truth that passes understanding				369
Westwood, Horace (1884 – 1956)				
Spirit of truth, of life, of power			146	403
Wile, Frances Whitmarsh (1878 – 1939)				
All beautiful the march of days	168	131	304	57
Wiley, Hiram Ozias (1831 – 1873)				
He leads us on bypaths we did not	264	240		

Hymnwriter & Hymn	NHTB	HOS2	HCL	SLT
Williams, Helen Maria (1762 – 1827)				
While thee I seek, protecting Power	304	255		
Williams, Rev. Theodore Chickering (1855 – 1915)				
As the storm retreating		145	430	
By law from Sinai's clouded steep	16	126		
Glory be to God on high		164		
God be with thee! Gently o'er thee		511	471	
Hast thou heard it, o my brother		540	476	
In the lonely midnight	531	173	292	242
Lord, who dost the voices bless	489	450		
My country, to thy shore	418	382		
Thou rulest, Lord, the lights on high	242	37		
To hold thy glory, Lord of all	493			
When the world around us throws	259	233		
When my heart, with joy o'erflowing	335	280	226	
Willis, Love Maria (1824 – 1908)				
Father hear the prayer we offer	122	85		
Wilson, Rev. Edwin H. (1898 – 1993)				
Where is our holy church		412	259	113
Wilson, Rev. Lewis Gilbert (1858 – 1928)				
O God our dwelling place	281	43		
O troubled sea of Galilee	266			
Wreford, Rev. John Reynal (British)				
Lord, while for all mankind we pray	425	390		
When my love to God grows weak		189	313	
Wright, Rev. Samuel Anthony (1919 –)				
We would be one				318
Young, Michael G. (1939 –)				
Mother of all (rewritten from "Father of all)				91

There is much to learn from such a list. It shows so clearly here, as we have said, the prolific output of our hymn writers. It is easy to see how more of our hymns could be in hymnals other than in our own, and that has been true for many years, suggesting a rate of change of theological and hymnodic taste far outstripping other denominations.

This also means, however, that the past for the most part is swiftly lost in our living hymnody. There are world reknown hymns and hymn writers from our past, vastly popular in other communions, but long since missing from ours. It is difficult not to mourn the waste and carnage, but we must be careful in interpreting this reality. It does not mean that we have carelessly trashed our past, though to some degree that is precisely true and needs to be unpacked and understood. It does not mean that we have tinkered with our hymnody to a degree unknown in the past. We have cut, pasted and amended in every generation, but it is true that today's tinkering often alters meanings as never before. It does not mean that nothing is sacred, nothing endures, for there is a continuity of faith and practice traceable through our hymns, especially the handful of long survivors. But we must acknowledge that there are very, very few survivors, works of our own long tradition, in *Singing the Living Tradition,* and that is troubling for it is not for want of greatness, depth, conviction or power in our older hymnody. And older hymns by women in our tradition have all but disappeared in *Hymns for the Celebration of Life,* and *Singing the Living Tradition,* making the title of the latter seem a strange misnomer.

Some simpler things may be garnered from this long list of hymns. The *New Hymn and Tune Book,* included almost every major British Unitarian hymnwriter of the day (Gill, Hawkes, Hopps, Tarrant, Taylor, Wreford and more). One wonders, given the then British Unitarian exclusion of music from their hymnals and the immense popularity of American Unitarian hymns there, whether the AUA's hymnbook commission in creating the 1914 hymnal thought that the *New Hymn and Tune Book* might have some currency on the other side of the Atlantic. It would in any event have been a futile hope given the extraordinarily different musical traditions on both sides of the Atlantic, since certainly American tastes, moving however strongly toward British cathedral music (not generally to British Unitarian tastes anyway), were (and are) too distinct from the cobelievers on the other side of "the great pond." Most of the British Unitarian hymns disappeared in *Hymns of the Spirit,* though *Singing the Living Tradition* brings a few of the new generation of British hymns into our hymnal.

Exceedingly little from our earliest hymn writers on these shores survives, many hymns and writers having already disappeared as early as *Hymns of the Spirit*. The greatest of our past hymnwriters are generally in this generation – though survivors – barely so, with few having more than a hymn or two in *Singing the Living Tradition*. Some continue in the hymnals from the last century to the present with one single hymn. Some appear with a single hymn in a single hymn book, and nevermore. A few writers and hymns appear and depart, only to appear again, rediscovered by a new commission. Some, like the excellent British hymnwriter, Sir John Bowring, and American Unitarian, John White Chadwick, disappear entirely in a single generation of American Unitarian Universalist hymnals. The pattern in our older hymnals is one of gathering hymns of good hymnwriters in our fellowship for a couple of hymnals, then a culling down to favorites, but this process seems aborted in our hurried generation, where a hymnwriter can be very popular in one hymnbook and gone or almost so in the next. This deserves study and reflection. *Hymns of the Spirit* put in the caboose of unfavored hymns, not "in the spirit" of the hymnal, several of immense public popularity, not daring to drop them outright. The subsequent hymnals chose the course of eliminating those that had been disfavored by that commission.

Sunday school and home and family hymn books deserve more than the passing mention they will get here. In 1868, when the *Hymn and Tune Book* was just coming from the press, another volume was also published, *Social Hymns and Tunes; for the Conference and Prayer Meeting and the Home with Services and Prayers,* also published by the American Unitarian Association. It is a small but tight packed little volume with hymns for every use, including children. There is little of the deadly sweet pandering that will be found later, but there is also not much for children to feel readily at home with. Some excellent and current hymns are here, and clearly this volume was created by women and men with many women's hymns, and did not speak down to children. It was followed in 1869 by the *Hymn, Tune, and Service Book for Sunday Schools,* published by the AUA, but created by a "subcommittee of the Ladies Commission" who obviously felt that *Social Hymns* wasn't good enough for children. The *Hymn, Tune and Service Book for Sunday Schools* printed music and words together and included some of the best Unitarian women's hymns and writers (Eliza Follen, Sarah Flower Adams, Love Maria Willis, Martha

Lowe, M.N. Meigs) and the best men too. "Silent Night" appears in an early, old translation. It even includes "Shall we gather at the river?" It was often reprinted until the Unitarian–Sunday School Society launched it's *A Book of Song and Service for Sunday School and Home*, compiled and edited by Edward A. Horton, AUA (Boston, 1895). Unfortunately, despite many grand new hymns, and interlined music, the editor was too enamored of his own work and included an obscene number of his own creations, which have not survived the test of time. But the wondrous variety of his selections from Fanny Crosby's "Rescue the Perishing" to a wonderful Jewish Hallelujah deserves praise.

Others were creating Sunday school songbooks, notably Charles William Wendte who published two:

> *The Carol, A Book of Religious Songs for the Sunday School and the Home*, John Church Co., (Cincinnati, 1888), music interlined. Wendte drew from popular Unitarian poets and hymnwriters, and traditionally popular hymns of many backgrounds. He drew music from classic, German and evangelical sources, declaring that he wanted hymns that could be enjoyed. His own hymns are sadly pedestrian and condescending for children.

> *Heart and Voice, A Collection of Songs and Services for the Sunday School and The Home*, George Ellis (Boston, 1908), a complete revision and extension of the earlier work, with still more attention paid to music, more subjects attended to and a better index.

These had wide use and undoubtedly encouraged the AUA to its own new efforts in the new century. The Universalists, long without an official Sunday school hymnal, published their *Songs of Work and Worship*, Edited by Stella Marek Cushing and Jason Moore Boston (Murray Press, 1923). With only 135 hymns it is an amazing collection, including little of classic Universalism, most of the best of the Unitarians, and a fascinating mix of evangelical and mainstream Christian hymns. It also shows the first recognition of sexism, in an added recasting of "Faith of our fathers," the second verse reading:

> Faith of our mothers, living still

> In love and life that ne'er shall die
> And children's children ever dear
> > Shall hold the faith that brings God nigh
> Faith of our mothers, holy faith
> > We will be true to thee till death.

Not many hymnals would have dared such heresy.

The *Beacon Hymnal* was next in 1924, edited by Religious Educator, Florence Buck, probably with too much of an evangelical gloss to long survive given the direction of Unitarian hymnody. It was, however, a serious attempt to put together worship and song for children and families, and it drew without apology from the best hymns and writers of the day, without heavy handed editing. It was followed by the *Beacon Song and Service Book* in 1935 a joint creation with the Universalists; Unitarian Vincent Silliman working with Universalist Katherine Yerrington. They also consulted vigorously with the commission already working toward *Hymns of the Spirit*, especially Henry Wilder Foote (II), its chair. *The Beacon Song and Service Book* previewed hymns later accepted by Foote for the new hymnal. It reached out to popular children's songs, to poets and hymnwriters as yet not included in "adult" hymnbooks. The next generation of children's hymnal was a long time coming.

Vincent Silliman, in reflecting on Arthur Foote's monograph on his father, remembered;

> Dr. Foote's vital part in the production of *The Beacon Song and Service Book*, 1935. This is a collection of hymns and service materials intended primarily for children and young people – a project which took several years of concentrated effort during the years in which *Hymns of the Spirit* was in preparation, and which involved religious, musical, and literary standards comparable with those of the other book. The editorial committee consisted of Ruth E. Bailey, music editor, Gertrude H. Taft, Katherine I. Yerrington, and the undersigned. Dr. Foote attended countless meetings of this committee, made available to us the evolving manuscript of *Hymns of the Spirit,* encouraged wholeheartedly our somewhat timid desire to include whatever we could lay our hands on that could give

devotional expression to the humanist phase of the Unitarian movement, and carried back to *Hymns of the Spirit* a number of our findings, choices of tune and texts set to tunes, including two of the hymns most cherished today in Unitarian Universalist churches.[11]

Vincent Silliman, who had worked twenty years before on the *Beacon Song and Service Book*, became editor of *We Sing of Life* in 1955, a very different songbook, done entirely in fresh calligraphy, drawing widely from Unitarian, Christian, world religious and secular traditions, and setting new words to music. The American Ethical Union cooperated in this creation, published by Starr King Press. Folk songs for the first time found their way into this songbook.

---

11 Quoted in Arthur Foote, footnote 22, p 23.

Hymns for the Celebration of Life – 1964

It was clear long before the new hymnal commission was created that *Hymns of the Spirit* no longer served for the entire denomination the fundamental gathering together in common expressions of faith function for which it was intended a quarter of a century before. The Association had grown more distinctly humanist, in majority, and a new hymnal to reflect the shift, and to respond to a new generation was in order. Churches throughout the country were mimeographing hymns and songs they valued from any and every source (mostly entirely illegally), and a few were publishing formal hymnbooks, most notably Waldemar Hille, First Unitarian Church of Los Angeles, *Hymns of Faith in Man*, much later reworked into *How can we keep from singing*. There was much discussion of a loose leaf hymnal among many who thought no fixed and printed book could ever meet the evolving needs of so disparate an Association of churches and fellowships. But it was clear that the issues of royalty and proper credit and remuneration due the artists would tie this proposal in a gordian knot of complexity.

The new hymnal commission appointed by the Unitarian Universalist Association Board was set to work in 1961. The commission set out to review and remake Unitarian Universalist hymnody. Its balance was humanist and its determination was, judging from its results, to let few prejudices of past use or affection for a particular hymn to sway the judgment of the commission. It meant to judge anew, as broadly and inclusively as its members knew how, and it did. The fury that attended its publication from those of more traditional religious taste, and the firestorm of feminist criticism in the years immediately following have obscured the very creative work the commission did, in fact, do.

The task of the commission, it must be stated, was impossible of achievement. The determination of the commission was to have texts entirely interlined, and printed clearly enough that all could be read. With the necessity of a wonderfully rich and diverse section of responsive readings and other worship materials, and the addition of a set of meticulous hymn and music notes, based in great part on the work of Henry Wilder Foote II, and a full usable set of indexes they had to limit the number of hymns to a manageable total that would not make the hymnal too heavy to lift or too expensive to buy. *Hymns for the Celebration of Life* has 327 hymns, a little over half the total in *Hymns of the Spirit*. If the commission had chosen to make as few changes in the corpus of Unitarian Universalist hymnody as possible from its predecessor it would, given the constraints, still have had a massive culling of hymns. It can be argued that, to a great degree, that is exactly what happened. *Hymns of the Spirit* had 39% Unitarian and Universalist hymns. Among its Unitarian and Universalist hymns, most had appeared in the *New Hymn and Tune Book* where the basic collection of acknowledged excellence in UU hymnwriters had already fairly conclusively been assembled, the additions mostly being more good hymns by the same authors. *Hymns for the Celebration of Life* had half the number of UU hymns, as would be expected from its size, and among its Unitarian and Universalist hymns 73% were carried over from *Hymns of the Spirit* (53% carryover from the *New Hymn and Tune Book*), meaning that few new UU hymnwriters and hymns were included and the commission was struggling to preserve a central body of UU hymnody. But critics bitterly complained of its excisions of hymns from the UU and broader traditions. The losses were across the board, but so were new inclusions from traditional sources. There were simply fewer hymns in almost every category.

The great change in *Hymns for the Celebration of Life* was in the vision of what new should be included. The commission was shaped by the humanist movement and the growing world religionist search and hunger. Shalom Havarim and the Hannukah Hymn joined Yigdal. Buddha, Confucius, a poem of the Baghavad Gita, even Horace were set to music. Poetry of Goethe, Tennyson, Erasmus Darwin, Alfred Noyes, Whitman, Edna St Vincent Millay, Mathew Arnold, S.R. Lysaught, William Blake, Christina Rosetti, Gilbert Chesterton, Algernon Swinburn, Lord Byron, Percy Bysshe Shelley became hymns. Ridgeley Torrence, Mary Howitt, Elizabeth Syle Madison, John Hall Wheelock, Helen Hoyt, John Burroughs, Archibald MacLeish, Laurence Binyon, Zona Gale, Sarah Henderson Hay, Robert Frost, Nancy Bird Turner and a host of others, many for the first time – few carryovers – were hammered into hymnodic form. John Holmes, son of a Unitarian minister, has four radiant hymns, and Jacob Trapp another new hymn. Sophia Fahs, thanks to the sunday school books, is here. A dozen more UUs are represented by their hymns.

The commission has been often called the Patton commission, and the hymnal, the Patton hymnal, after Kenneth Patton, minister of the Charles Street Meeting House in Boston. The label is not entirely wrong; but the assertion, based as it usually is on the number of Patton hymns in *Hymns for the Celebration of Life* – 13[1], it is blatantly false. The number is small and the quality varying but some excellent – as with most hymnwriters. The problem for a hymnbook commission when one of its members as author or composer submits a creation is, how do you say "No!" That has been a problem of all the Unitarian and Universalist commissions. Even if a commission rejects one submission, it cannot possibly reject all from a respected member, though that might be wise. Unless Unitarian Universalist hymnbook commissions develop a tiered structure for searching out and receiving hymns, with the final commission insulated from writers and composers, they cannot come close to impartiality, but other unfavorable characteristics would doubtless emerge. The entire process deserves to be rethought and reconfigured. The present (and past) system of an appointed commission creating a hymnal (regardless of extensive outside input, testing, previews, etc.) straight through to printing and distribution with no careful structures of denominational review at any level is an interesting and anacronistic mix of anarchy and autocracy unworthy of a "liberal" religious association. No other denomination eludes any review process, and the Unitarian Universalist Association claims to be a democratic association of congregations!

But *Hymns for the Celebration of Life*, in a fundamental way was the Patton hymnal. Patton was legendary for his "flimsies," the badly typed, through too many carbons, onion skin copies of the hymn collection of a lifetime. More of the hymnal's creative poetry came from the large collection of Ken Patton than any other source, indeed all other sources put together. But Patton had a quite limited, relatively classical, musical repertoir and sometimes a tin ear when it came to music so his matches of text and tune often had to be overturned, something the commission

---

1 Patton hymns in HCL are nos. 28, 56, 62, 66, 68, 138, 171, 181, 203, 225, 232, 256, and 320.

readily did, sometimes matching tunes he recommended with different words as well as the other way around.

Surely the presence of Frederick May Eliot's hymn ("O Thou to Whom the Father's Built") in *Hymns for the Celebration of Life*, the late American Unitarian Association President, is here out of respect to his long and devoted service. There was a respect for tradition notwithstanding later assessments, but it was joined to a drive to set to music the best, and as they envisioned it, the most spiritually moving and enlightening words of a world's literary culture. Musically the commission were still more inclusive than *Hymns of the Spirit*, struggling with new tunes, tunes from wider American religious traditions and tunes from other musical traditions and cultures. Chris Moore, talented and devoted minister–musician, lamented the many times the commission could not get permission to use newer American tunes they wished for some of their new matches[2]. Robert Saunders, a commission member, submitted several new compositions, only two of which (Adam's Song and Keith) survived in *Singing the Living Tradition*, actually an excellent survival rate for new compositions[3]. It is only quite rarely that new tunes catch the imaginations and hearts of congregations and clergy. The commission sought to recast Unitarian Universalist hymnody for a new world.

Hymns for the Celebration of Life, and especially Ken Patton, took heavy criticism for the "man" centered language from the reborn feminist movement in the years immediately following the publication. In fact it is quite possible to argue that the hymnal's language was so blindly "man" centered that it fed and fired the feminist fury that spread to target all the sexist institutions and practices of the Unitarian Universalist Association. Should the commission have seen it coming? Of course. It wasn't that invisible, especially among Unitarians and Universalists. A more nuanced structure of review might have forced a rethinking of the language, but even if the problem were seen Unitarians Universalists were not yet sufficiently conscious of the full implications to have moved

---

2 Personal conversations with Chris Moore in 1964. The Commission also expressed its gratitude to authors who "permitted or suggested changes" in their works, changes in flow and phraseology that made it "possible to include their work" in the hymnbook's Preface.

3 Saunders's tunes were Keiths, Adam's Song, Ganador, Pont Neuf, Binyon, Wheelock and Woodlawn, plus countless labors on other hymns as he had with the previous hymnal commission as well.

very far, especially with older hymns, and Ken Patton for years refused others' requests to allow a revision of his own language, preferring until late in life to do editing himself. How different the hymnal might have been if the commission had been more forsightful is impossible to judge. It must stand as created.

The commission was attacked from every quarter, not only traditionalists whose hymns were among the missing and the feminists who saw the language as more of the oppression too long endured, rightly I would say, both of them. It was also attacked from the center. Noone attacked them with more fire and flair than Clarke Dewey Wells (who had submitted a powerful hymn from a contemporary Christian author, which was put in the hymnal), then minister of St. John's Unitarian Church, in Cincinnati;

> We need a new hymnal to replace the new hymnal. The Blue Book, bulging with Ken Patton's grandiose try harder utopian mysticism, wears woefully. Phrases like "Man is the earth upright and proud" sound more desperate and declamatory every year. And my beloved Whitman can be wronger than Kennedy, like Number 429 announcing "sweet blooded youth" and "splendid savage old men."

> Quintessence of putrescence, friends, pure puke. Spender's "I think continually" is a triumph, and some new hymns and tunes, like 276, 111. But any hymnal with the guts to expunge The Battle Hymn of the Republic and perpetuate Abide With Me ought to be shot at dawn right in the clef, without blindfold or cigarette. U–Uers flying to Europe this summer instead of sailing ships should have their passports revoked. And get shot at dawn, with jet planes and Abide With Me playing in the background.... I buried a young soldier recently, in a full military committal (rifle volleys, flags, marching, bugle, all). this ceremonial offering by 20 officers and uniformed men was lean, comprehending, purging, sustaining, utterly sensitive, perfectly moving. Must the Christian Curch go to warriors to learn what great liturgy is about? (Try that one on for ambiguity.)

People who believe in God are infantile.
People who don't believe in God are narcissists[4].

This savage old man, Clarke Dewey Wells, somewhat of a luddite of course, targeted directly the shallow, rose colored glasses variety of humanism and theism that tinted so much of that hymnal to its detriment, not only in new hymnwriters and newly assembled hymns, but in the editing and altering old ones. In their defense it must be said that they acknowleged alterations that they made in detail in the thorough notes, though they missed noting some alterations earlier commissions had made in familiar hymns, and changes hymn authors made in their own hymns.

For the first time Orders of Service were absent from the hymnal. Readings were more likely to come from the secular or other religious worlds than our classsic Christian tradition. The king James language was preserved in most, hightly edited, psalms that appeared among the Responsive Reaings. The gathering of service materials was a heady and pungent collection, but the strong hand of tradition that had showed in previous hymnals was absent.

Some brutal mismatches of music – new music to "The Voice of God is Calling" – caused fierce objections. To what degree should any commission take a hymn, like that one, immensely popular (except with the commission for *Singing the Living Tradition*, which expunged it) sung in virtually every denomination's hymnal to "Kemm Seele" and change it? Such actions, by every commission of this century, presume that we live separated and isolated from the common world, and indeed work to perpetuate such isolation, unless the new match is so matchless that it becomes the standard, a rare occurence in recent years, not at all so rare in the days of the "Sams" who had the good fortune to create their hymnals when matches were not so fixed, or indeed with so many new hymns, not fixed at all. The outcry against *Hymns for the Celebration of Life* misses the fierce integrity of their vision and their determination to bring a world's moving poetry to song. The breadth and quality of the music

---

4   276 was "In the sweet fields of autumn," and 111 was "They cast their nets in Galilee" which Clarke submitted, and which *Singing the Living Tradition*, in the next generation, expunged.

also deserves praise, despite a few sour tunes that never could or would find place in people's hearts. It was, like its predecessors, a landmark hymnal with many more virtues than its detractors or the *Singing the Living Tradition* commission ever discovered.

A Songbook for a
New Millennium

Hymns *for the Celebration of Life* lasted for 30 years, with the late addendum of a non sexist amendment (the "Green Book") which declawed a few of the favorites. But it was a very small, limited hymnal, quite short on the older hymns from within and outside the movement, uncertain of moving too far into the folk genre, mostly unresponsive to the creative hymnody occurring in other denominations. The Roman Catholics were suddenly and explosively, in response to the opening of the doors of Pope John the 23rd, exploring a whole new world of congregational singing. The commission missed it, as well as the multi–ethnic push of some mainstream hymnody, notably then as now the Methodists. Its great strength was in its vigorous mining of the poetry of the century for wide ranging spiritual expression, and its breaking the stranglehold of traditional musical expectations in former hymnals in delightful new ways.

A new hymnal commission was appointed by the Unitarian Universalist Association Board in 1988. Its chair was Rev. Mark Belletini, a creative poet liturgist and hymn writer. T. J. Anderson, Ellen Johnson–Fay, Helen R. Pickett, Mark Slegers, Barbara L. Wagner and W. Frederick Wooden completed the commission, an excellent mix of musically literate clergy and active church musicians. Jacqui James was staff to the commission. Even full time, which she was not, she would have had more than she could possibly do. The UUA had forgotten the countless hours necessary for all the background, backstopping, and backbreaking labor involved. Henry Wilder Foote II chair of two commissions in this century lived, ate, slept, breathed those projects during their years, and still significant staff was required. But the UUA was deeply uncertain about the fate of the hymnal. Would there be enough trust and interest in enough congregations to purchase enough copies? All kinds of strategies were launched to involve people, to cover bills as they occurred, to heighten anticipation and interest. It worked and the hymnal, essentially sight unseen, sold like proverbial hotcakes when the commission's five years of labor hit the shelves. There were constituencies and congregations which "sat it out" until they could review the hymnal carefully, but they were few and mostly on the Christian end of the denomination, already knowing well that the hymnal could not serve their liturgical interests sufficiently. There was sadly no historian of hymnody on the commission, with the now long absence of Henry Wilder Foote II.

The Hymnbook Resources Commission well understood the diversity of interests, tastes, expectations that faced them. They sought to embrace "the riches of humanism, feminism, mysticism, natural theism, the Jewish tradition, many other world faith traditions, and the skepticism generated by this century's disillusioning woes and wars." Conspicuously absent from this list is Unitarian Christians. But the list was and is impossible of accomplishment in a hymnal of fairly small size, probably impossible in a hymnal double the size. That they covered so much of their intended territory, and in so many places well, is a tribute to their devotion and determination. The commission "sought to express the center and edges of our living tradition;"[1] and "found a wealth of music and poetry, wisdom and beauty"[2] from which they could choose. It is clear from the result that help was offered everywhere and accepted. New hymns, so many by women, and music so much composed, adapted and arranged by women, reveal a wondrous richness that reflects well on the commission and on the denomination's own creative juices. The sources and principles of the UUA and inspiration from "liberation philosophies, cross–cultural perspectives, and ecological awareness" opened up a "full range of spiritual imagery"[3] they were determined to express. Feminine images of the holy show everywhere in their labors, including in recast old formerly sexist hymns as well as fresh new ones.

The commission sought to establish a baseline of the use and popularity of hymns in current use among Unitarian Universalists. Thus a questionnaire, a very long questionnaire, was created and distributed asking ministers and musicians to cull *Hymns of the Spirit*, *Hymns for the Celebration of Life*, and *How can we keep from singing?* for hymns they

---

1 *Singing the Living Tradition,* UUA, Beacon Press (Boston 1993) Preface p.VII

2 Ibid

3 Ibid

used regularly and liked, hymns needed for special services and seasons, hymns the respondents would hate to see missing in a new hymnbook, etc. etc. The hapless respondent who followed the directions had to cull from more than 1000 hymns and their variations in three collections (if they were familiar with all three) repeatedly to respond to each of the several questions, and write out the name and number and hymnal for each one. No index of first lines or titles was given, no list that could be "checked off" in each category. It was an outrageous imposition on time and energy, and doubtless severely limited responses, and desperately complicated the tallying.

The Hymnbook Resources Commission clearly used this list, however badly gathered, to establish a corpus of hymns generally looked for in the new hymnal, a list of hymns known and favored. As I have said in my *Bibliography of Unitarian and Universalist Women Hymn Writers* using this list as the exclusive historic grounding of our hymnody was a significant mistake. Only rarely did this commission reach back beyond *Hymns of the Spirit*. They doubtless saw no need to, since *Hymns of the Spirit* included the largest gathering of Unitarian and Universalist hymns and hymn writers in a century. What could be missing? Unitarian and Universalist women's hymns; many hymns of the first generations of liberal Christians, early Unitarians and Universalists; hymn writers who were disfavored for their radicalism or freshness of expression, hymns badly matched to tunes earlier that fated them for the ash bin; and hymns from the mainstream and evangelical sources that were consigned to the same ash bin by the tastes of earlier commissions, among others. Two of the three of the hymnals referred to in the questionnaire were fundamentally sexist in much more than language. Unitarian and Universalist women's hymns, for example, were few in them not because they were not available, but because they were either not known, not sought and/or not valued. The Los Angeles hymnal, *How Can We Keep From Singing*? was small and of limited scope, and thus despite its greater inclusiveness, and recent language neutral revision could not make up this lack. So the new Hymnbook Resources Commission had a problem in its sources, a problem they never recognized, acknowledged or dealt with. Thus *Singing the Living Tradition* is a misnomer, despite its healthy new collection of women's hymns and songs. It should be called, perhaps, "singing parts of the living tradition," the hymnal having fewer UU women's hymns that reach back past its predecessor hymnal than any other denominational hymnbook in more than a century. The hymnal's lacks are visible in all the areas just listed above, suggesting that the commission did not seriously engage the larger resources of our heritage, or the heritage of Christian hymnody beyond the tastes of its predecessors. This was a critical error especially in an era when UU congregations are participating in more ecumenical endeavors and worship, and *Singing the Living Tradition* is impoverished in hymns from our Christian heritage that can be used on such occasions. Partly this is due to such hymns' absence. Partly it is due to odd matches of music to old words. And partly it is due to editing the hymnal for much more than the "isms." More of this anon.

Ministers and musicians were urged to send in any hymns and songs they would like to see included in the new hymnal. Thus, finally, the commission found itself with 8000 or so hymns to evaluate. It was an Augean task, but not very different from the task of all their predecessors, except that denominational tastes were broadening markedly and folk songs, civil rights songs, and popular songs were migrating from the popular culture into UU hymnody. There were no guides for the commission as it moved into this uncharted territory, except common use. And the Association itself was changing. Humanists found themselves faced with a diverse new feminist spiritualism that was "death" on the old humanist "man" centered faith, a resurgent and active Liberal Christian movement demanding a place in the sun, a congeries of new earth based "pagan" people and congregations, and a world religious consciousness that had yet, after more than a century of pleading and organizing, to find a real and solid place in UU hymnody. This commission faced, I believe for the first time, demands from the outset for assurances as to what the hymnal would contain. To please all of these was on the face of it, a hopeless dream! But to serve them all in some degree was clearly important; and to find hymns that bridged rifts and chasms between them – a critical goal. Creating *Singing the Living Tradition* was a five year process requiring uncountable hours, putting aside personal constituencies, working through tough tangles, holding always a larger and inclusive vision. No one should disparage the labor and love involved, on the part of this commission or any of its predecessors!

The commission early decided that sexist and hierarchical language, language that portrayed blackness as negative, evil, language that disparaged any category of people must be as completely as possible removed from the hymns and hymnal. No other denomination had yet attempted this, though the *New Century Hymnal* of the United Church of Christ, also moving toward publication at the same time, took some fundamental steps in removing "man" language, and some but not all of the regal masculine God language.[4] *Singing the Living Tradition* finally made its own compromises on the same ground. Hymns from Black origins did not have their God language changed, though some were heavily and not always sensitively edited, nor did our own Robert Collyer's "Unto thy temple, Lord, we come," though here too there are changes later in the hymn. Making such fundamental changes in dozens of hymns meant a more radical "tinkering" with hymns than any earlier commission had yet attempted, a more problematic and controversial alteration than ever before undertaken. The commission, no matter how well it did in serving its disparate and often conflicting goals, was bound to take heavy criticism from many quarters. But, the commission "held its cards close to its chest" in the long process of creating *Singing the Living Tradition*. They acknowledged early several results of their questionnaire and testing, one of which was a clear message to leave Christmas Carols alone. They chose not to, altering several to remove sexist man centered and disfavored theological language, but few indeed abroad in the denomination knew they had done so until the hymnal was in their hands.

The commission published in the spring of 1991 a list of first lines of hymns that they had decided to include in the new hymnal, but some first lines were so changed as to be unrecognizable. No music was included and alterations were in no way noted, including many alterations of the match of text and tune. Only a careful hymnodist could readily pick out new hymns and excisions in the list, and then not all of them. The Commission's 1991 spring "Update" noted that "45% of the music [is] from

---

4 It would be impossible to review here the tangled tale of the commission(s), controversies, furies that were unleashed in the process of the creation of this new UCC hymnal. The original commission was fired and a new team assembled to create the more traditional hymnal that they now have. The original commission's hymnal was published independently under a new title. I don't know another denomination that went through such "sturm und drang" in hymnal creation as the UCC did in this one, or came out worse!

Hymns for the Celebration of Life" and "64 hymns and songs are included from other existing UU hymn and song books," mostly *How can we keep from singing,* though not said.[5] Unstated was the fact that this represented another very extensive culling of older UU and other sources, as *Hymns for the Celebration of Life* had done before, making this hymnal a still more revolutionary document. The Commission went on to declare that;

> The new book will include 16 tunes and 15 texts commissioned especially for this book, a number of other newly created works, and material from a wide variety of sources.

> We have chosen a broad range of material, so that the new book will be suitable for use by all our congregations. There will be a hymn for every heart; a tune for every voice. There is something here for every musical taste: from Vietnamese folk songs to Duke Ellington, from the Bible to Holly Near, from chorales to gospel.[6]

> Hymns used by Unitarians and Universalists around the world – in England, India, Transylvania, Czechoslovakia, Nigeria and the Philippines – are included.[7]

The commission's excellent gathering of responsive readings from a world of sources, including international Unitarian Universalist sources, is not really duplicated in the hymns themselves, despite their assurance. Music is taken from one tradition and matched to words from another and visa versa. They struggled so hard to include music and once in a while a carefully edited hymn from other traditions, including our world wide tradition, but there is so little among the hymns that anyone from anywhere else would recognize in its entirety. They have edited and adjusted, cut and amended until little whole and real remains. Is there

---

5 Hymnbook Resources Commission, UUA, Update – Spring 1991, 6/91, xeroxed.

6 Despite the hyperbole the hymnal is still desperately American and Euro-centric. The Commission neglects to note that many folk songs, indeed almost all songs in other languages are untranslated in the hymnal. When the Commission was challenged on this they assured UUs that the companion volume of notes and biographical material (*Between the lines, Sources for Singing the Living Tradition,* Jacqui James, Ed., Skinner House [Boston, 1995].) would include the translations. It didn't.

7 There are no Transylvanian hymns, some Transylvanian music but no hymns!

truly so little even in the world wide Unitarian community's expression in song and hymns that could be included without such drastic change as to be unrecognizable?

The list and notes were clearly published for reassurance, but did not reassure. Nearly 200 hymns were missing from the small Hymns for the Celebration of Life, which had undertaken a radical culling. This was to be a new hymnal in a more fundamental way than any other denominational hymnal had been. The Unitarian Universalist Christian movement recognized from the outset that its interests, especially in hymns for many Christian liturgical services would not, could not, be met by the new hymnal. Hymn testing occurred across the country, but each test congregation received only a few hymns, some familiar with one or two possible new tune matches. Workshops were held at UUA General Assemblies, showcasing a few hymns at a time. "The singing gavel" at General Assemblies introduced some hymns. Concerts were held for the Hymnbook Resources Commission. But the commission's work was done, as was certainly necessary, basically in secret. Denominational anticipation, expectation and fears, were high. As well they might have been.

Though the Hymnbook Resources Commission never said so, they also edited hymns radically for theological content. To have openly admitted it would have created a firestorm of protest. But quietly hymns like John Coleman Adams's, "We thank thee God for harvests earned" became a humanist hymn, "Our praise we give for harvests earned." The process was repeated many times, sometimes masked by the removal of a "masculine" and/or "hierarchical" word with the substitution of a fudgy non specific expression. "Creation's Lord we give thee thanks" becomes "Creative love, our thanks we give" (with other like changes throughout). A host of hymns, by editing and excision, lost all references to any recognizable deity and/or to Jesus. The substitution for archaic theological language of new expressions for the presence at the heart of creation has a long history. Every generation sees the same words somewhat differently. Changes are inevitable, but changes that fundamentally gut both the theological point and the poetry as so many of the commissions changes do, it seems to me, are inappropriate. Further the commission betrays in this process, as they conducted it, a serious lack of theological understanding of the meaning of much they have removed and seems not to have tried fully the rich repertoire of other theological images that the UCC commission for the *New Century Hymnal*,[8] for example, wrestled with. It is my conviction that when faced with the judgement that a hymn requires fundamental theological revision, a new hymn should be sought instead, or written, and the old left in its integrity.

Elizabeth La Sonde Anastos points out a further editing of theology in Singing the Living Tradition. The commission in dozens of hymns removed Christian and theistic theological references, but they also removed references to "grace, salvation, atonement, sin, and forgiveness." That's not quite true. "Amazing Grace" survives, shortened but not changed otherwise, but there are indeed few of such hymns. Anastos' concerns point to a larger reality in the hymnal. Longfellow and Johnson, among the very best hymn writers in our long pilgrimage, wrote many hymns of prayer, of confession, of lamentation, of regret and contrition, of the personal spiritual life, of yearning and hunger for wholeness and comfort. They wrote hymns seeking to put aside the sins that beset, the wrongs we rush to do, the "world of sin," which the hymnal commission has so significantly removed. Hymns of the spiritual life are what is most painfully missing from *Singing the Living Tradition*, but our hardest hitting social action hymns are missing verses or simply missing as well.

Brian B. Noonan, a former theological student at Andover Newton Theological School, puts the issue powerfully and poignantly:

> Contemporary UU hymnody too often tries to sum up the entire UU outlook in four or five verses, each hymn so amorphous, so universal that the particular cannot shine through. The value of poetry is its concentration, its distillation of life into small, potent containers. In its clear lens one can see wide horizons.
>
> Rarely does the reverse work so well....
>
> There is too sweeping a view. It is not personal, it is not touching.

---

8   I do consider the *New Century Hymnal* an abject failure in meetng the needs of a new generation. The new Presbyterian hymnal, *Glory to God*, Westminster Press (Louisville, 20123) is advertised by some used booksellers as by God, as author. It is large, inclusive of a world Chrisitonity and avoids, where possible identifilable UU hymns.

There is a time and place for anthems that broadcast a whole ideology in meter; does almost every single hymn need to re–state an entire problem? [9]

A hymnal must serve many purposes and *Singing the Living Tradition* serves many well, especially those of general liturgical purpose, but it does not serve the inner and personal life in community which should be first and foremost among its interests.

There is other editing as well. It is hard to describe but it's driving conviction appears to be the commission's belief that it could improve the poetry of original authors. Vincent Silliman's building repetition of the word "fairer" in "Morning so fair to see" is attenuated, by the substitution of other words ("tall" and "deep"). "Light of ages" is heavily and ham handedly edited to no clear purpose. "Light" becomes "joy" later in "Joyful, Joyful, we adore thee." Harry Emerson Fosdick's "God of Grace and God of Glory" has no more "hosts of evil," but now "clouds of evil." "O Little Town of Bethlehem" no longer declares this a "world of sin" but affirms instead a "worldly din." There are many of these presumed "improvements" which only offend. They do not improve.

When *Singing the Living Tradition* appeared I sent three pages of corrections to the Hymnbook Resources Commission, mostly having to do with alterations in text, a few mistakes in attribution and elsewhere. Alterations tend to be cumulative, building from one hymnal to its successor. This commission, despite the detailed notes Henry Wilder Foote left for others to follow, missed many of the older changes, especially the long standing practice of culling verses.

Neither they nor any other of the Unitarian or Universalist hymnal commissions of this century note, for example, that the perennial favorite hymn of Samuel Johnson, "Life of Ages, richly poured," has been shortened by four verses in every hymnal. Who sings original verse 6:

In the touch of earth it thrilled;
Down from mystic skies it burned;
Right obeyed and passion stilled
Its eternal gladness earned.

---

9 "Theology Implicit in *Singing the Living Tradition*," by Brian Noonan, an unpublished paper for a class in UU Hymnody at Andover Newton Theological School, pp 1-2.

or verses 3, 4 or 5, all of which are missing? The Hymnbook Resources Commission, needless to say, missed many edits from earlier hymnals that Foote himself missed. Added to these, they missed noting dozens of their own alterations. There are very few hymns in the hymnal that have not been altered by someone. In proper respect to hymns' authors the next commission must return to the sources, and seriously and comprehensively note where alterations have been made from the originals. Given the resources of the present day it is nowhere near as difficult a task as it was so recently.

Singing the Living Tradition contains 415 hymns, roughly 90 more than its predecessor hymnal and nearly 175 less than its predecessor. But this doesn't, in truth, reflect the true size and shape of the hymnal.

> 59 out of 415 pieces of music are rounds or single verse hymns, making them useful for doxologies and responses, but not long enough for use as a hymn per se in most congregations. Added to this are 50 two–verse hymns ... ranging from very short (two lines) to short (six lines). This means fully 26% of the hymnal could be categorized under the broad rubric of "service music."

> Overlapping this group of one and two–verse hymns is the group of 24 texts which have one or more verses in a foreign language.... Not counted in these 24 are the several settings of "Alleluia."[10]

Functionally this hymnal is, in fact, no larger than its predecessor if the tremendous growth in "service music" is factored out. This makes the hymnal much more limited in terms of hymns themselves than it appears at first glance, and helps explain the high level of "losses" from earlier hymnals to be replaced by new hymns and songs.

About the same percentage of hymns by Unitarian Universalists are present as in the two predecessors, but only about a third are carryovers, a dramatic change in favor of new UU authors and new hymns. The greatest growth is in the new Unitarian Universalist hymns and hymn writers. Women are present in large numbers including Carolyn Mc-Dade, Shelley Jackson Denham, Mary Grigolia, Kendall Gibbons, Beth

---

10 Elizabeth LoSonde Anastos, "Report to the Council of Christian Churches within the UUA," unpublished.

Ide, and Alicia Carpenter. New hymns always involve guesswork on the part of the commission if they have not already found wide usage. In the case of *Singing the Living Tradition*, exempting commissioned hymns, almost all of the "new" hymns already had found an audience. This is both good and bad. Some of the best of the new hymn writers continued writing excellent songs and hymns, as they do today, but the Hymnbook Resources Commission never sat down with them to ask what they were working on, or, for example, to share the difficulty the commission had in finding sufficient appropriate memorial and nature hymns as they were struggling to close the book. Thus the commission missed good new hymns that were readily at hand. And now UUs openly wonder how they could have missed this or that song. They weren't looking.

The healthy change in hymns from beyond our denominational boundaries is reflected in a larger body of hymns from other religious sources than before. The close communication and sharing with other hymnbook commissions working toward new hymnals in other denominations, especially the UCC and Methodists, shows clearly in new hymns and writers, including a few excellent hymns by Brian Wren and several Black and Hispanic hymns.[11]

Nearly 25 familiar hymns have been matched to new tunes, 9 of them matched to different tunes in each of the last three hymnals, 6 altering matches that prevailed at least a century among us, surely some kind of a record for confusing congregations. There are three historic Universalist hymns, two edited almost beyond recognition, and not counting Ken Patton, now cut down to three old chestnuts, not counting service music. There are eleven hymns of Jewish origin, at last a workable set; seven civil rights songs, twenty five folk and gospel pieces, overlapping more than twenty hymns from Black sources, finally recognized in our hymnals. There are five Thanksgiving hymns, none traditional, six Easter hymns, a thin weak set, and thirteen Christmas hymns, well chosen, not always well edited, but missing several old UU favorites. All patriotic

---

11 *Singing the Living Tradition* shares 6 African American spirituals with The United Methodist Hymnal, The United Methodist Publishing House (Nashville, 1989), and more than twice that number with the previous African American Methodist Songs of Zion, Abington Press (Nashville, 1981). And SLT includes, at last, a few Hispanic hymns, SLT shares less with the UCC's *New Century Hymnal*, The Pilgrim Press (Cleveland, 1995) than ever before, reflecting significant change in their hymnody as well as ours.

hymns, and all hymns that praise war in any form have been intentionally excluded as unworthy of us, including the "Battle Hymn of the Republic."[12] It is strange to note that more excellent UU hymnody is in others' hymnals than in our own, but perhaps that is in part inevitable given the swift pace of change within the movement.

Responses to the new hymnal varied across the board as one might expect, from Betsy Williams; "From time to time great books come along as resources to help us 'consider and celebrate what is worthy.' One of these is the new UUA Hymnal."[13] To Anastos observation that despite the best of efforts there was "no way to provide what the Christian UU congregations needed" in *Singing the Living Tradition*. She cogently points, as well, to the music, some "excellent, some is mediocre and some is very difficult;" and to the excision of "light–dark imagery, militaristic images, and hierarchical images.... Where those images were actually racist, violent or oppressive, it is fitting and laudable that they be excised. Unfortunately, many rich and challenging images were removed under the above rubrics because of a misunderstood theology rather than any negative power in the images themselves."[14] This seems to be a point where illusions of some kind of ideological purity clouded the commission's vision. Surely it is easy to bring to mind many occasions, great public memorial and funeral services, worship services centering on major national events when "America the Beautiful," "O Canada" and the "Battle Hymn of the Republic" have been appropriately and powerfully used.

A distinguished elder minister, Ed Lane, called *Singing the Living Tradition*, "the most exciting event of our Unitarian Universalist movement in the forty years I have been a UU, and that covered a lot of territory". He did, however, have his concerns:

> I'm annoyed that they violated their commitment to "singable hymns" by including six composed by a member of the commission – some "unsingable" – and one of them replacing the lovely tune for "the World Stands Out on Either Side." ...I think they went

---

12 Just for the record, Julia Ward Howe believed it to be her great peace hymn!

13 Article by Betsy Williams in the Church of the Larger Fellowship Newsletter, November 1992.

14 Anastos, p ii, noting also the like comments of other reviewers, "John Corrado, Earl Holt, Arvid Straube, Joseph Bassett, among others."

overboard in being "politically correct," changing "Peace is the mind's old wilderness cut down" [to begin with the next verse] sacrificing a powerful metaphor because they thought giving "wilderness" a negative image was not environmentally PC.... I like the inclusion of the broader tradition but find it ironic that in a hymnal entitled Singing the Living Tradition we aren't permitted to know the meaning of the words we are singing.... But this is a superb hymnal that will enrich our worship and serve us well. [15]

The most savage criticism was, I believe, the earliest, that of the late Roy D. Phillips, then of Unity Church in St. Paul Minnesota in a column written for "First Day's Record" in November of 1988:

Where is this feeling coming from?

- that the Hymnbook resources Commission has become a tight little group with its own agenda

- that its agenda is increasingly governed by a wish to reform the way certain Unitarian Universalists worship by producing a book which is "pure" by the Commission's implicit (not explicit) view of purity

- that because of certain decisions made by the Commission early in its work – decisions at odds with the recommendations of the committee which designed the Commission's project – the development of the hymnbook project has now become a lower denominational priority than it was before the Commission began its work that the Commission "knows"

- that certain religious orientations among us are immoral and that the hymnbook project is an opportunity to rid the denomination of such points of view – and

- that the process of excluding such points of view is to be identified as being inclusive.

- that the Commission has convinced itself that there is no way to identify and involve significant numbers of creative minds

---

15 Ed Lane, "Lane's Lines" in the "Community Courier," Waltham, No 2 (nd). "PC" refers of course to "politically correct."

– in writing position papers, in commissioning texts using the much–needed feminine imagery for the Mystery, in locating a greater pool of writers of text and tune, and so on – and has burdened itself with too many of these tasks to do them as well as they might be done.

- Maybe all this is not exactly fact, but where are these feelings coming from? Is it something in the way the Commission has organized itself? Is it something in the way it chooses to express itself? Where is this feeling coming from?

Roy Phillips was not mistaken in most of his observations, a bit paranoid perhaps, but mostly correct. But the disabilities in closure, in setting a common agreed upon course, in seeking to shape the denomination's hymnody and worship are endemic to the structure, not a chosen and separate way of this particular commission. I sent a very long letter to the UUA before the Hymnbook Resources Commission was appointed urging that there be regional groups which could gather and submit materials feeding into a larger more inclusive process, a review process, and much more. The communication was rejected without response, before the commission ever existed. The answer to the issues raised by Roy Phillips lie in our long history of closed commissions which was simply continued without amendment. That has to be changed.

Having said that, there are several underlying assumptions that this Hymnbook Resources Commission held whether understood or not. The Commission clearly believed, judging from its work, that the hymnody of the Christian world is essentially irrelevant to us, beyond a few hymns for UU Christians and commonly accepted holidays. We may gather what pleases us old or new, change anything in any way, including the music however widely shared in the larger world we live in. We can borrow whatever we want and use it for our purposes without apology. There is no connection or continuity required. We are separate, unbeholden, without important hymnodic connections to the Christianity that birthed us and surrounds us. We don't have to sing anything they sing in the same words or to the same tune, because we never meet and worship together. Another implied assumption is that history is bunk. No historian of hymnody, like Henry Wilder Foote II, or Leo Capen on the Universalist side, is needed. There is nothing beyond the immediately popular, and pleasing to the commission and the denomination, that should be carried forward in the hymnody. Our greatest past hymnody may be simply be left there, and left to other denominations to pick through. Further they seem to have believed that, generally, women especially UU women before 1964 didn't write any important poetry, songs or hymns that deserve to survive. Women hymn writers for the most part don't need be asked to participate in creating new hymns, beyond recasting old ones. And fourth, whatever is commissioned must be fine, even if it isn't. There may be some degree of overstatement here, but the proof of most is in *Singing the Living Tradition*.

Unitarian and Universalist hymnals are not like those of other denominations in important ways. They draw more heavily from the living present. They draw texts broadly from the religious and secular world. Generally the music is of high and consistent quality, and increasingly of greater breadth in reaching out into the non Christian and secular worlds. The hymnals are expected to draw the movement in new directions, not simply reflect the worship and faith of the moment or of the past. These are great and enduring virtues. Singing the Living Tradition is a good and serviceable but not a great hymnal. There is too much heedless and unacknowledged tinkering, too little thought for the "living tradition," too little attention to the spiritual life in hymns, too much that is trivial, and insubstantial.

Postscript:
What Makes for Greatness ?

The first song of his happiness, and the song awoke
His heart to the darkness and into the sadness of joy.
Galway Kinnell — a piece of a poem

Music, potentially, has a depth and power that words alone cannot reach, a wordless realm too deep for words, too full of pain and fear, too full of formless joy and wonder. Hymns, at their best, allow the expression of deep personal feelings, anguish, struggle, that for many has few other forms of expression. Richard Jenkins in a vigorous review of two books on British hymnody for the "London review of Books" (11 December, 1997) declares:

> One might think that nothing could be further from the psychoanalyst's couch than the open spaces of the church nave, and yet both allow people to express what they would otherwise keep locked up. It is no accident that so many favorite hymns confess to human fear and frailty in the first person singular "The night is dark, and I am far from home," "Change and decay in all around I see," "Let me hide myself in Thee." To make these declarations in unison is at once to submit to a discipline and to be released from inhibition. Even the crowd singing "Abide with me" at the Cup Final unconsciously knows this; the words still matter, and the experience remains vestigially a spiritual one. Similarly [J .R.] Watson remarks that "Dear Lord and Father of mankind" is "probably as near as most people will ever get to the *vita contemplativa...*"

"One may regard," he quips, this "as either disheartening or hopeful." Either way the argument is correct, that hymnody is indeed as close as many people will ever get to cleansing, clearing and centering their souls, and that includes a whole lot of Unitarians and Universalists, even if they would never be caught with their mouths open in public on such a hymn as those above listed. Our best hymn writers of the past, by common consent the best, were all capable of writing hymns with that deep personal confessional character, and often did. I do not think for a minute that their being the most popular hymn writers among us and writing such hymns are unrelated facts. Any denomination's hymnody that misses this dimension, however differently expressed, is flawed.

There is another dimension of good hymnody that is almost impossible to put into words, but I think Garcia Lorca, Spanish dramatist poet, puts it as well as I've ever seen it said;

> All that has dark sounds has duende. It is not a matter of ability but of real live form; of blood, of ancient culture; of creative action. To help us seek the duende there is neither way nor discipline. All one knows is that it turns blood like powdered glass, that it exhausts, that it rejects all the sweet geometry one has ever learned, that it breaks with all styles."[1]

Hymnody must have a fierce and holy bite to it If it doesn't tear at flesh and bone, if it doesn't rend the heart as though it must break, if it doesn't stand four square against popular reigning evils it has missed its deepest calling. This may sound like overstatement but reading hymns from Adin Ballou's *Hopedale Hymnal* with an open heart one can feel in so many of its hymns that *duende* of which Garcia spoke. That one feels it almost nowhere"[2] in the newest denominational hymnal, *Singing the Living Tradition*, because in part, in relation to older hymns at least, it was edited out by the removal of biting words, verses and entire hymns, should cause a holy fear and trembling. Fear and trembling lost favor in our midst long, long years ago.

But hymnody has powers which burst forth even in highly controlled venues. Witness the moving and pungent words of Mark Belletini, chair of the Hymnbook Resources Commission that created *Singing the Living Tradition,* in February, 1990, reflecting on the Commission's meetings:

---

1 As quoted in Passages of the Soul, by James Roose-Evans, Element Books Limited (Shatesbury, Dorset, 1994), p 117.

2 Kendall Gibbons' sharp, "From the crush of wealth and power" being a delightful exception.

Our...meetings are rooted in music; we sing it, play it, hear it, discuss it, love it, praise it. It heals us when discussions about textual difficulties have worn us numb; it refreshes us when we get tired; it moves us when we are stymied. We get through our long meetings grateful for the power of music in our lives....

We cannot understand music, therefore, as simply a vehicle for the words. Music has integrity, its own character, that owes nothing to language.

....It leads us in power beyond words to the wordless, beyond names to the nameless, and beyond talking about love to expressing and experiencing something of love firsthand."[3]

Unitarian Universalist hymnody has moved, particularly in this century towards that loving gentleness of which Belletini speaks. In the earliest years of the century you have fierce social prophets crying in the hymnodic wilderness on both sides of our religious aisle, Universalist and Unitarian. Hymnbook commissions spoke proudly of the important social message of so much of our own hymnody, so missing in *Singing the Living Tradition,* except mostly for a few retrospective songs and hymns from the abolition and civil rights movements.

But the voices of propriety and political correctness were powerful a hundred years ago, too. In a 1909 *Unitarian Worship Handbook* the centrality of singing to worship had been forcefully underlined, as an expression "of a cheerful, earnest religious vitality" in a congregation with "true religious fervor which craves expression." They went on to urge that every congregation "should insist upon expressing its religious emotions only in noble verse set to noble music," though they admitted that this might be difficult considering the state of popular hymnody and hymnals. No serious challenge here (unless it's getting Unitarians to sing together in tune). This was the era of Teddy Roosevelt, of toughing it out and pulling yourself up by your own bootstraps, of physical culture and regnant masculinity. It was not a time for the virtues of gentleness and healing,

---

3 Mark Belletini, "Where words leave off music begins," a paper from the Hymnbook Resources Commission of the Unitarian Universalist Association, February, 1990.

of consolation and comfort of which Mark Belletini speaks so movingly.

Hymnody shapes itself to the spirit of every time and place, every hunger and hope, every human purpose however great or small, hurtful or full of life, good or ill. Thus hymnals are creatures of the time and place wherein they are set. No hymnal, and few hymns, however endearing, last forever, though some hymns which touch heart and soul do endure. Hymnody that does not embrace our lives, confront our evasions and evils, challenge our courage, lift the weary spirit, and make it possible for us to go on another week is no help at all.

But there is another potential to hymnody revealed beautifully in a refection of Elie Wiesel in his *Memoirs*. He tells of clandestine gatherings several years ago in Soviet Russia of young Jews, often in cemeteries, to study Hebrew and learn Israeli songs, of people in terror and courage singing and celebrating Jewish faith and hope on Arkhipova Street in Moscow. If, he declared, someday he is called before the heavenly tribunal and asked, "What did you do that was worthy of benevolence?" he will reply, "I was present at the dance of Jewish history in Moscow." They sang and danced against all fear. Wiesel tells of meeting a young woman, an enthusiastic young woman leading the Jewish crowd in chants of Jewish affirmation. He asks her why is she "so determined to be Jewish?" Her answer is simple, "Well, it's because I love to sing." "Her answer dazzled me," declares Wiesel who felt like embracing her. "Yes," he shouts,

> ...a Jew is someone who sings. He even sings a few steps from the Lyubianka Prison. And he sings when he is joyful and when he is not. A Jew is someone who turns suffering into a song, his solitude into a chanted prayer....It is through song that the Jewish soul expresses itself best.

And the song bonds past and present in one. If we but saw and understood it clearly the Unitarian Universalist tradition is also a tradition set in song, rising again and again in affirmation, rejoicing, grief, courage, compassion and outrage. What amazing voice we have given to people, ourselves and our world!

But what of us today? Do we remember our own stories, do we care'? Do we remember even so recently the martyrdom in the Philippines of Perfecto Siennes who gave Unitarians there hymns to sing in the face of life and of death?"[4] Do we recall the songs of Czechoslovakian Unitarian minister Norbert Cepek as he marched along the fences of the Death Camp of Dachau singing, lifting hopes of the hopeless?"[5] Did we ever know of the trail of tears of Polish Socinians expelled in the 17th century from their home and land, some of their communities still surviving and still singing in the hospitable hills of Transylvania? Do any British Unitarian hymns survive in our hymnals from their long years of persecution and trial, when to be a Unitarian carried a potential death sentence?"[6] Does anyone still remember the early Universalists whose journey to these freer shores rose in heartfelt song of gratitude and hope? Did anyone ever tell us of the ancient hymnody of our Transylvanian sisters and brothers that has carried them through centuries of oppression? The story, the struggle and the hymns go on. Surely no tradition has been more prolific in hymnody than our own, but I doubt that most Unitarian Universalists are even marginally aware of it. The truth is that hymns of this long struggle are not entirely but overwhelmingly missing from the new hymnal, *Singing the Living Tradition,* though they do exist. What Elie Wiesel found so moving was the living community bonded in song to the ancient tradition, the tale of long centuries of struggle and survival renewed in the suffering and courage of the living present in song. But what if the songs aren't remembered, aren't shared, and new songs don't bond the present with the past? The polarity here is the rift between some way in song to mark the milestones on the faith pilgrimage, to renew the story, and at the same time to welcome the heartfelt burst of new song in the living present. It is always an impossible task to deal creatively with this rift, which nonetheless every generation must undertake.

It is my conviction that this bond of past and present is in this generation significantly broken in our hymnody. The bond of song that could knit us, as well, to Unitarians and Universalists and others in the Global Village, that should tie their stories together with ours in our hymnody is seriously missing in our hymnbooks. A Transylvanian Unitarian organist can pick up *Singing the Living Tradition* and find nothing familiar save a

---

4 Bishop Toribio Quimada has a lovely and simple hymn in the hymnal.

5 We have Richard Boeke to thank for two of his hymns recast in *Singing the Living Tradition.*

6 "No" is the simple answer.

few snippets of tune and an old hymn by Martin Luther. Are Unitarian Universalists on these shores so terribly different that nothing of their hymnody can find voice in our own?

Appendix I

An incomplete list of Unitarian and Universalist hymn writers, with some resources for finding out more about each one. I have put in more women from many sources outside our official hymnals to balance the scale – a little bit – and recognize their contributions. Phebe Hanaford, for example hasn't been in an official Universalist or Unitarian hymnal for a century but the Hymn Society of America has a listing of 30 hymnals around the nation and the world where her hymns appear! How can we not include her and others of the forgotten women?

INDEX TO SOME RESOURCES ON HYMN WRITERS

Following this listing of resources are brief biographies of Unitarian and Universalist hymn writers, indexed to sources in this listing. Some of these are readily available; some frankly aren't. As you will notice the more unavailable resources are for a more obscure hymn writers. The listing may contain either the only resource for some writers, or the best resources even if not easily findable – thus they are here listed. Recent living hymnwriters are noted but no biographies provided.

2CD   *Two Centuries of Distinguished UU Women*, UU Women's Federation, (Boston, 1973). Brief sketches of UU women's lives.

AH   *American Hymns*, Vols. One and Two, Hymn Society of America, Columbia University Press, (New York, 1980). Volume One exhibits the best of American hymnody (according to the editors), words and music, denominationally identified. Volume Two contains biographical sketches of all the hymn writers, and occasional supplemental information.

AUH   *American Universalist Hymn Writers and Hymns*, Henry Wilder Foote, (Boston, 1979), and *American Unitarian Hymn Writers and Hymns,* Henry Wilder Foote, (Boston, 1959). Henry Wilder Foote for the most part gathered these brief lives of hymn writers from SSLF below (for the Unitarian authors) and CHNO below for the Universalist ones. In each such case the originals are generally more detailed. Foote also has included a listing of each author's hymns that were known to Foote (often far from a complete listing) with occasional notes on the hymns, and UU hymnals in which they appeared.

BTL   *Between the Lines; Sources for Singing the Living Tradition*, ed. Jacqui James, Skinner House (Boston, 1995).

CHNO *Church Harmonies, New and Old*, Universalist Church of America, (Boston, 1895). Not every edition has the full index of hymn writers, with the Universalists getting brief but useful biographies. Look for an edition with the biographies.

DUUB *Dictionary of UU Biography*, the online dictionary of prominent UU figures. Most biographies are of significant length and depth. DUUB listings mean the biography is finished, assigned or anticipated.

FMW   *Freedom Moves West*, Charles Little, Beacon Press, (Boston, 1952) This history of "Western" Unitarianism (read "Midwest") covers many church leaders not remembered in the East. It is written with passion, conviction and too many errors.

HAD   *Hymnal Amore Dei*, Velma C. Williams, George Ellis publ., (Boston, 1890) (this contains a helpful index of authors).

HCL   *Hymns for the Celebration of Life*, UUA, (Boston, 1964). There is a thumbnail sketch of each hymn writer and composer with occasional notes on the origins of the words and music.

HDUU *Historical Dictionary of Unitarian Universalism*, by Mark W. Harris, Scarecrow Press, (Lanham, Maryland and Oxford, 2004). This is precisely what it purports to be, a dictionary, including issues, institutions, people, chronology. One might hope for more attention to leading Universalists, women, more of the great hymn writers and books, more information in many areas, footnotes to find more, but it covers a great deal of ground and is immensely useful.

HLF & *Heralds of a Liberal Faith, The Prophets, The Pioneers, The Preachers*
HLF–4 (Three Volumes – index in Volume One, The Prophets), AUA, (Boston, 1910) and volume four, *The Pilots*, Beacon Press, (Boston, 1952) – all edited by Samuel Atkins Eliot. This is an amazing collection of brief biographies of a huge number of prominent figures in American Unitarian history, written by (mostly) close

colleagues with real appreciation – even of the difficult ones (skeletons tend to remain buried). The citation may be simply a reference, but the context may be relevant.

NAW *Notable American Women*, (Three Volumes) Belknap Press, (Cambridge, 1975). The biographies are wrought in a proper scholarly fashion with footnotes and bibliography.

NUUW *Notable UU Women*, UU Women's Heritage Society, WHS, (1989). These are brief life Sketches of outstanding UU women. They vary in quality, footnotes and bibliography. This volume is not fixed and finished, and may be expanded at any time. The WHS has many publications on UU women, and a library (at the Women's Industrial Union in Boston). Check the WHS for the latest information on their publications.

OWW *Our Women Workers*, Eliza Hanson, Star and Covenant, (Chicago, 1880) This is the rarest resource by far in this listing but it is the only one that touches on the lives of some Universalist hymn writers. It consists of relatively brief Victorian era biographies of leading Universalist women, with special attention to poets. In the back are biographies of Universalist women ministers.

ROS *Roots of Our Strength; A Heritage of Unitarian and Universalist Women*, Susan Gitlin–Emmer, (1980). Brief UU women's biographies – note denominational activity and connections which secular sources usually don't.

SBU *Standing Before Us*, Dorothy Emerson editor, Skinner House (Boston, 2000) This volume which includes writings of many well known UUs also includes brief biographies of all the authors in the volume. The biographies, though generally good, vary in quality, coverage, and useful footnoting.

STJ *Singing the Journey*, (a supplement to Singing the Living Tradition) UUA (Boston, 2005)

SOH *Singing Our History*, Gene Navias, UUA, (Boston, 1974). The Rev. Eugene Navias includes brief denominational biographies, the history of the hymn and often pithy and useful stories.

TLH *The Larger Hope*, (Two Volumes), Russell Miller, UUA, (Boston, 1985). This is the most Recent serious footnoted history of the Universalist Church of America. There are many useful biographical sketches, even whole chapters, on prominent leaders, not a few of which were hymn writers, especially in the early years.

TLT   *These Live Tomorrow,* Clinton Lee Scott Skinner House, (Boston, 1964). Twenty Unitarian and Universalist biographies.

UUWM *Unitarian Universalist Women Ministers,* Catherine Hitchings, (Boston, 1971–) Ms. Hitchings tries in all too brief sketches to cover the pulpits, and public and professional lives of UU ministers, with bibliography.

UIA   Universalism in America, ed, Ernest Cassara, Beacon Press, (Boston, 1971). This is a brief documentary history of American Universalism, with b rief biographical and contextual notes.

UNITARIAN AND UNIVERSALIST HYMN WRITERS

Adams, Rev. John Coleman, (son of Rev. J.G. Adams) (1849–1922) Graduated Tufts College, served Universalist churches in Newton and Lynn, Massachusetts before his three "great" congregations, Chicago, IL, NYC and Hartford, CT. He was a progressive Universalist thinker and hymn writer whose "We praise Thee, God, for harvests earned" survives in wildly altered form in SLT. AH, AUH, BTL, HCL, TLH, UIA

Adams, Rev. John Greenleaf, D.D., (1810–1887) Ordained in 1833, served Universalist congregations in Malden and Worcester, MA, Providence, RI, Lowell, MA, and Cincinnati, OH. Author of many hymns and editor with W.H. Chapin of *Hymns for Christian Devotion,* 1845 through many editions. His hymn, "Heaven is here; its songs of gladness" survived to HOS, AH, AUH, CHNO, TLH

Adams, Hon. John Quincy, (1767–1848) Graduated Harvard, was U.S. Minister to England, Netherlands, Prussia, later Russia. He was Secretary of State, President of the U.S., and member of the House of Representatives. Member of First Parish (Unitarian) Quincy he recast many psalms in new and freer language, 17 of which were included in Rev. William Lunt's *The Christian Psalmist* which also included 5 of Adams' hymns. After Adams' death his verses were gathered in a book entitled *Poems of Religion and Society,* NYC, 1848. All 22 psalms and hymns are noted by Foote.

None have survived.

Adams, Mrs. M.A., Author of the closing hymn at Phoebe Hanaford's ordination in 1868, "The harvest, Lord, is great."

Adams, Mrs. Sarah Flower, (1805–1848) An English Unitarian and Universalist actress and poet. Her church, founded by Elhanan Winchester Jr., for which she wrote a large number of hymns was very important in her brief life as was its minister, Rev. William Johnson Fox, who urged her to reflect on the Bethel story which became the foundation for her most famous hymn, "Nearer, my God, to Thee." Her story is retold in many popular volumes including NAW. BTL, DUUB, HCL, SOH, UUW

Alcott, Miss Louisa May, (1832–1888) American Unitarian, servant, governess, teacher, novelist of domesticity born in Germantown, PA. Early the basic responsibility for supporting the family fell on her. She was a strong suffragist, the first woman to vote in Concord. See SOH for a hymn and story. AH, AUH, DUUB, HDUU, HLF, NAW, NUUW, ROS, SOH, TCD, UUW

Alger, Rev. William Rounseville, (1823 – 1905) Graduated HDS, served in Roxbury, MA, Bulfinch Place Chapel, and 28th Congregational (Unitarian) in the Music Hall. He was a scholar, author, lecturer, poet, hymn writer. None of the hymns came into common use. HLF, HLF–4, SSLF

Alexander, Elizabeth, (1962 –) Poet, essayist, teacher and playwright. Author of "As We Sing of Hope and Joy" in STJ

Ames, Charles Gordon, (1828 – 1912) Free Will Baptist become Unitarian Minister in Illinois, Ohio, New York and California. For 24 years beloved minister of Church of the Disciples in Boston Author of one hymn in the NHTB.

Andrews, Miss Jane, (1833–1887) Lifelong resident of Newburyport, MA, except for college years at Antioch. Education writer for children, exponent of creative child centered education. She wrote the moving "Long, long ago, in manger low." DUUB, NAW, UUW

Appleton, Rev. Charles Francis Parker, (1822–1903) Two hymns of this Boston born HDS graduate survived into NHTB and one to HOS. AUH

Badger, Rev. George Henry, (1859 – 1953) This HDS graduate served churches in New England, Texas and Florida. Four of his hymns are in *The Isle of Shoals Hymn Book* of which he was editor, and one in NHTB. AUH

Baker, Miss Maria R., Vermont born Universalist public school teacher and poet. Lived and taught for many years in Chelsea, MA. Three hymns survived to CHNO. AUH, CHNO.

Balch, Emily Green, (1867–1961) Raised Unitarian, later Society of Friends, Professor of Economics at Wellesley College, founder of Women's International League for Peace and Freedom, prolific writer, 1946 Nobel Peace Prize recipient. She wrote "Now let us all arise and sing." DUUB, HDUU, NAW, NUUW, UUW

Ballou, Rev. Adin, (1803–1890) Universalist, later Unitarian minister, founder of Hopedale, author of *Practical Christian Socialism*, and editor of *The Hopedale Collection* of hymns, author of many hymns, one of which ("Years are coming – speed them onward") survives to SLT. AUH, BTL, DUUB, HCL, HDUU, HLF, HLF–4, HOS, SOH, TLH, TLT, UIA

Ballou, Rev. Hosea, (1771–1852) Ordained by Elhanan Winchester Jr. at the New England Convention of Universalists, Oxford, MA, in 1794. Preached widely in MA, NH, and VT, eventually settling at Portsmouth, NH, later Second Universalist in Boston. He was an inveterate and successful evangelist, editor of the "Universalist Magazine," author of *A Treatise on Atonement*, leader of the Universalists for more than a quarter of a century. With Sebastian Streeter, Edward Turner and Abner Kneeland he edited Hymns Composed by Various Authors, for the General Convention, and a few years later with Edward Turner edited, *The Universalist Hymn–Book; A New Collection*. His hymns at best were simple, evangelistic and pungent. Of the 189 Ballou hymns in the first collection, and others written later, only 5 survived to CHNO. AH, AUH, CHNO, DUUB, HDUU, HLF, HLF–4, SOH, TLH, TLT, UIA

Ballou, Rev. Hosea II, D.D., (1796–1861) (grand–nephew of HB above) Taught for several years, then served Universalist congregations in Stafford, CT, and Roxbury and Medford, MA, before his efforts for and Presidency of Tufts College. In 1852, editor with T. Whittemore of the *Universalist Magazine,* editor of the Universalist Expositor, later *Universalist Quarterly,* contributor to the Trumpet and more, author of *The Ancient History of Universalism.* Fierce advocate for education, served on the Massachusetts School Committee. Two hymns appear in CHNO. AH, AUH, BTL, CHNO, DUUB, HDUU, TLH, UIA

Ballou, Rev. Moses, (1811–1879) Ordained 1835, served Universalist churches in Portsmouth, NH, Bridgeport and Hartford, CT, Philadelphia, PA, and NYC. One hymn survived in CHNO. CHNO, TLH

Ballou, Silas, (1753–1837) Layman, "rustic poet" of Richmond, NH, edited New Hymns on Various Subjects in 1785. Two hymns are in AH. AH, AUH, TLH

Barber, Rev. Henry Hervey (1835–1923) MTS graduate and later Professor – one hymn was in the NHTB. AUH, HLF–4

Barbauld, Mrs. Anna Laetitia, (1743–1825) British Unitarian, wife of a minister, brilliantly educated writer, activist and hymn writer – doubtless the most prolific and popular UU woman hymn writer in the whole of our history. Her most famous, long surviving hymn was, "Praise to God, immortal praise," from her *Hymns for Public Worship,* 1772. Survives in NHTB and HOS. DUUB, HAD, SBU, UUW, WHP

Barnwell, Ysaye M., (1946–) Author and composer of hymns in STJ, translator of the famous "Woyaya" and more in STJ.

Barrows, Rev. Samuel June, (1845–1909) HDS graduate, minister in Dorchester, MA, editor of "The Christian Register," member of congress. One hymn in the *Isle of Shoals Hymn Book.* AUH, HLF, HLF–4

Bartol, Rev. Cyrus Augustus, D.D., (1813–1890) Born in Maine, HDS graduate, famous transcendentalist minister of West Church, Boston, an editor of *Hymns for the Sanctuary,* 1849. One hymn, sometimes attributed to him ("Be thou ready, fellow–mortal") appears in the Supplement to *Hymns for the Church of Christ.* AUH, DUUB, HLF, HLF–4, SSLF

Beach, Rev. George Kimmich, (1935–) Author of "Perfect Singer" in SLT. BTL

Beach, Rev. Seth Curtis, D.D., (1837–1932) Born in Wayne Co., NY, graduated from HDS, served churches in Augusta and Bangor, ME, and in Wayland, MA. His most famous hymn ("Mysterious Presence! Source of all.") survives in SLT. AH, AUH, BTL, DUUB, HC, HLF–4

Beardsley, Monroe, (1915–1985) Professor of Philosophy at Swarthmore College. Wrote "From all he fret and fever of the day" for the Unitarian Church of Delaware County, Springfield, PA. In HCL and SLT. BTL, HCL

Belletini, Mark L., (1949–) Hymnal commission chair for SLT, author of six hymns, co–author of one and translator of one in SLT. BTL

Bellknap, Rev. Jeremy, D.D., (1744–1798) HDS graduate, predecessor to William Ellery Channing at Federal Street, Boston, MA, editor of one of the most widely used hymnal in the pre and early Unitarian era, *Sacred Poetry: consisting of Psalms and Hymns adapted to Christian Devotion in Public and Private*, 1795 and many reprints. AH, AUH, DUUB, HLF

Benjamin, Thomas, (1940–) Benjamin, member of the commission that created SLT , and composer of many of its new tunes, also assisted in the creation of STJ, author and composer of "Calypso Alleluia" in STJ.

Bennett, Sanford Fillmore, M.D., (1836–1898) Physician–pharmacist, layman in Richmond, IL, he is credited with "In the Sweet Bye and Bye" in CHNO and countless other hymnals. AL, AUH, CHNO

Billings, Mary Charlotte Ward Granniss Webster Billings, (1824–1904) Frequent contributor in her mid–life to *The Rose of Sharon* and the *Ladies Repository*. Well known for her poetry and hymns, Vice President of the Woman's Centenary Association, frequent missionary preacher, long before marrying William Billings, Texas State Universalist Superintendent – whose labor she continued after his death in 1898. She is credited with 18 hymns, none in our hymnals – several in Woman in Sacred Song, ed. Eva Munson Smith, D. Lothrop and Company (Boston, 1885) OWW, UUWH

Bingham, Henrietta Adelaide Burrington, (1841–1877) Universalist teacher, editor, storyteller, preceptress at St. Lawrence University, Editor of the *Ladies Repository*, a brilliant, avid reader, a writer of grace and style. "The passing bell proclaims it here" is a stunning hymn. OWW, TLH

Blake, Rev. James Villa, (1842–1925) Born in Brooklyn, NY, HDS graduate, served Unitarian churches in Massachusetts and Evanston, IL, one of the editors of *Unity Hymns and Chorals*, Frequent hymn writer; two hymns survived to HOS. AUH, FMW, HLF–4

Boeke, Richard, (1941–) Author of the English version of two Norbert Capek's hymns in SLT. BTL

Bonney, Marye B., (1910–1992) Teacher in Louisville, KY. Author of four new verses for Baring–Gould's "Now the Day is Over" in SLT. BTL

Bornstein–Doble, Mimi, (1964–) Words and music for the lovely "Comfort Me" in STJ.

Bowles, Ada C., (1836–1928) Universalist minister, and wife of one, she served in MA, CA, RI and NC. Active in suffrage and a stirring evangelist, she was an organizer of the National and International Councils of Women. She addressed the World's Congress of Representative Women in 1893 in Chicago, where her powerful "Rise up, rise up, o women" was sung. DUUB, OWW, TLH, UUW, UUWM

Box, Howard, (1926–) Served Girard, PA, Newburgh, NY, Ottawa, Ontario and the Ethical Culture Society in Brooklyn, NY. Wrote "Bells in the high tower" for Christmas in the Ottawa congregation. In HCL and SLT. BTL, HCL

Briggs, Rev. Charles, (1791–1873) HDS graduate, minister of First Church, Lexington, MA, Secretary of the American Unitarian Association. One hymn with his attribution is in *Hymns for the Church of Christ*. AUH, HLF

Briggs, LeBaron Russell, LL.D., (1855–1934) From Salem, Harvard graduate, Professor and Dean. One poem ("God of our fathers, who has safely brought us") survives as a hymn, but not in any 20th century Unitarian hymnal. AUH

Brooks, Rev. Charles Timothy, (1813–1883) Born in Salem, HDS graduate, Minister of the Unitarian Church in Newport, RI. One hymn he partly authored survives ("God bless our native land") in HOS. Henry Wilder Foote says Julian unfolds its history. AUH, SSLF,

HLF

Bryant, William Cullen, (1794–1878) Famous lawyer, poet, journalist. Member of All Souls Unitarian Church, NY. Henry Wilder Foote identifies 26 hymns drawn from his poetry, two of which survived in HOS. AH, AUH, DUUB, HLF, HLF–4, SSLF

Budd, Daniel, (1951–) Author of "Be thou with us" in STJ.

Buehrer, Rev. Edwin, (1894–1969) Methodist become Unitarian, long minister of Third Unitarian Church of Chicago, IL, editor of the Journal of Liberal Religion, Western Conference President. His "Song of Thanksgiving" is in HCL and SLT. BTL, HCL

Bulfinch, Rev. Stephen Greenleaf, D.D., (1809–1870) Son of Cambridge, HDS graduate, served Unitarian churches in the South, East and Pittsburgh, PA. 13 of his hymns are identified by H.W. Foote, one of which survived to HOS. AH, HLF, HLF–4, SSLF

Bullock, Mary A.,(1839–1918) Appears only in the Unity Hymns – *Songs of Faith, Hope and Charity* out of Chicago.

Burleigh, William Henry (1812–1871) Editor and publisher in Pittsburgh, Hartford and Syracuse, later New York Harbor Master, member of Second Church in Brooklyn, NY. His anti–slavery and temperance convictions appear in his poetry. Two hymns survive, one ("Lead us, O Father, in the paths of peace") to HOS, and one ("Abide Not in the Realm of Dreams") to HOS and HCL. AH, AUH, SSLF

Canfield, Rev. Henry Lovell, D.D., (1828–1926) Served several Universalist churches in Ohio before taking congregation in Pasadena, CA and helping found the LA church. A founder of Buchtel College (today University of Akron). One hymn survives in CHNO. AUH, CHNO, TLH

Capek, Norbert, (1870–1942) Capek was founder of the Unitarian church in Prague, martyred in Dachau. The English version of three of his hymns in SLT owe their presence to Richard Boeke and Paul and Anita Munk. BTL

Carney, Mrs. Julia Abigail Fletcher, (1823–1908) Massachusetts born Universalist poet and writer, widely published in denominational (and other) journals, periodicals, often under a pseudonym. Editor and author of several journals Universalist and secular. Wife of Rev. T.J. Carney, mother of 9. She was known for her, "Think gently of the erring!" and a song written in late life called, "Fill your home with sunshine." AUH, DUUB, CHNO, OWW, UUW

Carpenter, Alicia, (1930–) UU singer and songwriter, author of eight hymns in SLT and recaster of two. BTL

Cary, Miss Alice, (1820–1871) Famous Universalist poet born near Cincinnati, Ohio, known for her nature poems, hymns, laments, ballads. Encouraged and supported by Whittier. In 1850 she and her sister, Phoebe, moved to New York City where soon their literary soirees became immensely popular among the literary set. Her poetry, timely, sweet and/or humorous, was often good but never great, as she herself acknowledged. Her hymns were many, well wrought and well received. Foote identifies 10 hymns clearly hers, some quite creditable. The author has identified 13 in our older hymnals but none in use lately. AH, CHNO, DUUB, NAUH, NAW, OWW, TLH, UUW (subsumed under her sister's listing below)

Cary, Miss Phoebe, (1824–1871, a few months after her sister Alice)A witty Universalist poet, satirist, whose conversation could "coruscate like pyrotechnics." She worked with Dr. Charles F. Deems on *Hymns for all Christians*. Threw off, after church, the most famous Universalist hymn, "One sweetly, solemn thought," a hymn very much like Adams, "Nearer, my God, to Thee" in CHNO. AH, AUH, CHNO, DUUB, NAW, OWW, SOH, TLH, UUW

Case, Mrs. Louella Juliette Bartlett, (1807–1857) New Hampshire born Universalist poet, the granddaughter of Gov. Josiah Bartlett, signer of the Declaration of Independence. Married at 21 to Rev. Eliphalet Case, she lived in Lowell, MA, and Cincinnati, OH, working and writing for Universalism. Her hymns are simple and elegant in expression. One survives in CHNO. AUH, CHNO, OWW, TLH.

Chadwick, Rev. John White, (1840–1904) From Marblehead, graduate of HDS, minister of Second Unitarian Church, Brooklyn, NY, He was biographer of Parker and Channing, and a prolific author of poem–hymns, friend of famous Unitarian hymn writers Hosmer and Gannett. Ten hymns survived to HOS, none beyond. AUH,

DUUB, FMW, HLF, HLF–4

Chapin, Rev. Edwin Hubbell, D.D., L.L.D., (1814–1880) Held churches in Richmond, VA, Charlestown and Boston, MA, and "Church of the Divine Paternity " in NYC. He was a winning preacher, lecturer, defender of the rights of the under class. His temperance hymn, "Now host with host assembling" is the most enduring of the 6 hymns Foote lists. AH, AUH, DUUB, CHNO, HDUU, HLF, SOH, TLH, UIA

Chapman, Maria Weston, (1806–1885) Born in Weymouth, MA, member of William Ellery Channing's congregation, teacher, reformer, founder of the Boston Female Anti–slavery Society, chief lieutenant of William Lloyd Garrison, editor of the National Anti–Slavery Standard, and according to Lydia Maria Child, "One of the most remarkable women of the age." One hymn, ("O God of Freedom! Hear us pray.") appears in *Hymns for the Church of Christ*. AUH, DUUB, NAW, SBU

Cheney, Mrs. Edna Dow Littlehale, (1824–1904) Unitarian writer, reformer, organizer, speaker, philanthropist, follower of Margaret Fuller. Black and women's rights were her focus. She was the author of several volumes of poetry and stories for children, and author of *The Life and Letters of Louisa May Alcott*. Her much altered hymn "At First I Prayed for Light" survives to HOS. AUH, DUUB, HAD, NAW, SBU, UUW

Chesbro, Caroline Frances Mayo, (1824–aft. 1902) Unitarian–Universalist poet, hymn writer, author of children's stories. Her hymns were written for special church occasions. She long lived with her father Rev. Amory Mayo in Gloucester, MA. SSLF

Church, Edward Alonzo, (1844–1929) Boston businessman who wrote a hymn for the dedication and the last service in the Church of the Disciples, led by Unitarian reformer and world religionist Rev. James Freeman Clarke. Both hymns appear in NHTB and HOS. AUH

Clapp, Eliza Thayer, (1811–1888) From Dorchester, MA, an author, poet, correspondent of *The Dial*, Sunday school writer. Her most remembered hymn ("All before us is the way") in *Hymns for the Church of Christ*, is misattributed to Emerson. AUH.

Clarke, Rev. James Freeman, D.D., (1810–1888) From Hanover, NH, graduate of HDS, minister of First Unitarian in Louisville and Church of the Disciples in Boston, lecturer in comparative religion at HDS. Reformer, activist and author of *Ten Great Religions* he gathered a *Service Book*, later enlarged to the *Disciples Hymn Book*, which included five of his hymns. H.W. Foote lists seven, one of which remained in HOS. AH, AUH, DUUB, FMW, HDUU, HLF, HLF–4, SSLF

Clute, Rev. Oscar, (1837–1902) From Bethlehem, NY, an MTS graduate he served Unitarian churches in New Jersey, Iowa and California, and is remembered for his support of women ministers in the Western Unitarian Conference. His hymn "Love of God most full" was in NHTB and HOS. AUH, FMW

Cobb, Rev. Sylvanus, D.D., (1798–1866) Universalist minister and evangelist, fiercely anti–slavery and pro temperance, a solid reformer a bit too outspoken for most church contemporaries, published his own journals, edited the *Trumpet* at the end of his life. One hymn survives in CHNO. AUH, CHNO, DUUB, HDUU, TLH, UIA

Colburn, Mrs. Mary Jane, (1827–1907) Member of Adin Ballou's Hopedale Community, young poet, worker, excellent hymn writer, especially in paralleling gracious, natural. Southern imagery with the horrors of slavery. *The Hopedale Collection* has 10 of her hymns.

Colegrove, Mrs. Minnie Ogsbury, (1867–1951) Universalist minister, wife of a minister in Ohio, Illinois, Iowa, Minnesota, religious educator, author and composer of numerous hymns and songs, compiler of *Lessons From Nature's Voices*, a children's songbook. UUW

Collyer, Rev. Robert, D.D. (1823–1912) Yorkshire born immigrant he became a blacksmith and a Methodist preacher in Pennsylvania. Befriended by William H. Furness, he became a Unitarian minister at Unity Church In Chicago, and later Church of the Messiah, NYC (today, Community Church). Stirring preacher, lecturer and beloved pastor, one hymn survives in HOS and SLT ("Unto thy temple, Lord, we come") . This hymn was written for the rebuilding of Unity Church (2nd Unitarian) in Chicago after the disastrous fire of 1870 that left only the walls standing. AUH,

BTL, DUUB, FMW, HCL, HLF, HLF–4, HDUU, SSLF

Comins, Sara, (1892–) Graduate of Smith College, author of the Young People's Religious Union's (later American Unitarian Youth) hymn, ("Forward, shoulder to shoulder") sung to "Pomp and Circumstance," leader in the Unitarian Women's Alliance. SOH, NUU

Corrado, Rev. John, (1940–) Author and composer of the moving "Voice still and small" in SLT and composer for another. BTL

Cranch, Christopher, (1813–1892) HDS graduate, one of the literati of the transcendentalist movement who tried their talents in the West, helped with the *Western Dial* before returning East, and occasional hymn writer. HLF

Crook, Margaret Brackenbury, (1886–1970) Ms. Crook was a teacher and author of the Beacon Press book, *Women and Religion.* She was also a very competent hymn writer, music often by her brother Waldo. None of her hymns appear in our hymnbooks.

cummings, e.e., (1894–1962) Poet, novelist, playwright and son of a Unitarian minister, cummings's poem "purer than purest" was adapted as a hymn for SLT. BTL

Cutler, Rev. Julian Stearns, (1854–1930) Graduated from Tufts Theological School, served churches in MA, NY and RI. Poet and hymnwriter, his "Motherhood, sublime, eternal" survives in HOS. AUH

Dall, Mrs. Caroline Wells Healey, (1822–1912) Born in Boston to a prominent merchant family, married Unitarian missionary Charles H. A. Dall. She was an abolitionist, staunch feminist, preacher, writer, educator, poet, biographer and scholar, and fiercely anti–slavery. DUUB, HDUU, SBU, SSFL, UUW

Dall, Rev. William Charles Healey, (1845–1927) (Son of above) Naturalist, explorer, surveyor of Aleutian Islands and Alaska, National Academy of Science. One hymn in SOH. HDUU, HLF, SSFL, SOH

Dana, Charles Anderson, (1819–1897) Born in New Hampshire, one of the leaders in Brook Farm, popular journalist for the New York Tribune, Asst. Secy. Of War (1863–64 – struggled with issues of Black freedom). He wrote a work hymn at Brook Farm which appeared in Hymns for the Church of Christ. AUH, HLF

Denham, Shelly Jackson, (1950 –) Denham, on of the movements bright

new stars authored and composed five of the hymn–songs in
SLT. BTL

DeWolfe, Rev. Mark, (1953 – 1988) Author of "Sing Out Praises for the
Journey" in SLT. BTL

D.S., (20th Century) Universalist author of "Holy, Holy, Holy" in HOS.

Dodd, Miss Mary Ann Hammer. (1843 –) Universalist, prolific writer
"though not of much genius" the editors of Church Harmonies,
New and Old noted. On the other side the Alliboni Dictionary
says a few poems are of "rare excellence." An early contributor
to Universalist womens' magazines. Married and "moved west."
AUH, CHNO, TLH

Dorian, Nancy (Christine Doreian Michaels), (1942 –) She wrote "Though
Gathered Here to Celebrate" after the death of a friend's husband
– in SLT. BTL

Dorr, Mrs. Julia Caroline Ripley (1825–1913) Prominent poet and prose
writer. Her "Heir of all the ages, I" was include in *Unity Hymns
and Chorals* published in Chicago in the late 1800s. Part of a larger
poem, "Heirship" it is a grand evocation of human and intellectual search with particular meaning as a woman's hymn. The
hymn survives in HOS, HCL. HCL

Dwight, Rev. John Sullivan (1812–1893) Graduate of HDS, tried ministry,
moved on to be for half a century editor of the *Journal of Music.*
He is best known for his rewrite of "God bless our native land"
by his friend Rev. Charles Brooks, in HOS. AUH, DUUB, HLF,
HLF–4

Eagleheart, Carole A., (1944–) Eagleheart authored the women's variant
on "Jacob's Ladder" – "We Are Dancing Sarah's Circle"– in SLT.
She has traveled widely in the UU world singing her songs and
more. BTL

Eliot, Rev. Frederick May, (1890–1958) HDS graduate, long minister at
Unity Church in St. Paul, MN, Chair of the 1936 Unitarian Commission on Appriasal, President of the American Unitarian Assn.
1937–1958. His hymn "O thou, to whom the fathers built" appears in HCL. DUUB, HCL, HDUU, HLF–4, TLT

Emerson, Ralph Waldo, LL.D., (1803–1882) Son of hymn writer Rev. William Emerson (A *Collection of Psalms and Hymns*, 1808), graduate

of HDS, minister Second Church of Boston, Unitarian, famous transcendentalist lecturer–poet. Many of his poems have been re-cast as hymns, two of which are in HCL, HDUU, SLT. AH, AUH, BTL, HLF, HLF–4, SOH, TLT

Everett, William, (1839–1910) Graduate of Harvard, Unitarian Lay Licentiate, Headmaster of Adams Academy in Quincy, MA, U.S. House of Representatives (1893–1895). Two hymns are remembered. AUH, DUUB, SSLF

Fahs, Rev. Sophia Lyon, (1876–1978) Cutting edge Religious Educator at Riverside Church, NYC. Congregational, then Unitarian Religious Educator, author of *Beacon Curriculum*, ordained in 1959. Her "Divinty is round us" is in HCL. Another, "For so the children come," is in STJ. DUUB, HCL, HDUU, UUW

Farmer, Mrs. M.G., Author of the ordination hymn at Phoebe Hanaford's ordination "Lay naught but holy hands on her" in Hingham, MA, in 1868.

Fay, Rev. Cyrus Hyde, D.D., (1815–1903) Served Universalist congregations in VT, MA, CT, PA, RI, and Washington, DC. Poet and hymn writer, one survives in CHNO. AUH, CHNO, TLH

Fernald, Woodbury Melcher, (1813–1873) Universalist, later Unitarian minister, still later Swedenborgian in Massachusetts. One abolition hymn appears in the *Unitarian Soldiers Companion*. AUH, TLH

Fields, James T., (1820–1881) Grew up with Thomas Starr King in Portsmouth, NH. Publisher, Ticknor and Fields, known as the poets and the transcendentalists publisher. Fields wrote and eventually published his poems. One hymn to Thomas Starr King for his ordination in 1846 is in SOH. DUUB, HLF, SSFL, SOH

Findlow, Bruce, (1922–) Findlow authored the beautiful "For All that is our Life" in SLT. BTL

Flint, Rev. James, D.D., (1779–1855) Congregational minister, later Unitarian minister to the East Church, Salem, MA. Flint published *A Collection of Hymns for the Christian Church and Home* in 1843, including several of his hymns. One survives ("In pleasant lands have fallen the lines") in NHTB and HOS. AH, AUH, HLF, HLF–4, SSFL

Follen, Eliza Lee Cabot, (1787–1860) Unitarian activist and poet, children's story (*Three Little Kittens*) and song writer, remembered for the power of her anti–slavery hymns. Also writer of very sweet and gentle lyrics for both children and adults. Married to abolitionist minister Charles Follen of Christmas tree fame. See hymn in SOH. The author has identified 12 others. AH, AUH, DUUB, HAD, NAW, SBU, SOH, SSLF, UUW, WHP

Foote, Rev. Henry Wilder (I), (1838–1889) Salem born, HDS graduate, minister of King's Chapel (Unitarian), an editor of the posthumous *Hymns of the Church Universal*. One hymn survives in the NHTB and HOS. AUH, DUUB, HLF, HLF–4

Foote, Rev. Henry Wilder (II), D.D., Litt.D. (1875–1964) HDS graduate, minister in Louisiana, Michigan, Virginia and Massachusetts, editor of the *New Hymn and Tune Book* (1914), and *Hymns of the Spirit* (1937). Also authored *Three Centuries of American Hymnody* which gives major attention to Unitarian hymn writers. One hymn survives in HOS ("Thou whose love brought us to birth") AUH, DUUB, HLF–4

Freeman, James, D.D., (1759–1835) Graduate of Harvard, as a lay reader at King's Chapel, revised *Prayer Book to Unitarian convictions in the revolutionary era*, became rector, edited *Psalms and Hymns for Public Worship* (1799) which was used till the Greenwood era (1830's). AH, AUH, DUUB, HDUU, HLF, SOH, SSLF

Frothingham, Rev. Nathaniel Langdon, D.D., (1793–1870) Graduate of Harvard, minister of the First Church in Boston (Unitarian). One hymn ("O God, whose presence glows in all") survives in SOH. That one and ("'Remember me,' the master said") were in NHTB. "Remember me..." went on to HCH. AH, AUH, DUUB, HCL, HLF, HLF–4, SSLF

Frothingham, Rev. Octavius Brooks, (1822–1895) Graduate of HDS, he became minister at North Church in Salem, MA, and Third Congregational Church (Unitarian and independent – the "artists church") He was an eloquent and outspoken speaker and author of several books including Boston Unitarianism, Recollections and Impressions [picking up where the former left off] and Transcendentalism in New England. His one great hymn ("Thou Lord of hosts") was in the *Book of Hymns,* by Longfellow and Johnson in 1846 and survives to HOS. There is a modern biography – but rather carelessly written. AUH, AH, DUUB, HDUU, HLF, HLF–4, SSLF

Fuller, Sarah Margaret, (1810–1850) Margaret Fuller's career as feminist, writer, editor (*The Dial*), her women's consciousness raising classes need no explication here. Her brilliant and outspoken feminism became a light to generations yet to come. Among her hymns, "Jesus, a child his course began" is not in any of the hymnals here detailed. AH, AUH, DUUB, HDUU, HLF, UUW

Furness, Rev. William Henry, D.D., (1802–1896) Graduate of HDS, ordained and settled at First Unitarian church of Philadelphia – remaining 71 years. He was a scholar teacher, preacher, reformer – anti–slavery where and when it was not popular. His *Manual of Domestic Worship* (1840) had several of his hymns. Foote lists 18 of his hymns of which only his famous vesper hymn ("Slowly by God's (thy) hand unfurled") survives in HOS. AH, AUH, DUUB, HDUU, HLF, HLF–4, SSLF

Gage, Mrs. Frances Dana, (1808–1884) Universalist author, editor, reformer, lecturer, abolitionist – had four sons in the Grand Army of the Republic. She was a novelist, poet of earth and farming, and love of natural things. Known as "Aunt Fanny." Radical who outdistanced her church in reform. Wrote hymns – none survive in current use. One is in SOH. DUUB, NAW, OWW, SBU, SOH, UUW, WHP

Gagne, Jeannie, (1944 –) She wrote words and music for one hymn–song, composed the music for one, and arrangements for five in the new STJ.

Gannett, Abbie M., (1845–) Unitarian poet and hymn writer, utterly overshadowed by her famous relative, William Channing Gannett. She was from the St. Louis Gannetts, related through William's uncle. Very capable and creative versifier whose work appears only in *Unity Hymns – Songs of Faith, Hope and Charity.*

Gannett, Rev. William Channing, D.D., (1840–1923) Born in Boston, worked for the New England Freedmen's Society on St. Helena Island, SC in the late Civil War. Graduated from HDS, had ministries in Milwaukee, St. Paul, Hinsdale, IL, and Rochester, NY. Gannett worked closely with the Western Unitarian Conference, authored a biography of Ezra Styles Gannett his father and successor to William Ellery Channing at Federal Street, Boston. With his friend Frederick Lucian Hosmer they published *The Thought of God* three collections of their hymns–poems – often challenging each other to create hymns for special occasions. Many of their best hymns are here, and in *Unity Hymns and Chorals* (1880 and several later and enhanced editions, including a section on revival hymns, recast for religious liberals). Foote identifies 11 of his great hymns, 8 of which survive in HOS, 3 in SLT and one in STJ. He was also asked by Rabbi Max Landsberg to take up the task that Gannett's predecessor Newton Mann had tried, to recast the ancient cantorial words to the tune Yigdal in more faithful metrical translation than then existed. The result is "Praise to the Living God" which endures in SLT and many popular hymnals including the Reformed Jewish. Gannett was one of our greatest hymn writers. AH, AUH, BTL, DUUB, HCL, HLF–4, HDUU, SSLF

Gibbons, Rev. Kendyl L.L., (1955 –) She wrote two strong hymns, "Lady of the Seasons' Laughter" and "From the Crush of Wealth and Power' in SLT. BTL

Gilbert, Rev. Richard, (1936–) He wrote the popular "Thanks be for These" – in SLT. BTL

Gilman, Mrs., Caroline Howard, (1794–1888) Born in Boston, settled after marriage in Charleston, SC. Prominent writer and publisher of short stories, verse, novels, woman's almanac and magazines for children. Tried to bridge breach of North and South before the civil War, then Southern supporter. The author has found 5 hymns which didn't survive into 20th century use. AUH, DUUB, HLF, NAW, SSLF, UUW

Gilman, Mrs. Charlotte Perkins Stetson, (1860–1935) Unitarian feminist, economist, author, lecturer, novelist, effective satirist, founder of the Women's Peace Party. Born in Hartford, CT, became celebrator of California in poems and song. A few of her hymns are in use today, but none in our hymnals. One is in SOH. 2CD, DUUB,

NAW, ROS, SBU, SOH, UUW, WHP

Gilman, Rev. Samuel, D.D., (1791–1858) Graduate of Harvard and student at HDS, ordained minister of the Unitarian church in Charleston, SC, which he served for life. He wrote popular literary and historical essays, and poems. He edited *Services and Hymns for the use of the Unitarian Church of Charleston, SC* which included three of his hymns and two by his wife Caroline. He also wrote "Fair Harvard" for Harvard's 200th in 1836. None of his hymns have survived into current use. AH, AUH, DUUB, HLF, SSLF

Goldsmith, Rev. Peter Hair, (1865–1926) Born in Greenville, SC, and educated at Southern Baptist Theological Seminary in Louisville, KY, he eventually converted to Unitarianism. His first Unitarian pulpit was the old First Church in Salem, later on to Yonkers, NY. One hymn by him was in the NHTB. AUH

Gould, Miss Hannah Flagg, (1789–1865) Newburyport poet, satirist, writer of epitaphs and elegant citations, known for her "piety, charity, hospitality, vivacity, wit." AH

Gray, Thomas Jr., M.D., (1803–1849) Graduated Harvard with M.D.. Traveled in Europe – first to popularly acquaint Americans with Pompeii and Herculaneum. Practised medicine and dentistry in Boston. Wrote several hymns, some in *Pray's Sunday School Hymn Book*, in 1833, and others. SSLF

Greeley, Dr. Dana Maclean, (1908–1986) Dr.Greeley, President of the AUA and UUA, and IARF wrote this simple tribute to life "Let All the Beauty We Have Known" in SLT. BTL

Greenough, James Bradstreet, (1833–1901) Graduated from Harvard where he was later Professor of Latin. He wrote a Latin hymn which appears in the *Harvard University Hymn Book* of 1926. AUH

Greenwood, Helen Woodward, (1880–1959) From Leominster, MA, long time secretary of the Unitarian Women's Alliance at the AUA. Her "Once again we gather here" is in the *Isle Of Shoals Hymn Book*. AUH.

Grigolia, Rev. Mary, (1946–) The lovely "I Know This Rose Will Open" is only one of her immense outpouring of words and music, but the only one in SLT. BTL

Guttormsson, Guttormur J., (20th century) This Icelandic farmer, poet wrote "Stillness Reigns" in SLT. BTL

Hale, Rev. Edward Everett, D.D., (1822–1909) Graduate of Harvard, tutored for the ministry, ordained at Church of the Unity in Worchester, MA, in 1846. He later served the South Congregational Church in Boston (Unitarian). He was a deeply loved pastor and storyteller ("Man Without a Country"). No hymn survives his day. One is in SOH. AUH, DUUB, HLF, HLF–4

Hale, Miss Mary Whitwell, (1810–1862) American Unitarian poet and hymn writer born in Boston where she taught (also taught in Taunton, and Keene, NH), several of the 25 carefully crafter hymns this author has identified appeared in the *Cheshire Collection and Universalist Hymns for Christian Devotion*, and *Church Harmonies*. AUH, SSLF

Hall, Harriet Ware, (1841–1889) Bostonian, member of King's Chapel, poet. Her "Lord, beneath thine equal hand" appears in the *Isle of Shoals Hymn Book*. AUH

Hall, Mrs. Louisa Jane Park, (1802–1892) She wrote several moving hymns (in other collections). Her fresh and thoughtful recasting of older expressions and understanding of faith are all in *Unity Hymns and Chorals*. Her hymns appeared, as far as this author can tell, nowhere else among us. SSLF

Ham, Rev. Marion Franklin, D.D., (1867–1956) Born in Harveysburg, OH, became a Unitarian in Chattanooga, TN, where he became a lay reader and eventually minister, later serving in Dallas, TX, Reading and Waverley, MA. In 1896 he published *The Golden Shuttle*, a book of verse. He then tried hymns, of which Foote records 12, but there were many more published in his 5 small collections. HOS included 9 of his well crafted hymns, HCL 3 and SLT 2, including the "merger hymn" "As tranquil streams that meet and merge" AH, AUH, BTL, DUUB, HCL

Hamilton, Dennis, (1944–) Hamilton wrote "I Know I Can" in STJ.

Hanaford, Mrs. Phebe Ann Coffin, (1829–1921) Universalist, born in Siasconset, Nantucket, voluminous writer of poetry and prose, editor of Universalist women's and children's magazines and papers, avid supporter of women's rights. Wrote lives of Abraham Lincoln and George Peabody. In 1868 became a Universalist minister. A founder of the Association for the Advancement of Women, author of *Women of the Century* recording the lives of public women. 2CD, AH, DUUB, HDUU, NAW, OWW, ROS, SBU, TLH, UUW, UUWM, WHP

Hanson, Rev. Heather Lynn, (1938–) Hanson composed and wrote "Gather Round the Manger" in SLT. BTL

Harris, Miss Florence, (1891–1933) (Mrs. Robert G. Hooke) American Unitarian whose "Like pilgrims sailing through the night" written for the 10th anniversary of Unity Church, Montclair, NJ, is an extraordinary hymn claiming the torch of freedom, especially when it is realized that she wrote it at the age of 16. It appeared for a quarter of a century in our hymnals before it was expunged by *Hymns for the Celebration of Life*. AUH.

Harris, Rev. Thaddeus Mason, D.D., (1768–1842) Harvard graduate, served First Church in Dorchester for more than 40 years. He was Librarian of the Massachusetts Historical Society. His *Hymns for the Lord's Supper*, original and selected, helped break the last stranglehold of psalms on old Puritan churches – since the psalms had no words for communion new words had to be written. It was a period piece! AUH, HLF

Harris, Rev. Thomas Lake, (1823–1906) British born Universalist minister who gradually moved into active spiritualism. He was a prolific writer on spiritual and religious subjects (collected works more than 2 shelf feet). He published his hymns in *Hymns of Spiritual Devotion*, one of which, "O earth, thy past is crowned and consecrated" in the caboose of HOS. AUH, DUUB, TLH

Hart, Connie Campbell, (1929 –) Hart recast the classic "What Wondrous Love" with new words – in SLT. BTL

Hayes, Mark W., (1949–) Hayes adapted a traditional Buddhist meditation, "Filled with Loving Kindness" in SLT. BTL

Hedge, Rev. Frederick Henry, (1805–1890) Graduated HDS, friend of Emerson. He served West Cambridge (today Arlington Unitarian), Bangor, ME, Westminster Unitarian Church, Providence, RI, and First Parish in Brookline, MA. (while also serving as a Harvard Professor). In 1872 he was appointed Professor of German Language and Literature at Harvard. He was a respected author, an editor of the *Christian Examiner,* briefly President of the American Unitarian Association, and one of the luminaries of the "Hedge Club" where transcendentalists met to converse. With Frederick Dan Huntington he edited *Hymns for the Church of Christ,* an inclusive hymnal drawing broadly from American and European sources. It included his famous translation of "A mighty fortress is our God" and his enduring "Sovereign and Transforming Grace" both of which in amended form survive in SLT. AH, AUH, BTL, DUUB, HCL, HDUU, HLF, HLF–4, SSLF

Higginson, Rev. Thomas Wentworth, (1822–1911) Born and died in Cambridge. In between he graduated HDS, served in Newburyport and Worcester. In the Civil War he commanded a Black regiment (later wrote his famous book, *Army Life in a Black Regiment*). He was a literary figure, remembered for his encouragement of and advice (not too good) to Emily Dickinson). Foote identifies 5 hymns, 2 of which were in HOS. One is in SOH. AH, AUH, DUUB, HDUU, HLF, SSLF

Hill, Rev. Thomas, LL.D., D.D., (1818–1891) Born in New Jersey, graduated HDS, minister in Waltham, MA, President of Antioch College following Horace Mann, President of Harvard University, and minister in Portland, ME. He wrote and edited several hymns none of which have survived in our hymnals. AUH, HLF, SSLF

Hodge, Rev. Dwight Munson, (1846–1906) Educated at St. Lawrence University, served churches in North Adams, MA, Danbury, CT, NYC, and at Franklin and Monson, MA. Active in local health issues, inveterate poet. One hymn survives ("Blow winds of God") in HOS. AUH, CHNO

Holland, Joseph Gilbert, (1819–1881) Massachusetts newspaperman, Editor of *Scribner's Magazine,* poet, author. AUH

Holmes, John, (1904–1962) Professor of English at Tufts University, elegant published poet, Unitarian–Universalist. One hymn (O Lord of stars and sunlight") and three recast pieces of poetry cum hymns are in HCL, only one ("The peace not past our understanding falls" – first verse removed) is in SLT. AH, AUH, BTL, DUUB, HCL

Holmes, Rev. John Haynes, D.D., Litt.D., (1879–1964) Graduate of HDS, served Dorchester (third), then Church of the Messiah, following Collyer, which under him became Community Church. Powerful reformer and founder of the NAACP, ACLU, FOR, all of whose concerns appear in his hymns (including a hymn against child labor). He left the American Unitarian Association after he was gaveled to silence, trying to speak against WWI, by William Howard Taft, Moderator. Foote identifies 36 hymns of which 8 were in HOS, 3 in HCL, 2 in SLT. One is in SOH. He published a volume of his own hymns and their stories, called appropriately, *The Collected Hymns of John Haynes Holmes*. His most famous hymn was "The Voice of God is Calling," not in SLT. Holmes also published an autobiography, *I Speak for Myself*. AH, AUH, BTL, DUUB, HCL, HDUU, HLF–4, SOH

Holmes, Oliver Wendell, M.D., LL.D., (1809–1894) Graduated Harvard, Professor of Anatomy at Harvard Medical school he became best known for his poetry, prose and biographical sketches. He wrote two hymns for his church, King's Chapel, and several more, 4 of which appear in NHTB and HOS, 1 in HCL ("Lord of all being, throned afar"), none since HCL. AH, AUH, HDUU, HLF, HLF–4, SSLF

Horton, Rev. Edward Augustus, (1843–1931) Graduated from Meadville, ministries in Leominster, Hingham and Second Church n Boston, MA. He was active in the Unitarian Sunday school Society. One hymn in NHTB. AUH, HLF, HLF–4

Hosmer, Frederick Lucian, D.D., (1840–1929) Born In Framingham, MA, he served Unitarian churches in Northborough, MA, Quincy, IL, Cleveland (First), OH, St. Louis (Unity), MO, and Berkeley, CA. Beginning while in Quincy he started writing hymns and poems. Between 1885 and 1918 he and William Channing Gannett published three small volumes of their poem–hymns (no music) under the title, *The Thought of God*, which were republished in many nations and languages. Hosmer is usually regarded as the better hymn writer, perhaps the best of his time. It is certain that Gannett and Hosmer produced hymns of such excellence and beauty that they form a central corpus of Unitarian Universalist hymnody to this day. Of the 44 Hosmer hymns that Foote lists 18 were in HCL and 8 survive in SLT, including "Forward through the ages," "When courage fails, and faith burns low," "We pray no more, made lowly wise," "One thought I have, my ample creed" and favorite Easter hymns. Hosmer and Gannett's efforts to bring popular moving gospel tunes into liberal hymnody were not successful in their time, but are reflected in *Singing the Journey*. AH, AUH, BTL, DUUB, HCL, HDUU, HLF–4

Howe, Mrs. Julia Ward, (1819–1910) Women's Club–and suffrage leader. Founder of the Unitarian Women's Ministerial Association. A woman of aggressive, eclectic interests, from Goethe to gala parties. Author, playwright of caustic wit, lecturer, advocate of values and ideals swamped by the gilded age. Author of the "Battle Hymn of the Republic." One hymn is in SOH. 2CD, AH, AUH, DUUB, HDUU, HLF, HLF–4, NAW, ROS, SOH, UUW, WHP

Huntington, Rt. Rev. Frederick Dan, D.D., (1819–1904) Graduated from HDS he served South Congregational Church (Unitarian), Boston, and then Professor of Christian Morals and University Preacher at Harvard (1855–1859). In 1853 he and Frederick Henry Hedge edited *Hymns for the Church of Christ*, including 3 of Huntington's hymns. (Huntington was ordained an Episcopal Priest in 1859 and consecrated Bishop of Central New York in 1869.) None of his hymns continue in usage among us. AUH, HLF

Hurlbert, William Henry, (1827–1895) Graduated from HDS, tried preaching, returned to Harvard Law school then tried Journalism in NYC. He contributed three hymns to the hymnals by Johnson and Longfellow. AUH

Hutchinson, Abby, (1829–1892) Abby and brothers Judson, John and Asa made up the original "Singing Hutchinsons" who began in a Universalist choir, often sang for Universalist events, known for their great singing and anti–slavery work. Abby's signature song was "Kind words can never die." AH

Ide, Beth, (1921–) Beth Ide has completely recast the classic "Creation's Lord, We Give Thee Thanks," into "Creative Love, Our Thanks We Give" in SLT. BTL

Issacs, Rev. Robert Eller, (1951–) Issacs has given us "We Begin Again in Love" – in STJ.

Jackson, Helen Hunt (Holm, Saxe), (1830–1885) Massachusetts born poet, essayist and scholar, she is remembered for her novel *Ramona* which revealed the American Indian's plight, and her fiery *Century of Dishonor* which established her as a fierce defender of Indian rights. Only a single hymn of hers appears, that only in *Unity Hymns and Chorals*, but it is an exquisite hymn. NAW

Jerauld, Charlotte A. Fillebrown, (1820–1845) Cambridge born Universalist friend of Sarah Mayo. Wrote "as a bird sings, from a full heart." Untrained, untutored, a poet of straightforward feeling and sparkling images. The single hymn "Where shall the kingdom come?"is a magnificent creation, quite different in expression from most other hymnody. OWW, TLH, UUW, WHP

Johnson, Rev. David A., (1935 –) He has altered John Haynes Holmes' "This Land of Bursting Sunrise" to fit long vistas on land as well as Star Island for which it was written, and Sarah Flower Adams' "Part in Peace" for current acceptance – both in SLT. BTL

Johnson, Rev. Samuel, (1822–1882) Graduated HDS, minister of the Independent Religious Society, (Unitarian before and after) Lynn, MA, author of Oriental Religions and while still students at HDS with Sam Longfellow authored their *Book of Hymns*. The book includes a few of their own hymns but it is notable mostly for its drawing widely on untapped poetic sources, including Whittier. Foote identifies 13 hymns by Johnson (later he added three built around brief quotes of others Johnson was reluctant to claim). The Most beloved of his hymns are, "Father (Savior) in Thy mysterious presence kneeling," "City of God, how broad, how far," and "Life of Ages, richly poured." Only the last survives in SLT. Historians speak of the hymns "lyrical quality" but they also plumb the depths of sorrow, confession and repentance, which seem notably absent in recent UU hymns. AH, AUH, BTL, DUUB, HCL, HDUU, HLF, HLF–4, SSLF

Jones, Sarah Dan, (1962–) Music and Words to "Meditation on Breathing" in STJ.

Kapp, Dr. Max, (1904–1979) Dr. Kapp was Dean of the Theological School at St. Lawrence University, and a long supporter of Ferry Beach Camp and Conference Center. His "I Brought My Spirit to the

Sea" and "Far Rolling Voices," in SLT, are but two of the prolific songs and hymns he wrote. BTL

Kimball, Richard S., (1934–) His "Winds be Still" is in SLT. BTL

Kneeland, Rev. Abner, (1773–1844) Universalist editor (with H. Ballou and others) of *Hymns Composed by Different Authors*, of 1808. He contributed 138 hymns. Only one survived to CHNO. He moved on to freethinking and creating the intentional community of Salubria. His convictions caused a "conviction" in Boston on the charge of blasphemy. Universalists were slow to defend his freedom of thought, but W.E. Channing did. One hymn is in SOH. AUH, CHNO, DUUB, HDUU, SOH, TLH, TLT, UIA

Larned, Augusta, (1835–1924) American Unitarian author, critic, mythologist and creator of "exquisite, fugitive poems " whose lovely," In quiet hours the tranquil soul" appeared in Unity Hymns and Chorals, NHTB and HOS. AUH, HAD.

Larsen, Rev. Tony, (21st century) Tony has become one of the most creative parodists of UU hymnody, so good, in fact that a few of his parodies may cross the line into accepted hymns ("This is my story, This is My Song," "The Spirit of this church," "I love to tell the story").

Lathrop, Rev. John Howland, D.D., (1880–1967) Graduated Meadville, AB Harvard. He was minister of First Unitarian in Berkeley, and First Unitarian of Brooklyn. His "Hosanna in the highest!" is in SLT. AUH, BTL, DUUB, HCL

Laurie, Rev. Alexander Gretton, (1816–1891) Scotch born, Laurie served churches in PA, NY and MA, taking on the task of evangelizing the southeast border Canada for a time. His "The golden clouds that float along" is still exquisite, in CHNO and SOH. AUH, CHNO, SOH, TLH

Lehman, Rev. Robert, (1913 –1997) His "Within the Shining of a Star" in SLT is a humanist Christmas Carol from this minister, who long served First Unitarian Church in Minneapolis. BTL

Leland, Mrs. E.H., Well known as a children's poet, two of her calm and gentle hymns appear in *Unity Hymns – Songs of Faith, Hope and Charity*; one is quite contemporary in feel.

Leonard, Ellen T., Only one hymn of hers appears, that only in *Unity*

Hymns – Songs of Faith, Hope and Charity.

Leonard, Rev. Henry Codman, (1818–1880) Preacher on Cape Ann, MA, several churches in ME before becoming Chaplain to Maine companies in the Union Army. After the Civil War he served in Philadelphia, PA, Deering, ME (while Professor of Belles Lettres in Westbrook Seminary) and Annisquam and Pigeon Cove, MA. He was an editor of the *Gospel Banner, and Universalist*, as well as much nature poetry. Two Christmas hymns survive in CHNO. AUH, CHNO

Lewis, Mrs. Abby Goodwin Davis, (1843–.   ) Vermont Universalist writer, musician correspondent to several periodicals. Followed her husband, Rev. J.J. Lewis from South Boston to Chicago. One hymn survives in CHNO. AUH, CHNO.

Lewis–McLaren, Grace, (1939–) Author and composer of "Touch the Earth, Reach the Sky" and "When We are Gathered" she also arranged or harmonized three other hymns in SLT. BTL

Livermore, Rev. Abiel Abbot, D.D., (1811–1892) Born in New Hampshire and returned there after graduating HDS, to Keene Unitarian Church. Later he served First Unitarian in Cincinnati, then as President of Meadville Theological School. He wrote books and hymns, and was prime editor of what is known as the *Cheshire Collection*, a noteworthy, theologically inclusive, broadly drawn collection of some of the best hymnody for religious liberals in the Western world at its time – went through 60 editions. One of his hymns survived in NHTB and HOS. AUH, DUUB, HLF, HLF–4, SSLF

Livermore, Mrs. Mary Ashton Rice, (1821–1905) Universalist lecturer, reformer, "Queen of the platform," author, editor and hymn writer. An organizer of the Western Sanitary Commission's fairs during the Civil War and the Universalist Women's Centenary Association, powerful speaker on women's rights and suffrage, encourager of women in the ministry. Received honorary LLD from Tufts. One hymn is in CHNO and one in SBU, SOH. 2CD, AUH, CHNO, DUUB, HDUU, NAW, OWW, ROS, SOH, SOH, TLH, TLT, UUW, WHP

Livermore, Sarah White, (1789–1874) Unitarian schoolteacher from Wilton, NH, aunt of A.A. Livermore above. Two of her hymns were in the Cheshire Collection. AUH, SSLF

Lombard, James, (1815–) Poet, educator and compiler of *Sunday School Liturgy* (containing some of his hymns) and *A Liturgy with a Collection of Hymns and Chants for the use of Sunday schools*. Two hymns are in CHNO. AUH, CHNO

Long, Hon. John Davis, (1838–1915) Governor of Massachusetts, Secretary of the U.S. Navy, member of Old Ship Church (Unitarian) Hingham, MA, and author of a hymn appearing in NHTB. AUH, HLF–4

Long, Lilly Augusta, (1890–1927) Bright resourceful hymn writer two of whose hymns appeared in *Unity Hymns – Songs of Faith, Hope and Charity.*

Longfellow, Henry Wadsworth, D.C.L., (1807–1882) Graduated from Bowdoin College, returned to be Professor of Modern Languages. On to Harvard as Professor of Modern Languages and Belles–Lettres. Beloved American poet, whose verse was culled for use as hymns. 11 are identified by Foote, the most famous of which are, "I heard the bells on Christmas Day," and "All are architects of fate." He claimed his brother Samuel (below) was the real poet. Both of these hymns are in SLT. AH, AUH, BTL, DUUB, HCL, HDUU, HLF, SSLF

Longfellow, Rev. Samuel, (1819–1892) Born in Portland, ME, graduated HDS with Sam Johnson. Served Unitarian Church of Fall river, MA, Second Unitarian Church in Brooklyn, NY, and the Unitarian Church in Germantown, PA. With Sam Johnson he published the *Book of Hymns*, which went through 12 editions. Longfellow discovered that other Brooklyn churches were drawing crowds at vespers services. He couldn't use popular vespers hymns threatening perdition or God coming in the night to take the unrepentant, so he published his own Vespers, in 1859, and a year later *A Book of Hymns and Tunes for the Sunday School, the Congregation and the Home* (Hymnals with music on the same page were rare.), and in 1864 published with Sam Johnson *Hymns of the Spirit* which at last included a good collection of their own work. (The volume, revised, with music came out in 1876.) Foote lists 52 hymns by Longfellow. 9 survive in SLT including two beautiful vespers hymns. He was one of the greats! AH, AUH, BTL, DUUB, HCL, HDUU, HLF, HLF–4, SSLF

Loring, Louisa Putnam, (1854–1924) Unitarian hymn writer and compiler of *Hymns of the Ages* (1904), whose taste in hymns was inclusive and faultless, but did not embrace the musical currents of the times. Her "O Thou who turnest into morning" appeared in NHTB, 1914. AUH.

Loring, William Joseph, (1795–1841) A Unitarian layman, businessman, President of the Washington Benevolent Society and member of the Boston Horticultural Society. His one known hymn appears in *Hymns for the Church of Christ*. AUH

Lowe, Mrs. Martha Perry, (1829–1902) Born in Keene, NH, married the secretary of the AUA, published poet and correspondent. HLF, SSLF

Lowell, James Russell, LL.D., (1819–1891) Succeeded Longfellow as Professor of Belles Lettres at Harvard, later editor of *The Atlantic Monthly*, still later of *The North American Review*. His editorial work, essays and poems led to many published volumes and a stellar reputation. He served as U.S. Minister to Spain, followed by Great Britain. His poetry was culled for hymn material, but he only wrote two for that purpose ("Our house, our God, we give to Thee" for a church dedication in "Watertown, MA, and "What means this glory round our feet?") The three culled from his poems include "Men whose boast it is that ye," and "Once to every man and nation," the only two to survive, altered, in SLT. AUH, BTL, DUUB, HCL, HDUU, HLF, HLF–4

Lowell, Mrs. Lucy Buckminster Emerson, (wife of Judge John, 1824– 1897) Brookline, MA, Unitarian who put the tragedy of three children's death into a long and striking hymn of comfort for others. Included by her minister, transcendentalist Frederick Henry Hedge in his hymnal, *Hymns for the Church of Christ*.

Lunt, William Parsons, D.D., (1805–1857) Graduated HDS and ordained as minister of Second Unitarian Congregational Society, NYC. His second and final church was Quincy, MA. His The *Christian Psalter* for the Quincy church was widely used. (containing several hymns by and psalms recast by John Quincy Adams. AUH, HLF, HLF–4, SSLF

Lyon, Carrie Ward, (1879–1965?) Unitarian, member of the Summit, NJ, church. New hymn "Praise ye, praise ye" appears in HCL. HCL

Lyttle, Charles H., (1884–1980) Unitarian minister in Brooklyn, NY, and Omaha, NB, before becoming the James Freeman Clarke Professor of Church History at Meadville, and along the way rescued and then ministered to the First Unitarian Society of Geneva, IL. Author of *Freedom Moves West*. His 3 hymns in HCL and SLT are humanist but not narrowly so. BTL, HCL

MacKinnon, John, (1903–1983) Long minister of All Souls Church in Indianapolis, he gave SLT "Ye Earthborn Children of a Star." BTL

Maki, Jeanne, (1943 –) Maki is the translator of the Finnish "Has Summer Come Now Dawning?" in SLT. BTL

Mann, Newton, (1856–1926) Was head of the Western Sanitary Commission in the Civil War . Organized and ministered to Kenosha, WI, church, then served in Troy and Rochester, NY, and Omaha, NB. Rabbi Max Landsberg in Rochester asked him to create a properly metered and translated Emglish version of the hymn we know by the music Yigdal. His labors are reflected in William Channing Gannett's final version we sing today. AUH, HCL, HLF–4

Marean, Emma, (1854–1936) Massachusetts poet and editor of the Christian Register (Unitarian) early in this century. Three of her simple hymns for family worship were included in *Unity Hymns – Songs of Faith, Hope and Charity* and in *The Isle of Shoals Hymn Book*. AUH.

Markham, Edwin, (1852–1940) Well known poet and teacher, his "We men of earth have here the stuff" has been recast into "Here on the Paths of Everyday" in HCL (with two other poems) and alone in SLT. BTL

Martineau, Miss Harriet, (1802–1876) Famed British Unitarian poet, abolitionist, sociologist, journalist, author, traveler and also hymn writer. Her most enduring hymn is, "All men are equal in their birth." It is a moving, elegant and well–constructed hymn. Not in any recent UU hymnal. AUH, DUUB, UUW, WHP

Marvin, Mrs. Anna Lippit, (1834–1880) This New York born Universalist poet was eclipsed by her more famous sister, Jane Patterson (below). Only one hymn survives in Universalist hymnal CHNO. AUH, CHNO, OWW

Mason, Caroline Atherton Briggs, (1823–1890) Born in Marblehead, MA, correspondent, author poet. She had two published volumes of poetry, and at least 13 hymns to her credit. One hymn, "O God, I thank thee for each sight" was widely popular, survives in NHTB and HOS. AUH, SSLF

Masten, Richard Taylor (Ric), (1929–2008) His "Let is Be a Dance We Do," which along with much of Ric's poetry and song has entranced audiences in colleges and churches for a generation, is in SLT. BTL

Mayer, Peter, (1963–) Mayer's radiant "Blue Boat Home" is in STJ.

Mayo, Mrs. Sarah C. Edgarton, (1819–1848) Universalist, born in Shirley Village, MA, wife of minister A.D. Mayo. Nature poet of passion and style, publisher of the short lived Universalist women's journal, *Rose of Sharon*. She and Charlotte Jerauld published, alternately, a separate hymn for each phrase of the Lord's Prayer from beginning to end. DUUB, OWW, SBU (under Edgarton), TLH, UUW, WHP

McDade, Carolyn, (1935–) McDade's songs and poetry have captivated audiences since the Women's Caucus at Arlington Street Church more than a generation ago, down to her major labors on "Gaia." Only three of her song–hymns are in SLT including "Spirit of Life." One more, "Rising Green," is in STJ. BTL

Miegs, Mrs. M.N., Author of hymns "There's a Wonderful Tree" and "Hark! A Burst of Heavenly Music." Only one verse of one hymn survives, (in *Unity Hymns and Chorals*, and *Sacred Songs for Public Worship*) but it is a very good one, "Now the joyful Christmas Morning."

Mikelson, Rev. Thomas, (1936–) Mikelson's "Wake Now My Senses" has become a UU favorite, especially for ordinations and installations. It and "Sing of Living, Sing of Dying" are in SLT. BTL

Miles, Sarah Elizabeth Appleton, (1807–1877) Born in Boston, died in Brattleboro, VT. Some of her hymns appeared in the Longfellow – Johnson *Hymns of the Spirit* of 1864. AUH, SSLF

Mitchell, Rev. Stanford A., Universalist minister and traveling troubador, the Universalist "Ira Sankey" whose tenor voice awakened the sleeping and raised the dead (churches that is). Published little chapbooks of hymns including *Goodwill Songs*. One commemorative hymn survives in CHNO. AUH, CHNO

Moore, Berkley L., (1932 –) Moore's "Let Love Continue Long" expands on Hosea Ballou's words on "Brotherly love" – in SLT. BTL

Morgan, Rev. John Hanley, (1918–) Morgan, long a UU minister wrote the moving "Let Christmas Come" – in SLT. BTL

Morn, Mary Katherine, (1961 –) With Jason Shelton Moore created "The Fire of Commitment" in STJ.

Mott, Rev. Frederick B., (1856–1941) British born, ordained in Salem, MA. Third Religious Society in Dorchester (Unitarian) was his final American settlement before returning to serve the Southport Unitarian Chapel in England. Two hymns appear in Church Harmonies. AUH

Murray Rev. John, (1741–1815) London born, follower of James Relly, fled to the colonies in 1770. Served the Gloucester, MA, congregation and First Universalist Church of Boston. A founder of the Universalist Church in America, he reprinted Relly's hymnal in 1776, again in 1782 including 5 of his hymns. None has survived in any of our hymnals for over a century. One hymn is in SOH. AH, AUH, DUUB, HDUU, SOH, TLH, TLT, UIA

Murray, Mrs. Judith Sargent Stevens, (1751–1820) Gloucester born Universalist author, dramatist, feminist, poet. Supporter of human rights and liberties. Her "Marriage Hymn" is doubtless the longest, most detailed of (men's or women's') hymns I have ever found. One hymn is in SOH. HDUU, NAW, OWW, ROS, SBU (under Stevens), SOH, TLH, UUW, WHP, UIA

Navias, Rev. Eugene, (1928 –) Navias added two verses to the classic "Come Thou Fount of Every Blessing" – in SLT. He has helped edit and reshape countless hymns and shaped the Singing, Shouting and Celebrating programs for GAs and more. BTL

Newell, Rev. William, D.D., (1804–1881) Graduated HDS, ordained to First Parish, Cambridge – for life. No poem–hymns appear in American UU hymnals. One hymn is in SOH. AUH, HLF, SOH, SSLF

Norton, Ada R., One of three Universalist sister poets and hymn writers (Ida Carnahan and Lucy Thomas were the other two), all intellectually gifted. They were nieces of Alice Cary who declared that Ada had more poetical genius than she did. –Ada's hymn "It is easier in this world" in Eliza Hanson's "Our Women Workers,"is an excellent example of the creative women's hymns men have ever let slip by. OWW

Norton, Prof. Andrews, (1786–1853) Graduated Harvard and appointed Tutor there, later Librarian and Lecturer on the Bible, finally at HDS Professor of Sacred Literature. Noted author of Biblical scholarship and commentary, and self chosen Unitarian spokesman to combat "The latest form of Infidelity" (Emerson). He authored 6 hymns of which two survive in NHTB and 1 in HOS. AH, AUH, DUUB, HDUU, HLF, HLF–4, SSLF

Page, Nick, (1952–) Page's infectious enthusiasm has motivated even non singers to try. He co–authored with Nita Penfold "When Will the Fighting Cease?" in STJ and helped with arranging one hymn in STJ and SLT. BTL

Palfrey, Sara Hammond, (1823–1914) Popular, widely published poet, daughter of a distinguished Unitarian Minister. Nom de plume – "E. Foxton." This author has identified one hymn "Along time's river, – like a soul unborn." SSFL, UUW

Palmer, Phillip, (1980 –) Palmer's "Winter Solstice Chant" is in STJ.

Parker, Theodore, (1810–1860) Born in Lexington, studied at Harvard and HDS. Ordained in West Roxbury, MA, moved on to the church created for him in Boston, 28th Congregational Society (Unitarian) until his death. His collected works (Centennial edition) encompassing theological issues, non–western faith, and responses to the bitter issues of his time including slavery comprise nearly 2 and 1/2 shelf feet (including a volume of prayers). He sparely and carefully edited a poem to create "O thou great Friend of all the sons of men" in 1846 which survived to HOS and HCL. Another is in STJ and one in SOH. AUH, DUUB, HCL, HDUU, HLF, HLF–4, SOH, SSLF

Patterson, Adoniram Judson, D.D., Litt. D., (1827–1909) Graduated Tufts College, served churches in Girard, PA, Portsmouth, NH, Roxbury, MA.. One hymn survives in HOS ("In Thee, O Father, are we all at home"). AUH, CHNO

Patterson, Mrs. Jane Lippit, (1829–1919) Ostego, NY, born Universalist scholar, teacher, lyric poet, novelist (*Victory*, on the civil War), author, editor (*Christian Leader*), preacher who trained several young folk for the Universalist ministry, and wife of Adirondam (above). Her sermons were "faultless" according to a contemporary. Her hymns are primarily for children. Three are in CHNO. AUH, CHNO, OWW, UUW

Patton, Kenneth, (1911–1994) Disciples of Christ minister, later Unitarian at First Unitarian, Madison, WI (while they built the Frank Lloyd Wright building), then Universalist minister at Charles Street Meeting House in Boston (his *Religion for One World*, is a record of that religious experiment, museum, publishing venture and church). Patton published several volumes of poetry and *Hymns for Humanity*. He was a member of the hymnal commission for HCL which included 13 of his hymns. 5 survive in SLT. BTL, DUUB, HCL, HDUU, UIA

Peabody, Miss Elizabeth Palmer, (1804–1894) Unitarian, one of the three Peabody sisters (Mary Mann and Sophia Hawthorne were the other two). Women's rights advocate, bookstore owner, activist, editor (*The Dial*), best known for her late life initiative in the Kindergarten movement. One hymn found its way into one hymnal, Hedge's *Hymns for the Church of Christ*. 2CD, DUUB, HDUU, HLF, NAW, ROS, SBU, UUW, WHP

Peabody, Ephraim, (1807–1856) Graduated HDS, was Tutor to the Huidekopers in Meadville, PA, before taking on the new frontier Unitarian congregation in Cincinnati, OH. Not prepared for the rough life of the Queen City he became co–minister in New Bedford, MA, from which he moved on to King's Chapel. He was a thoughtful, reflective, persuasive preacher and occasional poet. His hymn "Lift aloud the voice of praise" appeared in *Hymns for the Church of Christ*. AUH, DUUB, HLF, HLF–4

Peabody, Oliver William Bourne, (1799–1847) Born in Exeter, NH, graduated Harvard, he practiced law briefly. He became Professor of Literature at Jefferson College in LA. before being licensed to preach. He served the Unitarian Church in Burlington, VT his last two years. One hymn survives "God of the rolling orbs" in *Hymns for the Church of Christ*. AUH, HLF, SSLF

Peabody, William Bourne Oliver, D.D. (twin of above), (1799–1847) Ordained to his one and only church, the Unitarian Church of Springfield, MA, in 1820. Published a *Poetical Catechism* for the Young, including hymns, and The *Springfield Collection of Hymns for Sacred Worship*, including several of his hymns. Foote identifies 5 worthy hymns of which "Who is thy neighbor?" survives in NHTB. AUH, HLF, SSLF

Penfold, Nita, (1950 –) Penfold co-authored "When Will the Fighting Cease" in STJ with Nick Page.

Perkins, James Handasyde, (1810–1849) Educated in Massachusetts, he entered the bar in Cincinnati, later becoming Minister–at–Large to the Unitarian Church there, still later the settled minister. Co-operated in editing the *Western Dial*, he was a literary and reform figure in the Ohio Valley. No hymn survives to the 20th century. HLF

Perkins, Wendy Luella, (1966–) The words and music of "We Give Thanks" in STJ are hers.

Pierpont, John, (1785–1866) Born in Litchfield, CT, educated Yale and HDS, became minister of the troubled Hollis Street Church in Boston. His abolition and temperance work put him on a collision course with the Church which he left in 1840. He published his *Temperance Hymns*, a fierce little pamphlet, and his *Poems and Hymns* later, including temperance and abolition hymns and verse. He served churches in Troy, NY, and Medford, MA, then became a Union Army Chaplain, later working for the U.S. Treasury. His hymns were passionate and timely; a few made *Hymns for the Church of Christ*. 4 were in NHTB, 2 ("Gone are those great and good" and "O Thou to Whom in ancient times") in HOS. AUH, DUUB, HLF, HLF–4, SSLF

Poley, Joyce, (1941–) "One More Step" has become familiar to all protesters for peace – in SLT. BTL

Pray, Lewis Glover (1793–1882) A Boston businessman, Member of the Boston Board of Education and the State Legislature. He was Superintendent of the sunday school at 12th Congregational, Boston, for 33 years. Published several sunday school hymn books. One hymn survived to *Hymns of the Ages,* 3rd Edition, 1864. AUH, SSLF

Price, Mrs. Abby Hills, "Poet Laureate" of Adin Ballou's Hopedale Community, friend of Mary Colburn. Frequent and popular hymn writer (at least 10 hymns) in *The Hopedale Collection.*

Putnam, Alfred Porter, D.D., (1827–1906) Educated at Brown and HDS, he served Unitarian churches in Roxbury (First), and Brooklyn (Church of the Savior). His great gift was *Singers and Songs of the Liberal Faith: being selections of hymns and other sacred poems of the Liberal Church in America,* with biographical sketches of the writers, here known as SSLF. AUH, HLF, SSLF

Rayner, Menzies, (1770–1850) Episcopal convert, served Universalist churches in Hartford, CT, Portland, ME, and Schnectady, NY., edited regional Universalist journals. One hymn survives in CHNO. AUH, CHNO, TLH

Reese, Curtiss Williford, D.D., (1887–1961) Executive of the Unitarian Western Conference, editor of *Unity,* the Midwest Unitarian journal. Reese is credited with the composite form of "From all that dwell below the skies, Let songs of hope and faith arise; Let peace, good–will on earth be sung Through every land by every tongue" in HOS, but not in HCL or SLT. BTL, DUUB, HLF–4

Reynolds, Malvina, (1900–1978) Surely she needs no introduction to peace, environmental and women's activists. Her "O What a Piece of Work We Are" with the sexist "man" removed appeared at last in SLT. BTL

Richards, George, (c1744–1814) Teacher, Navy Chaplain (and Purser), became Universalist minister, poet, "florid preacher" in Portsmouth, NH and Philadelphia, PA. He edited, with Oliver Lane the *Hymns and Spiritual Songs, for use in Universalist Churches,* (49 of his) Boston, 1792, and 9 years later *A Collection of Hymns,* Dover, NH, containing, by the second edition, 32 of his hymns. AH, AUH, CHNO, TLH

Robbins, Chandler, D.D,. (1810–1882) Graduated HDS and ordained to Second (Unitarian) Church, Boston, where he published *The So-*

cial Hymn Book (1843), and *Hymn Book for Christian Worship* (1854). Only one hymn ("Lo! The day of rest declineth") survived in NHTB. AUH, HLF, SSLF

Robbins, Samuel Dowse, (1812–1884) Graduated HDS – served the Unitarian churches in Lynn, Chelsea, Framingham and Wayland, Massachusetts. Wrote several poems and hymns. None survived to the 20th century. AUH, HLF, SSLF

Rogers, George, (1805–1846) London born, with a wide religious pilgrimage, then Universalist minister in Brooklyn, PA, later Cincinnati, OH, and evangelist in much of the Ohio and Mississippi Valleys, and Canada. He published his own small hymn book, *Universalist Hymn Book*, to fit in an itinerant's saddlebags. Four of his hymns are in CHNO. AH, AUH, CHNO, DUUB, TLH

Russell, Byron, (c1850–1930) Graduated Tufts Theological School, served in Universalist church in Standing Stone, PA. One hymn survived to HOS. AUH, CHNO

Safford, Mary Augusta, (1851–1927) Born in Illinois she became one of the great leaders of the Iowa Sisterhood, Unitarian women ministers in the state. Church organizer, missionary, a Director of the AUA, she fought the sidetracking of women out of the ministry. I've found only one hymn used in an Iowa Installation Service. Doubtless there are other hymns by Ms. Safford and others of the Iowa Sisterhood, but being women and radical Westerners they had two strikes against them. DUUB, HDUU, HLF–4, SBU, UUW

St. John, Mrs. A.R. Monroe, (1805–) Born in Boston, a quiet poet and hymn writer whose compositions punctuated special occasions at Church of the Savior (Unitarian) in Brooklyn and elsewhere in the mid 1800s. SSFL

Sargeant, Epes, (1813–1880) Layman, journalist he translated "Dies Irae" into English verse, and wrote one hymn, "All Souls are thine," which is in HOS. AUH, CHNO, TLH

Sargent, Lucius Manilius, (1786–1867) Layman and Temperance advocate. His famous temperance hymn (revised) appears in *Church Harmonies* (1895). AUH, TLH

Savage, Minnie Stebbins, (1850 –) *Unity Hymns – Songs of Faith, Hope and Charity* included one hymn by her "Is there a human soul despairing?'

Savage, Minot Judson, D.D., (1841–1918) Graduated Bangor Seminary – served Congregational churches in several states before becoming Unitarian Minister for two years of Third Unitarian Church in Chicago. Then he served Unity Church in Boston before moving on to New York City's Church of the Messiah. Popular author and speaker, popularizer of evolutionary thought and religion he published many books including *Sacred Songs for Public Worship; a Hymn and Tune Book* (1883) with 42 of his own hymns. 4 survived to HOS, 3 to HCL and 2 to SLT ("Seek not afar for beauty" and "O star of truth"). AUH. BTL, DUUB, HCL, HDUU, HLF, HLF–4

Sawyer, Mrs. Caroline Mehitabel Fisher, (1812–1894) A Universalist from Newton, MA, she spent most of her life in New York, until moving to MA where her husband was Dean of Tufts University. She was among the best–educated women of her day, an editor, and popular author and poet, well known among her contemporaries. Her hymns are directed at youth. Two are in CHNO. AUH, CHNO, DUUB, NAW, OWW, TLH, UUW

Schermerhorn, Martin Kellogg, Late 19th – 20th century Unitarian minister who created the *Universal Worship: the Catholic Gospel* – "Our Father..." hymnal, writing and editing hymns to speak only of the "Father" – no other religious figure – believing that this hymnal would have universal appeal. It didn't and doesn't.

Scott, Jim, (1945 –) Long known separate from the Paul Winter Consort, especially among UUs this composer writer, performer finally appeared with three song–hymns in SLT, and three more in STJ. BTL

Scudder, Miss Eliza, (1821–1896) American Unitarian – Episcopalian, (niece of Rev. E.H. Sears) one of America's greatest, most profound and passionate hymn writers. Many of her hymns from her mid (Unitarian) years survive in a host of hymnals. 3 of the 10 Foote identifies are in HOS ("I cannot find Thee...," "Thou Grace divine, encircling all," and "Thou Life within my life..."). AH, AUH, DUUB

Seaburg, Rev. Carl, (1922 –1998) Known for his liturgical works on communion, and everything from dedications to memorial services.

Seaburg wrote five hymns in SLT, including the favorite "Find a Stillness." He also masterfully edited "Once in Royal David's City" and "Rank by Rank Again We Stand" both in SLT. BTL

Sears, Edmund Hamilton, (1810–1876) Graduated HDS, ordained minister in First Parish (Unitarian), Wayland, left to serve Lancaster, returned to Wayland. He was a progressive, anti–slavery minister, gradually turning inward, writing many hymns. Two famous ones survive, both extraordinarily beautiful Christmas hymns ("Calm on the listening ear of night" and "It came upon the midnight clear") in SOH. The former was expunged in HCL, the latter continues in HCL and SLT. AH, AUH, BTL, DUUB, HCL, HDUU, HLF, HLF–4, SSLF

Senghas, Dorothy, (1930–2002), and Senghas, Robert, (1928 –) They jointly recast "We Gather Together" in SLT. BTL

Seymour, Almira, Author of an elegant Christmas hymn sung at Phoebe Hanaford's ordination in 1868.

Shelton, Jason, (1972–) Shelton arranged or wrote the music for eleven song–hymns, and wrote both words and music for two, including the favorite "Standing on the Side of Love," in STJ.

Sigourney, Mrs. Lydia Howard Huntley, (1791–1865) Connecticut born, well known writer and poet, author of children's stories. 2 hymns of hers appear in *Hymns for the Church of Christ*. AH, AUH

Sill, Edward Rowland, (1841–1887) Graduated Yale, studied at HDS., Wrote "Send down thy truth, O God" for HDS's visitation day in 1867, one of many good poems. Became Professor of English Literature at the University of California. AUH, HLF–4

Silliman, Vincent Brown, D.D., (1894 – 1979) Graduated Meadville, served Unitarian congregations in Buffalo, NY, Portland, ME, Hollis, NY and Beverly Church in Chicago, IL. He was a team member in creating *The Beacon Song and Service Book*, successor to the *Beacon Hymnal* for families and children, and he edited *We Sing of Life* with its lovely calligraphy and several Silliman songs. 6 of his hymns are in HCL. His "Morning so fair to see" has been a staple in all subsequent UU hymnals. AUH, BTL, DUUB, HCL

Skinner, Rev. Otis Ainsworth, D.D., (1807–1861) Universalist minister, first preached in small town New Hampshire, later Woburn,

MA, Baltimore, MD, 5th Universalist in Boston, Orchard Street Church in NYC, Elgin, IL, Galesburg, IL where he became President of Lombard College. He was editor of a continuous stream of Universalist regional periodicals, successful fund raiser for Tufts, and Lombard as well, and author of one of the great controversial works, *Universalism, Illustrated and Defended,* 1842.One hymn endured to CHNO, "Thou fount of love and grace." AUH, CHNO, DUUB, TLH

Small, Fred, (1952 –) This musician minister's moving "Everything Possible " is in STJ.

Soule, Caroline, (1824–1903)   Founder of the Universalist Centenary Association, Universalist missionary to Scotland (first woman minister there), forceful figure in denominational life. She wrote a "Centennial Hymn" for the Universalist Centennial in Gloucester, MA, in 1870. Neither it nor she appeared in any denominational hymnals.

Spencer, Anna Carpenter Garlin, (1851–1931) Massachusetts born Unitarian minister, writer on ethical and social problems, reformer ¬especially in child labor, criminal justice and women's rights issues. Professor of Sociology and Ethics at Meadville Theological School, lecturer at University of Chicago and Columbia. Her "Hail the hero workers" appears in HOS. AUH, DUUB, HLF–4, NAW, SBU, UUW, UUWM

Sprague, Charles, (1791–1875) Unitarian businessman poet. Ticknor and Fields published two volumes of his poetry. One hymn appears in Hymns for the Church of Christ. AUH, SSLF

Streeter, Sebastian, (1783–1867) Tried law, taught school, settled in small New Hampshire churches, on to Haverhill, MA, Portsmouth, NH, and long itinerant labors in Maine, before 30 years at Hanover Street Universalist, Boston. Worked on the first General Convention hymnal in 1808 (writing 48 of its hymns). In 1829 he and brother Russell edited *The New Hymn–Book designed for Universalist Societies,* an indexed, popular, diverse hymnal. Four of his hymns survive in CHNO. AUH, CHNO, DUUB, TLH

Streeter, Sebastian Ferris, (1810–1864) (Son of S. Streeter above) A layman, teacher, scholar, wrote one surviving hymn, "How gracious the promise, how soothing the word," in CHNO. AH, AUH, CHNO

Streeter Russell, (1791–1880) There are 7 of his hymns in the Streeter brothers' hymnal of 1829. Several are for children, but theologically they are universalist and good for their time. DUUB, TLH

Sumner, Samuel Barstow., (1830–1891) Businessman, Sunday school teacher at First Unitarian Church in Louisville, KY, and later Bulfinch Place Chapel in Boston. Perennial hymn writer, gentle sweet, personal. SSLF

Sweetser, Paul Hart, (1807–1872) Teacher, editor, writer, anti–slavery and pro–temperance, deeply involved in education and community issues – retired to his home "Greenwood." He left one hymn in CHNO. AUH, CHNO

Tagore, Rabindranath, (1861–1941) Tagore's lyrical, mystical poetry is known to generations. Three are hymns, one with Tagore's own music, in SLT (Two were in HCL), including the favorite "Now I Recall My Childhood When the Sun." BTL

Taylor, Emily, (1796–1872) Traveler, essayist, writer, especially of children's stories – a rich profusion of her well crafted hymns appeared in most of our hymnals of the last century. One, of 11 identified, "God of the changing year," appears in NHTB.

Thomas, Abel Charles, (1807–1880) Quaker teacher and printer became Universalist minister and editor., Served centrally the Lombard St. Universalist Church in Philadelphia, wrote a moving history of Universalism in the environs. Edited and published the first American hymnal with words and music on the same page, *Hymns of Zion,* Philadelphia, in 1839, The *Gospel Liturgy,* and *Hymns of Devotion,* in 1857. His hymns were personal and pungent. 5 survived in CHNO. AUH, CHNO, DUUB, TLH, UIA

Thorne, Emily, (1915 –) Thorne's "Do You Hear O My Friend" made the rounds of conferences, churches, surreptitious songbooks before finding a home in SLT. BTL

Torrey, Hiram, (1820–1900) Born in Ravenna, OH, Universalist minister in PA, NY, MA, became editor, left one hymn written at 14, "Heavenly Father, we desire" in CHNO. AUH, CHNO

Trapp, Jacob, S.T.D., (1899–1992) Graduated Pacific School of Religion (now Starr King) Served congregations in Salt Lake City, UT,

Denver, CO, and Summit, NJ, before retiring to his beloved Southwest – New Mexico. He was a moving, mystical poet, especially of the desert. Published a hymnal for his Salt Lake City congregation, *Songs and Readings* in 1931 (There was a second and larger edition.) It included excellent hymns, many of which appeared in HOS; one had to wait for HCL. It included Trapp's hymn "Wonders still the world shall witness" which survives to SLT, where his "Let freedom span both east and west" appears for the first time. HCL also had "The art, the science and the lore" by Trapp. AUH, BTL, DUUB, HCL

Tuckerman, Joseph, D.D., (1778–1840) graduate of Harvard, licensed to preach and ordained in the Chelsea Church. 25 Years later he became the Minister–at–Large for Boston, under the AUA, later the Benevolent Fraternity of Unitarian Churches (today the UU Urban Ministry). He worked with a series of chapels for the poor and unchurched, with youth and family programs. He is called a founder of American Social Work. One hymn ("Father divine! This deadening power control") appeared in *Hymns for the Church of Christ*. AUH, DUUB, HLF

Turner, Edward, (1776–1853) Universalist minister, restorationist, who became Unitarian in the battle with Ultra Universalists. He was an editor of the first General Convention hymnal in 1808. and joined in Ballou's Collection in 1821. Two hymns are in CHNO. AUH, CHNO, DUUB, TLH

Udis–Kessler, Amanda, (1965–) "Mother Earth, Beloved Garden" is hers, both words and music – in STJ

Very, Jones (1813–1880) Graduate of Harvard became tutor of Greek there. He preached occasionally, but his life was a literary one, publishing Essays and Poems in 1839, frequent contributor to Unitarian magazines. Foote identifies 10 of his hymns; 2 are in *The Isle of Shoals Hymn Book* and one in HOS ("We go not on a pilgrimage"). AH, AUH, DUUB, SSLF

Very, Lydia Louisa.Ann, (1823–1901) Prominent poet, writer – four hymns survive but none in our hymnals.

Very, Washington, (1815–1853) Graduate of HDS, briefly preached, conducted a private school in Salem. No hymns survive to the 20th century. AUH, SSLF

Ware, Henry, Jr., D.D., (1794–1843) Graduated Harvard, taught at Phillips Exeter Academy, licensed to preach, ordained as minister Second Church (Unitarian), Boston. In 1830 became Professor of Pulpit Eloquence and Pastoral Care at HDS. He edited The Christian Disciple wrote many books and beautiful hymns. Foote identifies 14 of which two survived to HOS ("All nature's works His praise declare" and "Great God, the followers of thy son"). AH, AUH, DUUB, HDUU, HLF, SSLF

Waterston, Mrs. Anna Cabot Lowell Quincy, (1812–1899) .Poet, grand–daughter of Josiah Quincy of Revolutionary Boston. This author has identified 4 hymns by her, none in any recent UU hymnal.

Waterston, Robert Cassie, (1812–1893) Studied at HDS, ordained to the Ministry–at–Large in Boston, served in two chapels, then minister of the Church of the Savior in Boston, followed by First Religious Society of Newburyport, MA. Poet, author, member of the Boston School Committee, he wrote many hymns. Foote lists 11. None survive. AUH, HLF, SSLF

Weir, Robert Stanley, D.C.L., (1856–1926) He was a prominent Canadian Judge who translated from the French the hymn, "O Canada, our home, our native land," the Canadian national anthem. Appears in NHTB. AUH

Weiss, John, (1818–1879) Graduated HDS, ordained to ministry of First Church (Unitarian), Watertown, MA. Moved on to New Bedford, First Church, and back to Watertown. He was a mystical theist who wrote widely on non-western faith, and was fiercely anti–slavery – demanding such a declaration from the New Bedford church before he would be their minister. Foote identifies three hymns, one of which appears in *Hymns for the Church of Christ* and another in *Church Harmonies*. AUH, DUUB, HLF, SSLF

Wendte, Charles William, (1844–1931) Graduated HDS and served Fourth Unitarian in Chicago, First Unitarian in Cincinnati and Channing Memorial in Newport. He worked for the AUA in California and the coast, and became Secretary for Foreign Affairs of the AUA. He published *The Carol, for Sunday School and Home, Jubilate Deo* (for children), *Heart and Voice, a Collection of Songs and Services for*

Sunday School and Home. These were in great part his own hymns and songs. None have survived. Hardly any were ever reprinted. But one hymn "Not given to us from out the sky" endures in NHTB and HOS. DUUB, HDUU, HLF, HLF–4

Weston, Caroline, (1808–) One of the outspoken Weston sisters who opposed slavery so forcefully. She was a teacher in Boston and a founder of the Boston Female Anti–Slavery Society. She wrote hymns as did her sister Maria Weston Chapman.

Weston, Robert Terry, (1898–1988) Weston was an irrepressible liturgist, especially in shaping responsive readings. It is good to see a hymn of his even if it has only one verse in SLT. BTL

Westwood, Horace, D.D., (1884–1956) British born he served Methodist churches for years. Later he served Unitarian churches in Youngstown, OH, Winnepeg, Manitoba, Canada and Toledo, OH, and as an extension preacher. He published hymns and poems, but only one endures, "Spirit of truth, of Life, of Power" in HOS, HCL, SLT. AUH, BTL, HCL

Whitney, Frederick Augustus, (1812–1880) Graduated HDS, was a Missionary for the American Unitarian Assn. in Massachusetts, and South and West, them minister of the Unitarian Church in Brighton, MA. Wrote many creditable hymns for special church occasions. HLF, SSLF

Whittemore, Benjamin Ballou, (1829–) Universalist businessman, member of the Boston School Committee. One hymn survived to CHNO. CHNO, TLH

Whittemore, Thomas, (1800–1861) Boston born, won by Hosea Ballou's preaching (he played the bass viol for services) he trained for the Universalist ministry. Whittemore served churches in NH and MA. He and Russell Streeter bought *The Universalist Magazine,* merging it into *The Trumpet and Universalist Magazine*, the leading Universalist paper. Whittemore did much controversial writing and speaking, and wrote *The Modern History of Universalism.* Hosea Ballou II had done *The Ancient History of Universalism.* Whittemore was a composer and hymn writer. He published *Songs of Zion, The Gospel Harmonist, Conference Hymns,* and *The Sunday School Choir and Superintendant's Assistant.* He wrote The Life

170

of Hosea Ballou, and was an extraordinary businessman, and a member of the MA state legislature. Three of his hymns are in SOH. AH, DUUB, HDUU, SOH, TLH, UIA

Wile, Frances Whitmarsh, (1878–1939) From Bristol Center, New York, encouraged by her Rochester minister, William Channing Gannett, she crafted the masterpiece, "All beautiful the march of days" in 1907, which appears in NHTB, HOS, HCL and SLT . AUH, BTL, HCL

Wiley, Hiram Ozias, (1831–1873) Lawyer and poet in Peabody and Danvers, MA. His "He leads us on by paths we did not know" endures in HOS and HCL. AUH, HCL

Willard, Emma C., (1787 –1870) Educational missionary, chronographer, peace and woman's rights activist. Only her "Rocked in the cradle of the deep" appears in our hymnody, and that only in Louisa Adams Beal's, *Hymns for Christian Worship.*

Willard, Samuel, (1776–1859) Graduated Harvard, served First Church (Unitarian) Deerfield, MA. He published a volume of 158 of his own songs, and a more inclusive *Sacred Music and Poetry Reconciled,* a hymnbook – used at Third Church in Hingham, some wider use. AUH, HLF, SSLF

Williams, Helen Maria, (1762–1827) British Unitarian hymn writer, and much honored poet whose "While thee I seek, protecting Pow'r" appeared in a dozen of our hymnals, latest HOS, and continues in many others' hymnals. An outspoken figure she was imprisoned during the "reign of terror" in France, during which time she wrote the above hymn, giving it particular poignancy and power. DUUB, HAD

Williams, Sarah, (1805–1868) British Unitarian whose gentle but strong "Because I knew not when my life was good" hymn (alone) survives in *Unitarian hymnal Hymns for Church and Home,* 1903.

Williams, Theodore Chickering, (1855–1915) Born in Brookline, MA, graduated HDS. He was ordained to the Unitarian church in Winchester, MA, moved to All Souls, NYC the next year. Later he was Headmaster of Hackley School in Tarrytown, NY. He was a scholar of the classics, a fine poet and hymn writer. Foote lists 14 of his hymns, most of which are in the NHTB and HOS, 2 are in HCL ("When thy heart with joy o'erflowing" and the lovely Christmas hymn "In the lonely midnight"). The latter alone is in SLT. AH, AUH, BTL, HCL, HLF–4

Williams, Velma Curtiss Wright, (1852–1941) Wife of Rev. Theodore Chickering Williams. She published *Amore Dei,* a hymnal of great quality and inclusivity in 1890. She didn't write hymns.

Willis, Love Maria, (1824–1908) American Unitarian editor and author whose work is more familiar to others than to ourselves. Author of several hymns, her "Father hear the prayer we offer" is a gracious and strong hymn, in HOS. AH, AUH

Willis, Nathaniel Parker, (1807–1867) Graduated from Yale, wrote for the *American Monthly* and the New York Mirror and was an editor of *The Corsair.* He wrote prolifically including *Sacred Poems* in 1843. One hymn appears in *Hymns for the Church of Christ.* AUH

Wilson, Edwin Henry, D.D., (1898–1993) Graduated Boston University and Meadville, received his MA at the University of Chicago. He served Third Church, Chicago, IL, and churches in Schnectady, NY and Salt Lake City, UT. He was the Executive Director of the American Humanist Assn. almost until his death. One hymn survives, "Where is our holy church?" to SLT. AH, AUH, BTL, DUUB, HCL

Wilson, Lewis Gilbert, (1858–1928) Graduated Meadville, ordained in Leicester, MA, later serving the Hopedale Unitarian Church. Was also Secretary of the AUA 3 hymns are recorded by Foote, "O God, our dwelling place" surviving in HOS. AUH, HLF–4

Winchester, Elhanan, II, (1751–1797) Born in Brookline, MA, Calvinist, become, Baptist, become Universalist. He was a powerful and persuasive preacher carrying most of his Philadelphia Baptist congregation into Universalism. He often spent time in England, and founded the Parliament Court Chapel which later became Unitarian, (and is today the Ethical Culture Society). He published a hymnal for his Philadelphia congregation in 1786 including some of his own hymns. No hymns are in our hymnals, but a couple from the Revolutionary era are in SOH. AH, DUUB, HDUU, SOH, TLH, UIA

Witt, Elsie, (1953–) Witt, inspired by a Georgia Sea Island spiritual, wrote and composed "Open the Window" in STJ.

Wooley, Celia Parker, (1848–1918) Born in Toledo, OH, she became a leader in the literary and civic life of Chicago. Woman's Club President, brought in African-Americans. Active in suffrage and reform. On the Editorial staff of Unity for 34 years, writing articles especially on human rights. Ordained a Unitarian minister in 1894. Her one hymn in our corpus of hymnody, "On bent, misshapen lines of faith" in *Unity Hymns and Chorals* is a powerful and personal evocation of the struggle for faith. HDUU, HLF–4, SBU, UUW, UUWM, DUUB

Wright, Samuel Anthony, (1918–) Wright wrote "We Would be One" for the formation of Liberal Religious Youth in 1953 (from the youth organization of the Universalists and Unitarians). It has only been altered for inclusion of all folks. BTL

Young, George H., One hymn appears in *The Isle of Shoals Hymn Book.* AUH

Young, Michael, (1939–) "Mother of All" is a complete recasting of Alexander Pope's famous Universal Prayer in SLT. BTL

Zala, Elsie, (1925–) Three song–hymns owe their clear English translations to Elsie Zala in STJ.

Appendix II

1. A listing of some proto Unitarian and pre–organized Universalism hymn books.
2. Some but not all Unitarian and Universalist hymn books.
   A complete list is doubtless impossible but this has almost all of the hymn and song books that had more than a local usage (in some cases – despite their local titles). They are listed in alphabetical order.
3. Followed by an alphabetical listing of Sunday school, youth, children's and family hymnals and song books.

Early Liberal Christian Hymnals
Proto–universalist

Das Gesang der Einsamen un Verlassenen Turtel–Taube, ed. Johann Conrad Beissel (1690–1768), Ephrata Press (Ephrata, PA, 1747)

Proto–unitarian

A Collection of Hymns, more particularly designed for the Use of West Society in Boston, ed. Simeon Howard (1733–1804), T.& J. Fleet (Boston, 1782–1813)

A Collection of Hymns for Publick Worship, ed. William Bentley (1750–1819), (Salem, 1788)

A Collection of Psalms and Hymns, ed. William Emerson (1769–1811), Munroe, Francis and Parker (Boston, 1808)

A Collection of Psalms and Hymns for Public Worship, James Freeman (1759–1835) and Joseph May, (Boston, 1799); Second Edition (1813)

A Collection of Sacred Musick, [West Church, Boston], Buckingham and Titcomb (Boston, 1810)

A New Version of The Psalms of David, contains a collection of hymns for the use of West Society, Boston, ed. Tate and Brady (1783 & 1803)

A New Version of The Psalms of David, contains a collection of hymns for the use of The Church in Brattle Street, ed. Tate and Brady, Boston (1808 & 1812)

Columbian Harmonist, ed. Timothy Flint, (1816)

Hymns for Public Worship, (Part Two of Brattle Street Collection above) ed. Joseph Stevens Buckminster, (Boston, 1812)

Hymns for the Lord's Supper, Thaddeus Mason Harris (1768–1847), Thomas, Andrews,

West and Greenleaf (Boston, (1801– 1821) Often bound with *Belknap's Sacred Poetry*)

Psalm and Hymn Tunes, Selected for the Use of the Hollis Street Society, J.T. Buckingham (Boston, 1811)

Sacred Poetry Consisting of Psalms and Hymns, Adapted to Christian Devotion, in Public and Private, ed. Jeremy Belknap (1744–1798), Joseph Belknap (Boston 1795–1820)

The Brick Church Hymns, Gardner Spring (1823)

The First Church Collection of Sacred Music, J.T. Buckingham (Boston, 1805–1815)

Unitarian and Universalist, and Unitarian Universalist Hymnbooks:

A Book of Hymns for Public and Private Devotion, ed. Samuel Johnson (1822–1882) and Samuel Longfellow (1819–1892), Metcalf and Co. (Cambridge, 1846 [12 editions in 2 years]) UN

A Book of Prayer for the Church and the Home: with selections from the Psalms and a collection of hymns, ed. Charles Leonard, A. Tompkins (Boston, 1864); Second Edition: Universalist Publishing House (Boston, 1865) UV Universalist Publishing House (Boston, 1919) UV

A Choice Collection of Hymns, ed. Elhanan Winchester, (Philadelphia, 1782–1787) UV

A Collection of Hymns, ed Samuel Willard, (1830) UN

A Collection of Hymns: designed for the use of the Universal Churches: and adapted to public and private devotion, ed. George Richards (Dover, NH, 1801) Second Edition: Samuel Bragg (Dover, NH, 1806) UV

A Collection of Hymns for the Christian Church and Home, ed. James Flint [East Church, Salem](and William Bentley?), James Munroe and Co. (Boston, 1843) UN

A Collection of Psalms and Hymns for the use of Universalist Societies and Families, ed. Hosea Ballou II, Benjamin B.Mussey (Boston, 1839) With Second Edition in 1853 – went to 18 editions] UV

A Collection of Psalms and Hymns for Christian Worship, ed. Francis William Pitt Greenwood, Carter and Hendee (Boston, 1830 [50 editions]) UN

A Collection of Psalms and Hymns, for social and private worship, Henry D. Sewall, (NYC, 1820–1845) UN

A Collection of Psalms and Hymns for Social and Private Worship, compiled by a committee of the West Parish in Boston, ed. John Russell (Boston, 1823) UN

A Collection of Psalms and Hymns for the Sanctuary, ed. George Ellis (1814–1894), (Boston, 1845) UN

A liturgy for the Use of the church at King's Chapel in Boston, [with Liturgy], ed. Francis William Pitt Greenwood, (Boston, 1831) UN

A Manual of Prayer for Public and Private Worship, William Greenleaf Eliot (Boston, 1842) [For the newly formed St. Louis Society] UN

An Appendix to Universalist Hymn Books: ed. George W. Montgomery, Grosh and Hutchinson (Utica, NY, 1838) UV

Anti Slavery Hymns, ed. George N. Stacy, Hopedale (1844) UV & UN

A Selection of Sacred Poetry, Consisting of Psalms and Hymns from Watts, Dodderidge, Merrick, Scott, Cowper, Barbauld, Steele and others, for the Use of the Unitarian Church in Philadelphia, ed. Ralph Eddowes (1751–1833) and James Taylor (1769–1844), William Fry (Philadelphia 1812–1846) UN

A Selection from Tate and Brady's Version of the Psalms: with Hymns by various authors [for Brattle Square Church], Richardson and Lord (Boston, 1825) UN

Blessed Life, Mary Wilder Tilletson (1843–1934), (?) UN

*Book of Worship; Being Selections, Chiefly from the Psalms...*Prepared for the Third Congregational Society of Springfield, Massachusetts, Ticknor and Fields (Boston, 1866) UN

Celebration of Life, Hymns of Humanity [in Meeting House Series: Religion for our Time, ed. Kenneth R. Patton, Meeting House Press (Boston, 1951) UV

Chapel Hymnbook, ed. Charles Francis Barnard (1842) UN

Christian Chorals: a hymn and tune book for the congregation and the home, ed. J.W. Hanson (1823–1901), Western Universalist Publishing House (Chicago, 1879–1887) UV

Christian Hymns Adapted to the Worship of God our Savior, in Public and Private Devotion, Central Universalist Society, Charles Crocker (Boston, 1823) UV

Christian Hymns for public and private worship. A Collection compiled by a committee of the Cheshire Pastoral Association, [known popularly as *The Cheshire Collection*], ed. Abiel A Livermore (1811–1892), Levi W. Leonard (1790–1864), William A. Whitwell (1804–1865), Curtis Cutler (1806–1874 [all New Hampshire ministers], (Boston, 1845 [went to 60 editions]) UN

Christian Hymns, Poems and Spiritual Songs, sacred to the praise of God, our Savior, James and John Relly, John Melcher (Boston, 1774); (Burlington, NJ, 1776) and John Melcher (Portsmouth, 1782) UV

Christian Worship, Samuel Osgood (1812–1880) and Frederick Farley (1800–1892), (NYC, 1862) UN

Church Harmonies, A Collection of hymns and Tunes for the Use of Congregations, Published under the direction of the Universalist Publishing House, (Boston, 1873 – 1911) UV

Church Harmonies New and Old: A Book of Spiritual Song for Christian Worship; Complete Edition with Psalms and Chants, ed. Charles R. Tenny and Leo R. Lewis [Some printings include biographies of hymn writers, especially Universalist], Universalist Publishing House (Boston, 1895–1909) UV

Church Pastorals, ed. Nehemiah Adams, Ticknor and Fields (Boston, 1864) UN

Church Worship: in Readings, Songs and Prayers, Third Church Publishing Committee (Chicago, 1892) UN

Collection of Psalms and Hymns for Christian Worship, ed. Francis William Pitt Greenwood, Carter, Hendee and Co. (Boston, 1835), New Edition edited by Robert Cassie Waterston. UN

Coldwater Melodies, ed. John Pierpont, (1943) UN

Come Sing a Song With Me, compiled and edited by Melodie Feather, UU Musician's Network, (2008) This is a compilation of 25 songs from SLT and Singing the Journey with simple arrangements and commentary.

Communal Songs and Hymns, Original and Selected, Reed (Hopedale, 1805–1806) UV

Conference Hymns and Tunes,I, ed. Thomas Whittemore (1800–1861), James M. Usher (Boston, 1842–1857) UV

Conference Hymns and Tunes, II, ed. Thomas Whittemore (1800–1861), James M. Usher (Boston, 1843–1857) UV

Contemplations of the Savior, ed. Samuel Greenfield Bulfinch, Carter and Hendee (Boston, 1832) UN

Devotional Melodies, Adapted to Social Worship, Universalist Publishing House (Boston, 1876–1880)

Evangelical Psalms, Hymns and Spiritual Songs, Selected from Various Authors; and published by a committee of the convention of the churches, believing in the restitution of all men. Met in Philadelphia, May 25, 1791. General Convention of Universalists of the New England States and Others. Thomas Dobson (Philadelphia, 1792) UV

Familiar Hymns and Tunes: for congregational singing, ed George L. Perin, Universalist Publishing House (Boston, 1886) UV

Family Manual for the Broad Church...Hymns, William D'Arcy Haley (1828–1884), O. Hutchinson (NYC, 1859) UN

Gems of Sacred Poetry, William Brigham Tappan (1794–1849), H. Dayton (NYC, c1846) UN

Gloria Patri: Prayers, Chants, and Responses for Public Worship ed. L.J. Fletcher and Thomas B. Thayer, Universalist Publishing House (Boston, 1886–1894); Revised and expanded edition: (1903–1909) UV

Good–Will Songs; A Compilation of Hymns and Tunes Original, Selected and arranged for Praise and prayer Meetings and Stated Church Services, ed. Stanford Mitchell, Universalist Publishing House (Boston, 1882–1894) UV

Gospel Melodies New and Old: for Use in the Universalist Church, ed. Chester Gore Miller, Universalist Publishing House (Boston, 1904) UV

How Can We Keep From Singing!, ed. Waldemar Hille, The Hodgin Press (Los Angeles, 1976) UN

Hymnal, ed. Frank Hall and Edward Thompson, for the Unitarian Church

(Westport, CT, 1987) UN

Hymnal: Amore Dei, ed. Velma Williams (?), (Boston, 1890, revised, 1897) UN

Hymn and Service Book, ed Frederick Augustus Farley, Samuel Osgood and Seth Low, (1862) UN

Hymn and Tune Book, for the Church and the Home, primary ed. Leonard J. Livermore (1822–1886), American Unitarian Association, (Boston, 1868); Revised Edition, ed. Rush R. Shippen (1828–1911), AUA (1877–1889); Revised Edition, AUA (Boston, 1895) An abridged edition called *Social Hymn and Tune Book: for the Vestry and the Home* was published by the AUA (Boston, 1880) UN

Hymn Book for Christian Worship, Chandler Robbins (1810–1880), Boston, 1854) UN

Hymn, Tune and Service Book, ed Leonard Jarvis Livermore (?) UN

Hymns Adapted for Communion Service, Universalist Conference, John Mann (Dover, NH, 1834) UV

Hymns, composed by different authors, at the request of the General Convention of Universalists, ed. Hosea Ballou, Abner Kneeland and Edward Turner, Samuel T. Armstrong (Charlestown, MA, 1810) UV

Hymns, composed by different authors, by order of the General Convention of Universalists of the New–England states and others: adapted to public and private devotion, ed. Hosea Ballou, Abner Kneeland and Edward Turner, George W. Nichols (Walpole, NH, 1808) UV

Hymns for All Christians, ed. Charles Deems and Phoebe Cary, Hurd and Houghton (NYC, 1869) UV

Hymns for Christian Devotion, Especially Adapted to the Universalist Denomination, ed. John Greenleaf Adams and Edwin Hubbel Chapin, Abel Tomkins (Boston, 1846–1867 [63rd Edition]); New Edition 1870–1875; [As this popular hymnal had no music a supplementary volume was published: *The Musical Supplement and Congregational Melodist,* John G.Adams, B.F. Tweed and J.S. Barry, Tompkins and Co. (Boston, 1864)] UV[1]

Hymns for Christian Worship With Music, ed. Louisa Adams Beal, Stan-

---

1   There are many local hymn books that edit and copy the popular, as: *A Selection of Hymns for the use of the Universalist Church, Upper Lisle,* [selected from *Hymns for Christian Devotion,* B.S. Hoag (Upper Lisle, NY, 1876)

hope Press (Boston, 1909) UN

Hymns for Church and Home, Mary Wilder Tilletson and Arthur Foote, American Unitarian Association (Boston, 1895 [Several Editions and Printings including an Abridged Edition in 1902]) UN Robert Sanders and Vincent B. Silliman, Beacon Press (Boston, 1964) UU

Hymns for Public Worship, ed. George W. Briggs (1810–1895), [of Plymouth, MA], (Boston, 1845) UN

Hymns for Social Worship and Private Devotion, ed Edward Brooks Hall, Providence (1837) UN

Hymns for the Celebration of Life, ed. Arthur Foote II, Lorraine Bays, Henry Leland Clarke, Ida, M. Folsom, Christopher Moore, Kenneth Munson, Kenneth L. Patton

Hymns for the Christian Church, [First Church, Boston], ed. Rufus Ellis (1819–1885) Little Brown and Co. (Boston,1869) UN

Hymns for the Church and Home; with a Selection of Psalms: Portland Collection, ed. E.C. Bowles and Israel Washburn Jr., Universalist Publishing House (Boston, 1865–1870) UV

Hymns for the Church of Christ, ed. Frederick Henry Hedge (1805–1890) and Frederic Dan Huntington (1819–1904), Crosby, Nichols and Co. (Boston, 1853–1865 [10,000 copies]) UN

Hymns for the Use of the Unitarian Church in Washington, D.C., W. Cooper (Washington, 1821) UN

Hymns in Harmony with Modern Thought, [commonly called "The Tacoma Hymnal"] ed. Alfred W. Martin, First Free church of Tacoma (Tacoma, WA, 1901) UV

Hymns of Humanity, ed. Kenneth L. Patton [New and final edition of *Celebration of Life...* There were intervening editions of smaller hymn books, also called *Hymns of Humanity],* Meeting House Press (Ridgewood, NJ, 1980) UU

Hymns of Joy for Christian Worship, ed. Alexander Streeter Arnold (1829–1923), Alexander S. Arnold (Valley Falls, RI, 1879) New Edition 1886. UV

Hymns of Spiritual Devotion, Thomas Lake Harris (1859–1861) UV

Hymns of the Ages, ed. Louisa Putnam Loring (1854–1924), The University Press (Cambridge, 1904) [Henry Wilder FooteII says: based on

University Hymn Book (Harvard) of 1895²] UN

Hymns of the Church, with Services and Chants, ed. Charles Conklin, Stephen L. Roblin and Cornelius A. Parker, Universalist Publishing House, (Boston, 1907–1920) UV

Hymns of the Church Universal, compiled by Henry Wilder Foote (1838–1889), ed.and revised by Mary Wilder Tilletson and Arthur Foote, (Boston, 1890) UN

Hymns of the Sanctuary, ed. Cyrus Bartol (1813–1900) and others, (Boston, 1849) [a Revised and Enlarged version of *A Collection of Psalms and Hymns for Social and Private Worship,* West Boston] UN

Hymns of the Spirit, ed. Samuel Longfellow (1819–1892) and Samuel Johnson (1822–1882), Ticknor and Fields (Boston, 1864–1868); New Edition: James Osgood and Co. (Boston, 1875) UU

Hymns of the Spirit, ed. Henry Wilder Foote (1875 –), Edward P. Daniels (1891–), Curtis W. Reese (1887 –), Von Ogden Vogt (1879 –), L.Grisword Williams (1893 –), Alfred S. Cole (1893 –), Edson R.Miles (1875–1958) and Tracy M. Pullman (1904–19), Beacon Press (Boston, 1937) UN & UV

Hymns of Zion, with appropriate music: designed as an aid to devotion in families, social circles, and meetings for public worship, Abel Charles Thomas (1807–1888), Cowperthwait and Co. (Boston, 1839 [Several editions of this first American hymnal to print music and words on the same page throughout were published.]) UV

Hymns Original and Selected: With Responsive Services for Private and Public Use, ed. R.C. Waterston (John Wilson and Co. (Cambridge, 1893) UN

Hymns on the Universal restoration, ed. Elhanan Winchester, R. Folwell (Philadelphia, 1795) UV

Hymns Used in the Universal Church, James Relly, B. Larkin (Boston, 1791) UV

Isle of Shoals Hymn Book and Candle Light Service, ed. George H. Badger (1859–1954), Isle of Shoals Association (1908) UN

Jubilate Deo: A Hymn and Service Book, ed. Charles W. Wendte, George H. Ellis Co. (4th Edition, Boston, 1900) UN

---

2 *University Hymn Book* was used by some Unitarian churches, including New Bedford.

Lessons from Nature's Voices, ed. Minnie O. Colegrove, Colgrove (Greenville, OH, 1912) UV

Melodies of Heaven, A Collection of Hymns and Tunes for Social Worship, for the use of Universalist and other Liberal Christian Churches, ed. Thomas Eliot St. John, Williamson and Cantwell (Cincinnati, OH, 1863–1874) UV

National Hymns, Original and Selected; for the use of those who are "Slaves to no Sect." Ed. Abner Kneeland, The Investigator (Boston, 1832–1852); later edition: J.P. Mendum (1870)) UV

Matins and Vespers, ed. John Bowring, Ticknor and Co. (Boston, 1844) UN

New Hymns of Joy, Sacred Songs of perfect faith for Christian Worship, ed. Alexander Streeter Arnold, Arnold (Valley Falls, RI, 1885) UV

New Hymns on Various Subjects, viz: On the Creation of the World; and the Formation of Man – the State wherein He was Created, and his Sad and Shameful Fall. On the Early and Extensive Promises of God – the Coming of Christ, and the Completion of the Father's Promises: or, the Eternal Redemption and Victorious Salvation of Mankind through Him, ed. Silas Ballou, (Worcester, MA, 1785); also Nathaniel Coverly (Newbury, VT, 1797) UV

Poems and Hymns, ed. John Pierpont, 1840 (temperance and anti–slavery)

Prayers and Hymns for the Church and Home, with selection of psalms, ed. Edwin C. Bolles, New England Universalist Publishing House (Boston, 1865–1873) UV

Psalms, Hymns and Spiritual Songs: Compiled for the use of Universalist churches, associations and social meetings, ed. Holden Ryan Nye, Nye and Demarest – later Williamson and Cantwell, (Cincinnati, 1861–1870 [six editions]) UV

Psalms, Hymns, and Spiritual Songs, Selected and Designed for the Use of the *Independent Christian Church of Gloucester,* Munroe, Francis and Parker (Boston, 1808) UV

Psalms, Hymns, and Spiritual Songs, Selected and Original, Designed for the Use of the Church Universal in Public and Private Devotion, I. Thomas and E.T. Andrews (Boston, 1792) [A Revision of Relly for First Universalist in Boston] Also published by Monroe and Francis (Boston, 1802). Edition with appendix (Boston, 1808); New and corrected edition ed. George Richards and Oliver W. Lane, I.

Thomas and E.T. Andrews (Boston, 1818)

Psalms, Hymns and Spiritual Songs; selected and designed for the use of the Independent Christian Church in Gloucester, Monroe, Francis and Parker (Boston, 1808) UV

Psalms and Hymns, for social and private worship: carefully selected from the best authors, ed. David Pickering Ashbel Stoddard (Hudson, NY, 1822). Later Edition: Marshall and Brown (Providence, RI, 1832) UV

Sabbath Worship; Prayers, Chants, and Responses, ed. R.A. Ballou, Universalist Publishing House (Boston, 1870) UV

Sacred Poetry and Music reconciled, or a Collection of Hymns original and compiled, ed. Samuel Willard, L.C. Bowles (Boston, 1830) UN

Sacred Songs, ed. L.S. Everett [minister Universalist Society of Salem, Massachusetts],Tomkins (Boston, 1843) UV

Sacred Songs for Public Worship: A hymn and Tune Book, ed. Minot J. Savage (1841–1918) and Howard M. Dow, (Boston, 1883) UN

Service and Hymn Book: for the Unitarian League of Lay Centers, ed. L.G.W., American Unitarian Association (Boston, c1900) UN

Service Book: for the Church of the Savior, ed. Robert Waterston (1812–1893), Jenks and Palmer [essentially A Collection of Psalms and Hymns for Christian Worship – "Greenwood's Collection" with additions] (Boston, 1845) UN

Services and Hymns for Alliance Meetings: prepared for The Alliance of Unitarian and Other Christian Women, (Boston, 1922) UN

Services and Hymns for the Use of the Unitarian Church in Charleston, S.C., ed. Samuel Gilman and C.M. Taggart, (Charleston, SC, 1854) Second Edition: Joseph Walker, Agt. (Charleston, SC, 1867)

Services and Songs for the Celebration of Life, ed. Kenneth L. Patton [few hymns – no music], Beacon Press (Boston, 1967) UU

Signature Songbooks, One and Two, Unitarian Universalist Association in cooperation with the UU Musicians Network (Boston, 1990) [These were test songbooks for *Singing the Living Tradition*, as was *Signature Songbook*, Three – primarily for children so it's listing is under Sunday School Hymnals. UU

Singing the Journey, (Supplement to *Singing the Living Tradition*) ed. Barbara Wagner, Leon Burke, Jeannie Gagne, Dennis Hamilton,

Kenneth Herman and Jason Shelton, Unitarian Universalist Association (Boston, 2005) UU

Singing the Living Tradition, ed. Mark Belletini, T.J. Anderson, Ellen Johnson–Fay, Helen R. Pickett, Mark Slegers, Barbara L. Wagner, W. Frederick Wooden, Jacqui James [ex–officio], Beacon Press (Boston, 1993) UU

Social Hymns and Tunes for the Conference, American Unitarian Association (Boston c. 1868) UN

Songs and Readings, ed. Jacob Trapp (1899–1992), Porte Publishing Co., (Salt Lake City, 1931) (There was a second enlarged edition.) This small book introduced many hymns later to be found in HOS, HCL and SLT. UN

Songs of Faith in Man, ed. Waldemar Hille, The Hodgin Press (Los Angeles, 1960; second edition, 1969) UN New edition – see *How Can We Keep From Singing!*

Songs of the Free and Hymns of Christian Freedom, Maria W. Chapman, Issac Knapp (Boston, c. 1836) UN

Songs of Work and Worship, ed. Stella Marek Cushing and Jason Moore, Universalist Publishing House (Boston, 1923) UV

Songs of Zion, or the *Cambridge collection of sacred music designed for the church, for the social meetings of Christians, and for family worship,* ed. Thomas Whittemore (1800–1861), The Trumpet Office (Boston, 1837–1839) UV

Souvenir Festival Hymns, Edna Dow Cheney, Free Religious Association (Boston, 1899) UN

Sunday Services: ed. Charles G. Ames, Printed for the Spring Garden Unitarian Society (Philadelphia, 1890) UN

Sursum Corda, Mary Wilder Tillotson (1843–1934) (?) UN

The Chapel Hymn Book, [Warren and Pitts Street Chapels, Boston], S.G. Simkins (Boston 1836–1839) UN

The Century Hymnal, [Universalist edition ed. Henry R. Rose], ed. H. Augustine Smith, Century Co. (NYC, 1921) UV

The Christian Psalter: A collection of Psalms and Hymns for Social and Private Worship, ed. William Parsons Lunt, [for First church in Quincy, MA] (Boston, 1841) UN

The Disciples Hymn Book: A Collection of Hymns and Chants for Public and

Private Devotion, prepared for the use of the Church of the Disciples, ed. James Freeman Clarke (1810–1888), Benjamin Greene (Boston,1844); New Edition: Horace B. Fuller (Boston, 1852–1869) UN

The Family Singing Book, ed. Sylvanus Cobb, S. Cobb (Boston, 1848–1856) UV

The Gospel Harmonist: a collection of sacred music, consisting of tunes of all metres, and also sentences, anthems for a variety of occasions, chants, etc. to which is prefixed a familiar introduction to the art of singing, on the Pestzlozzian system, ed. Thomas Whittemore (1800–1861), Whittemore (Boston, 1841–1845) UV

The Gospel Hymn Book: being a selection of hymns composed by different authors, designed for the use of the church universal, and adapted to public and private devotion, ed. Abraham Maxim, Maxim (Maine, 1879) UV

The Gospel Liturgy: a Prayer–Book for Churches, Congregations, and Families, prepared under the direction of the General Convention of Universalists, ed. Abel Thomas, G. Collins (Philadelphia, 1857–1871); also published by Woman's Centenary Association (Philadelphia, 1887) UV

The Gospel Psalmist a collection of Hymns and Tunes, ed. John Greenleaf Adams and S.B. Ball, James M. Usher, Universalist Publishing House (Boston, 1861) UV

The Gospel Psalmist: A Collection of Hymns for Public and Private Devotion, ed. John Greenleaf Adams and S.B. Ball, J.M. Usher (Boston, 1861–1869) UV

The Harp and the Cross; A Collection of Religious Poetry, ed. Samuel Greenleaf Bulfinch, American Unitarian Association (Boston, c 1857) UN

The Hopedale Collection of Hymns and Songs, for the use of practical Christians. Ed. Adin Ballou, A.A. Ballou (Hopedale, MA, 1849–1850) UV & UN

The New Hymn and Tune Book, ed. Samuel A. Eliot (1862– 1950), Henry Wilder Foote (1875 –), Rush R. Shippen (1828–1911), Lewis G. Wilson (1856–1928), American Unitarian Association (Boston, 1914) UN

The New Hymn Book Designed for Universalist Societies: Compiled from

Approved Authors, with Variations and Additions, ed. Sebastian and Russell Streeter, Marsh and Capen (Boston, 1829–1845 [35 editions including other publishers]) UV

The Philadelphia Hymn Book: or a selection of sacred poetry, consisting of Psalms and Hymns, from watts, Doddridge, Merrick, Scott, Cowper, Barbauld, Steele, and others; adapted to public and private devotion; compiled for the use and benefit of Christians of all denominations, ed. Abner Kneeland, Clark and Raser (Philadelphia, 1819) UV

The Social Hymn Book, consisting of psalms and hymns for social worship and private devotion, ed Chandler Robbins (1810–1882) [Second Church, Boston], James Munroe and Co. (Boston, 1843) UN

The Soldier's Companion: Dedicated to the Defenders of their Country in the Field, by their Friends at Home, Published as an Edition of *The Monthly Journal,* Boston, Oct. 1861, No. 10 UN

The Soldier's Hymn Book for Camp and Hospital, University Press (Cambridge, 1863) UN

The Soldier's Hymn Book, containing a supplement of *Antional Songs for the use of chaplains and soldiers in the army and navy of the United States,* ed. J.G. Forman, (Alton, IL, 1863) UN

The Springfield Collection of Hymns for Sacred Worship, W.B.O. Peabody, Samuel Bowles (Springfield, 1835) UN

The Universalist Church Companion: prepared by the Merrimac River Ministerial Circle for the use of its members and others; and by order of said circle Revised and Enlarged by Issac Dowd Williamson, A Tomplins (Boston, 1853) UV

The Universalists' Hymn Book: A New Collection of Psalms and Hymns, for the use of Universalist Societies, ed. Hosea Ballou and Edward Turner, Munroe and Francis (Boston, 1821– 1844) ; also by B.B. Mussey (Boston, 1844) UV

The Universalist Hymn Book: founded on the principles of Universalist logic: containing psalms, hymns and spiritual songs, original and selected, Origen Bacheler and J.B. Whitcomb, J.B. Whitcomb (Boston, 1829) UV

The University Hymn Book, ed. Charles F. Russell and Samuel A. Eliot,

University Press (Cambridge, 1898) UN3

The Western Universalist Hymnbook: designed for public and private worship: compiled from various authors, ed. M.A. Chappell and S.A. Davis, W.F. Stewart (Pittsburgh, 1837) UV

Tunes with Hymns for Use in King's Chapel, (Boston, 1878) UN

Twenty–five Hymns for Use in Time of War, [WW1] Beacon Press (Boston, 1916) UN

Unity Hymns and Chorals, ed. William Channing Gannett, James Vila Blake, Frederick Lucian Hosmer, (Chicago, 1880 [several variations, additions and editions over more than a generation, the 1911 edition significantly revised and added to]) UN

Universal Worship: The Catholic Gospel – "Our Father…" by Martin Kellogg Schermerhorn, (Cambridge, 1906), NABU Press Reprints *Universalist Church Companion,* A Tompkins (Boston, C 1850); Revised and Enlarged 1855 UV

Universalist Hymn Book: Psalms, Hymns and Spiritual Songs: Selected and original, [52 hymns by George Richards] (Boston, 1792) UV

Universalist Hymn Book; comprising a Great Variety of Sacred Effusions, Original and Selected; suitable to the livelier as well as the graver purposes of devotion, ed. George Rogers (1805–1846), R.P. Brooks (Cincinnati, 1842–1844); New Edition: John A Gurley (Cincinnati, c1848 [6 editions]) UV

Vesper Service An Order of Evening Worship. Especially arranged for Universalist Churches, ed. J.A. Seitz, James Miller (NY, 1876) UV

Vestry Harmonies: A Collection of Hymns and Tunes for all occasions of Social Worship, ed. John Greenleaf Adams, Universalist Publishing House (Boston, 1868 – 1872) UV

Vestry Hymn Book: Designed for Universalist Conference Meetings, compiled by a Friend to Devotion, J.T. Gilman (Bath, 1843) UV

Voice to Universalists ed Hosea Ballou, J.M. Usher (Boston, 1849) UV

Washington Pocket Companion, Temperance Hymns, Songs Etc., ed. A.B. Grosh, Grosh (Utica, 1832–1845) UV

---

3   This Harvard University hymn book is included for four reasons. Its editors were both Unitarian. It contains a stunning collection of Unitarian hymnody, with much else. It has excellent end notes on hymn writers, their hymns and the composers. It was used by Unitarian congregations as their hymnal – New Bedford, MA – for instance.

Sunday School Hymnals:

A Book of Hymns and Tunes for the Sunday School, the Congregation, and the Home, ed Samuel Johnson (New York, 1860) UN

A Book of Song and Service: for the Sunday School and Home, Ed. Edward A. Horton, The Unitarian Sunday school Society, AUA (Boston, 1895) UN

A Catechism for the Use of Children, W.B.O. Peabody, Tannatt (Boston, 1823) UN

A Collection of Hymns for the Sunday School, Compiled for the use of the Boston Chapel Sunday School, Green (Boston, c 1842) UV?

A Manual for Sunday Schools to Which is Added a Collection of Hymns, ed. William S. Balch, A Tompkins (Boston, 1839–1851) UV

A Service Book; with a Selection of Tunes and Hymns for Sabbath Schools, ed. Henry Bacon, A Tomkins (Boston, 1849–1860) UV

A Year of Worship for Sunday Schools and Homes, G.L. Demarest, Universalist Publishing House (Boston, 1873–1899) UV

Book of Hymns for Young Persons, Charles Eliot Norton, Bartlett (Cambridge, 1854) UN

Good News Songs, Compiled and Edited from the Sunday School Hymnal, ed. Mrs. L. Weston Atwood, Murray Press (Boston, 1912) UV

Heart and Voice: A Collection of Songs and Services for the Sunday school and the Home, ed. Charles W. Wendte, George H. Ellis Co. (Boston, 1909–1910) UN

Hymn and Tune Book for Sunday Schools, American Unitarian Association (Boston, 1869) Bound with Services, 1880, UN

Hymn Book Designed for the Use of the Universalist's and Restorationist's Sabbath Schools, ed. David Pickering, Wheeler (Providence, 1834 third edition) UV

Hymn Book for Sunday Schools, published under the patronage of the Providence Association of Universalists, Marshall and Hammond (Providence, 1829) UV

Hymns and Exercises for the Federal Street Sunday School, I.R. Butts (Boston, 1839) UN

Hymns for Children and Young Persons, [Warren Street Chapel, Boston], Little Brown and Co. (Boston, 1854) UN

Hymns for Children, Selected and Altered with Appropriate Texts of Scriptures,
ed. Dorothea Linde Dix, Munroe and Francis (Boston, 1825) UN

Hymns Prepared for the Scholars of the Marblehead Universalist Sabbath School,
ed. Henry Bacon (1840) UV

Hymns, Songs and Fables for Children, Eliza Lee Cabot Follen (1787–1860),
Carter, Hendee and Babcock (Boston, 1831); New Edition: Leonard C. Bowles (Boston, 1833); New Edition: William Crosby and H.P. Nichols (Boston, 1852) UN

May this Light Shine, A Songbook for Children and Youth, UU Musicians
Network, (2008)

Our Sunday School, ed. John Eliot Trowbridge, J.M. Russell (Boston, 1879)
UN

L.R.Y. Sings, ed. Christopher Moore for Liberal Religious Youth, Cooperative Recreation Services (Delaware, OH, 1960) UU

Poetical Catechism for the Young, ed. W.B.B. Peabody (a selection of hymns
in the back)

Praise and Thanks, Number One, A Hymn Book for the Young People's
Christian Union of the Universalist Church, ed. Grace F. White,
Universalist Publishing House (Boston, 1895–1911) UV

Praise and Thanks, Number Two, A Hymn Book for the Young People's
Christian Union of the Universalist Church, ed. Grace F. White,
Universalist Publishing House (Boston, 1903–1911) UV

Sacred Songs: adapted to social religious meetings, Sabbath schools and
family worship, ed. Linus Smith Everett, A. Tompkins (Boston,
1843) UV

Sacred Songs for Sunday schools, Original and Selected, Eliza Lee Cabot Follen, B.H. Green (Boston, 1839) UN

Select Hymns for Sunday schools: compiled for the use of Universalist Sunday schools, ed. John H. Gihon, Gihon and Fairchild (Philadelphia, 1842) UV

<u>*Signature Songbook,*</u> Three, Unitarian Universalist Association in cooperation with the UU Musicians Network (Boston, 1990) UU

Social Melodies: a collection of hymns for the use of prayer–meetings, Sabbath–schools, Bible–classes and families, ed. C Chauncey Burr,
S.H. Colesworthy (Portland, ME, 1841) UV

Songs along the Way, Murray Press (Boston, 1915) UV

Songs of Faith, Hope and Love: for Sunday Schools and Devotional Meetings, ed. Albert J. Holden, William A. Pond and Co. (Chicago, 1883) UV

Songs of Joy, for Sunday Schools and Homes, ed. G.L. Demarest, Universalist Publishing House (Boston, 1870) UV

Songs of Work and Worship, ed. Stella Marek Cushing and Jason Moore, Universalist Publishing House (The Murray Press) (Boston and Chicago, 1923) UV

Sunday School Harmonies, Number one, Universalist Publishing House (Boston, 1879–1882); Number two, UPH (Boston, 1885); Numbers one through four, UPH (Boston, 1914) UV

Sunday School Hymn Book, ed. Lewis Glover Pray, 1833 UN

Sunday School Hymn and Service Book, (revision of above) ed. Lewis Glover Pray, 1844 UN

Sunday School Hymnal: with offices of devotion, ed. Mary S. Attwood, Universalist Publishing House (Boston, 1895) UV

Sunday School Liturgy, ed. James Lombard, c1800 (including hymns) UV

The Altar: A Service Book for Sunday schools, ed. J.G. Bartholomew, Universalist publishing House (Boston, 1865) UV

The Beacon Hymnal: for Church Schools, Young People's Services, Day Schools and the Home, ed. Florence Buck, Beaon Press (Boston, 1924) UN

The Beacon Song and Service Book for children and Young People, ed. Ruth E. Bailey, Vincent Silliman, Gertrude H. Taft and Katherine I. Yerrington, Beacon Press, (Boston, 1935–1966) UU

The Carol: A Book of Religious Songs for the Sunday School and Home, ed. Charles W. Wendte, The John Church Company (Cincinnati, c1890) UN

The Children's Program Lyceum [Hymns and Songs], Second Edition, ed. Andrew Jackson Davis, Bella Marsh (Boston, 1867) UV

The Child's Offering, or, Flowers for all seasons consisting of hymns, oratorios, dialogues, colloquys, and single pieces for the use of Sabbath schools, ed. James M. Usher, J.M. Usher, Universalist Sunday School Depository (Boston, 1850) UV

The Child's Universalist Companion: consisting of stories, hymns, etc., designed to illustrate the nature and tendency of the doctrine of Universal salvation, ed. Daniel D. Smith, D.D. Smith and A. Tompkins (Boston, 1836) UV

The Family Singing Book: a collection of hymns and tunes for the use of families and social circles, ed. Sylvanus S. Cobb, s. Cobb (Boston, 1848–1861) UV

The Junior Star, ed. Mary Grace Canfield, M.G. Canfield – The Young People's Christian Union (Boston, 1895–1905) UV

The Life Hymnal: A Book of Song and Service for the Sunday School, Stanford and Emma Talbot Mitchell, Universalist Publishing House (Boston, 1904–1910) UV

The Manual and Harp, for the Use of Sunday Schools, ed. L.J. Fletcher, New England Universalist Publishing House (Boston, 1861–1867) UV

The New Altar: A service Book for Sunday schools, Compiled primarily by John Glass Bartholomew; newly arranged with additions by Charles L. Hutchinson, published by J.G. Bartholomew and Charles L. Hutchinson; Universalist Publishing House (Boston, 1906) UV

The Prayer and Hymn Book of the West Boston Sunday School, S.Nikinson (Boston, 1843) UN

The Redeemer: a series of opening services for the Sunday school, founded on the life of Jesus Christ, ed. John Hay Lewis and Eeo Rich Lewis, Universalist Publishing House (Boston, 1888) UV

The Sabbath School Melodist: a collection of hymns and tunes designed for the Sabbath School and the home, ed. John Greenleaf Adams, R.A. Ballou (Boston, 1866), also Universalist Publishing House (Boston, 1867–1870) UV

The Sunday School Choir and Superintendent's Assistant: consisting of servies, prayers, and lessons for the opening of Sunday Schools, with services for Christmas, Independence, for the death of teachers and pupils and Sunday School exhibitions, etc. with a great variety of tunes and hymns for the use of Sunday Schools, ed. Thomas Whittemore (1800–1861), Curtis (Boston, 1844–1846) UV

The Sunday School Hymnbook: Designed for Universalist Sunday Schools Throughout the United States, ed. Clement Fall LeFevre, P. Price (New York, 1837), Universalist Union Press (1838–1841) UV

The Sunny Side, Charles William Wendte, William A. Pond (NYC, c. 1875) UN

The Sylphid's School, ed. Lewis Glover Pray (poems and hymns) UN

Unity Services and Songs, (a revision with substantial additions and revisions of next listing), Western Sunday School Society (Chicago, 1894) UN

Unity Songs and Services for the Sunday School, Part One, ed. James Vila Blake (1879) UN; Parts One and Two, Western Sunday School Society (Chicago, c1889) UN

We Sing of Life: Songs for Children, Young People, Adults, ed.Vincent Silliman, Beacon Press (Boston, 1955) UN

We Sing Together Universalist Youth Fellowship and American Unitarian Youth (Boston, c. 1953) UU (printed by Cooperative Song Service, successor to American Unitarian and Universalist Youth Fellowship CSS songbooks)

ABOUT THE AUTHOR

Rev. David A. Johnson (BA, BD, MA) has researched the stories of the development of Unitarian and Universalist hymnody for decades, and taught UU Hymnody in theological schools — primarily Andover Newton Theological School. Following in the footsteps of Henry Wilder Foote's lifelong labors to put liberal hymnody into the larger story of the development of American Hymnody, his labors to record it for Julian's masterful *Dictionary of American Hymnology*, and his own leadership in the creation of two landmark Unitarian hymnals, *The New Hymn and Tune Book* (1914) and *Hymns of the Spirit* (1938), Johnson has continued the story to the present, noting movements in and the faith pilgrimage of Unitarians and Universalists that shaped the hymnals of each new generation. He has, with Rev. Eugene Navias, and on his own, created several "Singing Our History" programs for national, regional, and local meetings. He continues to work on hymn stories — for every hymn has a story behind it, why, through what experience and for what faith purpose it was written and the music composed.

Rev. David Johnson is a semi-retired UU minister, living in North Providence, Rhode Island, living with his wife of 37 years Julie Coulter, and following the burgeoning lives of eight grandchildren.

www.ingramcontent.com/pod-product-compliance
Lightning Source LLC
Chambersburg PA
CBHW070349090426
42733CB00009B/1348